DO
NOT
GO
GENTLE

Also by Kathleen Stock

Material Girls

KATHLEEN STOCK

DO NOT GO GENTLE

THE CASE AGAINST ASSISTED DEATH

The Bridge Street Press

THE BRIDGE STREET PRESS

First published in Great Britain in 2026 by The Bridge Street Press

1 3 5 7 9 10 8 6 4 2

Copyright © Kathleen Stock 2026

The moral right of the author has been asserted.

All rights reserved.
No part of this publication may be reproduced, stored in a retrieval system, or transmitted, in any form or by any means, without the prior permission in writing of the publisher, nor be otherwise circulated in any form of binding or cover other than that in which it is published and without a similar condition including this condition being imposed on the subsequent purchaser.

A CIP catalogue record for this book
is available from the British Library.

Hardback ISBN 978-0-349-13664-6
Trade Paperback ISBN 978-0-349-13665-3

Typeset in Sabon by M Rules
Printed and bound in Great Britain by
Clays Ltd, Elcograf S.p.A.

Papers used by The Bridge Street Press are from well-managed forests and other responsible sources.

The Bridge Street Press
An imprint of
Little, Brown Book Group
Carmelite House
50 Victoria Embankment
London EC4Y 0DZ

The authorised representative
in the EEA is
Hachette Ireland
8 Castlecourt Centre
Dublin 15, D15 XTP3, Ireland
(email: info@hbgi.ie)

An Hachette UK Company
www.hachette.co.uk

www.littlebrown.co.uk

In memory of
Russell and Mary Spear
and
Tommy and Dorothy Stock

Contents

	Introduction	1
1.	Give Me Liberty and Give Me Death	21
2.	Better Off Dead	45
3.	Suffering What You Fear	74
4.	Worse Than the Disease	104
5.	A Few Grannies	133
6.	A Humiliating Dependency on Others	158
7.	Human Beings as Units	186
8.	Slippery Slopes and Bottomless Pools	215
	Conclusion	239
	Notes	255
	Acknowledgements	281
	Index	283

Introduction

We are all going to die: a phrase uttered in blind panic during many a disaster movie, but which also expresses a basic and incontrovertible truth. In a book that is partly about death – though also about life – we might as well look difficult things in the face. So let's do it together.

About 650,000 people die every year in the UK, around 44% of them in hospital.[1] For many of us – perhaps even most – the thought of being faced with a difficult death is extremely disturbing. The fear might be for the self or a loved one, or both. Perhaps you are frightened of terrible pain, or of having to depend upon others during the final stages. Perhaps you find the prospect of losing control of your body humiliating. Some will have seen close relatives die in the grip of awful suffering and wish to avoid that at all costs.

To worry about death is deeply human. In most countries, the feelings wax and wane depending on circumstances and mood, but don't result in any drastic action; for, practically speaking, there are few drastic actions available to take. Most people would not dream of attempting a solo suicide in the face of terminal illness. Short of this option, all they can do is seek out whatever palliation is available from the medical profession, and get on with what is left of their natural life.

In these places, assisting or encouraging someone else's

suicide is still a crime – an attitude most people would agree with. There is something deeply wrong with encouraging another person to self-destruct, let alone helping them carry it out. Pro-suicide websites, where depressed visitors are urged to take their own lives, are abhorrent. But as soon as grave illness or significant disability enters the picture, feelings tend to get a lot more mixed.

In some jurisdictions, there are official systems that allow people to channel their disturbed feelings about bodily deterioration into self-extinction. Should you be diagnosed as terminally ill, or perhaps even just incurably disabled, there is an established route to help you orchestrate your own death. It is nearly always described as 'medical', though its business is far from the traditional stuff of doctors' to-do lists. The process starts by making an appointment or calling a special hotline. It ends with a health professional helping you take poison, your breath ceasing, and your heart coming to a stop.

Each of us will face death at some point, whether assisted or not. But particular deaths are not the main topic of this book. This is a book about *organised* death, or what I will be calling 'assisted death services': formal structures dedicated to helping consenting people to die with the aid of clinicians. They are embedded within wider health systems and set up and sustained by the work of politicians, civil servants, and lawyers as well as doctors, nurses, and pharmacists.

Some believe that helping another person to die is always deeply immoral; in which case, assisted death services automatically count as immoral too. This is not my approach. I allow that in some rare situations, where physical suffering is genuinely intense enough and cannot be remedied otherwise, helping someone to die can be the right thing to do; though equally, many assisted deaths are profoundly wrong. So I am not against the act in principle. When it comes to the question of an entire assisted death *service*, however, its introduction into the real world is bound to have unacceptably harmful consequences. So to adopt a phrase from historian Kevin Yuill, I am against the 'institutionalisation of death'.[2] By the end of this book, I hope you will be too.

There is a difference between establishing a death service and mere legalisation. Take Switzerland. Assisted suicide was made legal there in 1937 and was not defined as a medical procedure. Anyone is permitted to help with another person's suicide as long as it is not for 'selfish reasons'. It was only in the 1980s and 90s that non-profit organisations such as Dignitas emerged, offering death with the aid of doctors.

Still: in most places, the doctor-delivered route is the only one available. There are established or emerging 'medical' assisted death services in Austria, Belgium, Columbia, Luxembourg, and the Netherlands; in Canada and New Zealand; in twelve US states or jurisdictions; and in seven Australian states or territories. Assisted death legislation is also part-way advanced in Ecuador, Italy, Portugal, and Spain. It is under discussion in Germany and France, and it looks like New York will soon pass a bill too.

Despite the growing popularity of such services, they are far from alike. The variety can seem bewildering at first. Some jurisdictions only legalise assisted suicide. Others permit voluntary euthanasia as well (i.e. where the doctor administers the lethal substance directly, rather than helping you take it yourself). In some places, a doctor stays with you as you die; in others, you may take lethal substances without the prescribing doctor present.

There is also significant variation in eligibility: who exactly is to be helped to die and for what reason. Most countries or states confine it to citizens, but Switzerland allows foreign nationals. Most offer assisted death only to mentally competent adults; but in Quebec and Benelux – that is, Belgium, the Netherlands, and Luxembourg – an assisted death can be given to adults with dementia if they have indicated their consent in advance. Also in Belgium and the Netherlands, non-voluntary euthanasia is practised on a few extremely ill babies and young children, as long as their parents agree.

Most services require a terminal diagnosis beforehand, but there are different definitions of 'terminal'. Sometimes this is defined in terms of death being 'reasonably foreseeable', while other places make mention of a specific number of remaining months (e.g. six or twelve). Another important difference concerns whether terminal illness is the only real criterion for eligibility. Some services – for instance, in Australia and New Zealand – formally require, alongside a terminal diagnosis, the simultaneous presence of unbearable suffering that cannot be remedied. Others, such as in Oregon, simply ask for the former and don't mention suffering at all.

In Canada and Benelux the focus is *only* upon relieving severe suffering, and a terminal diagnosis is not required. Physically disabled people with long lives ahead of them can opt for an early death, assuming their suffering is deemed intense and unrelenting enough. Also in Benelux, it is legal for a doctor to supply an assisted death to a person who suffers unbearably from a psychological illness or cognitive disorder but has no underlying physical illness. This practice, ratified a few years ago but then postponed, is also due to be introduced in Canada in 2027.

In the UK there have been numerous attempts to get assisted death onto parliamentary statutes – for instance in 1997, 2003, 2006, 2013, 2014, 2016, and 2021 – and until recently all of them failed. But in October 2024, Labour MP Kim Leadbeater won a ballot to introduce a private member's bill in Parliament, and she chose the cause of assisted death for England and Wales. The result was the Terminally Ill Adults (End of Life) Bill.

Like the Oregon law upon which it was based, this new bill did not mention suffering as necessary for eligibility, let alone suffering of any particular intensity or duration. Essentially it proposed offering a doctor-assisted suicide to nearly every adult with a terminal diagnosis, for whatever personal reason they liked. Terminal illness was defined as 'an inevitably progressive illness or disease which cannot be reversed by treatment', where 'the person's death in consequence of that illness or disease can reasonably be expected within six months'.

From the point of view of supporters of assisted death, this was a golden opportunity. Strongly behind the bill was the lobby group Dignity in Dying, whose well-funded campaigning now stepped up a gear. Leadbeater's entry in the parliamentary Register of Interests makes clear she received thousands of pounds from Dignity in Dying for printing out bill briefings for fellow MPs and other relevant parties.[3] Here, finally, was a real chance to usher in a compassionate practice which from their perspective simply extended a terminally ill person's right to self-determination. Many were delighted when, after a free vote was permitted, the bill passed its second reading in the Commons in November 2024: 330 for and 275 against.

But from the perspective of critics, such a momentous proposal – carrying with it huge implications for the National Health Service, and for society more generally – should not have been brought in via backbench legislation. The truncated format meant there was no time for the sort of prolonged scrutiny of surrounding issues that would have preceded a government-sponsored bill. And it also meant that Leadbeater could hand-pick the people charged with looking at those details after the bill's second reading. Indeed, the committee she eventually chose was stacked with a majority of MPs who agreed with her, meaning that very few critical amendments got through.

On Friday 20 June 2025, the bill came to its third and final reading in the Commons, by which time the issue was dominating front pages. After a passionate debate the bill again passed, although this time with a reduced majority: 314 in favour, 291 against. It caused obvious divisions across every political party. Even within the Cabinet, the Health Secretary and the Justice Secretary voted no, while the Prime Minister and the Chancellor of the Exchequer voted yes.

I am finishing this manuscript one week after the third vote. Within the next few months, Leadbeater's bill will go to the House of Lords. Given that assisted death was not a Labour manifesto commitment, there is a small possibility the Lords might reject the bill in its entirety; otherwise, it may face substantial amendment. Assuming the bill passes, it is predicted to receive Royal Assent by the end of 2025, and come into effect by 2029 at the latest.[4]

At the same time, a separate assisted death bill is making its way through the Scottish Parliament. Rather than specifying eligibility in terms of a terminal diagnosis of six months or less, as Leadbeater's does, it refers more vaguely to offering assisted death to someone with an 'advanced and progressive disease, illness or condition from which they are unable to recover', which can 'reasonably be expected to cause their premature death'. At the time of writing it has passed its Stage One vote 70 to 56, but there is some doubt as to the life expectancy of the bill, given the competing one down south.

So assisted death is very much in the air; and the moment provides us with a good opportunity to take stock. Leadbeater's bill is by far the most successful attempt there has ever been to bring organised assisted death to the UK. The contents of the bill, and the contested process that led up to it, offer a window into current progressive-badged thinking about assisted death: what it should look like, why societies should have it, who it should be for, and what consequences there are for others. Despite the lack of a government-backed process, there has still been a significant amount of debate carried out in public, which gives us a rich seam of evidence and argument upon which to draw. Supplemented by looking at how services abroad are working, we can build a detailed picture of the ideological and practical currents shaping the visible tide.

You will have noticed I am using the term 'assisted death' rather than 'assisted dying'. I do so because the word 'dying' obscures important issues. To a casual glance, presenting doctors as engaged in 'assisted dying' might imply they are providing beneficial treatment for seriously ill people, helping them live out their final days with less suffering – a bit like assisted shopping, daily help to wash and dress, or the delivery of pain-relieving drugs. In fact, though, a doctor who helps you end your life is not assisting you to better withstand dying. They are bringing the period of your dying to a complete halt.

'Assisted death' encompasses both assisted suicide and voluntary euthanasia. Though the prospective UK system is aimed only at legalising assisted suicide, voluntary euthanasia is permitted in many international jurisdictions where assisted suicide is allowed too. There are plenty of supporters in the UK who would admit – at least privately – that they eventually wish to see voluntary euthanasia legalised as well. They don't see a significant ethical difference between a doctor helping someone to take lethal substances orally and administering them intravenously with that person's consent. Indeed, Leadbeater's bill would allow doctors to 'prepare a medical device which will enable that person to self-administer the substance', or to 'assist that person to ingest or otherwise self-administer the substance', both of which sound closer to euthanasia than suicide. So it seems important to discuss voluntary euthanasia too.

Even though Leadbeater's legislation was aimed only at legalising assisted suicide, there was still heated debate about language. Critics of the bill, keen for people to understand exactly what was at stake, wanted to call a spade a spade and a suicide a suicide, assisted or not. But Leadbeater and fellow bill-defenders baulked at the term, describing 'suicide' in the assisted context as highly offensive. One supportive member of the bill committee, Conservative MP Kit Malthouse, declared that 'suicide is a healthy person taking their life, but what we are talking about is somebody who is seeking to take control of their inevitable death in these circumstances'.

A Labour MP, Rachel Hopkins, agreed: 'a healthy person taking their own life by suicide is different from a terminally ill person, who is facing their death, ending their life by shortening their death'. An Australian committee witness speaking in favour of the bill, Alex Greenwich, followed this line of thinking to its conclusion. A doctor helping a person to take lethal substances was, according to him, a form of 'suicide prevention' in that it stopped people taking their lives on their own – the only version of suicide he apparently was willing to recognise as such. 'If someone wishes to end their life, voluntary assisted dying is not the process they are going to take.'[5]

The tendency to obfuscate about suicide has a long history. Medieval chroniclers and coroners, trying to avoid referring to an act perceived as sinful and shameful, would write euphemistically about someone dying 'of an excess of grief', or 'by the temptation of the Devil'.[6] In his groundbreaking book about suicide published in 1897, the French sociologist Émile Durkheim criticised those who insisted that no suicides were ever committed by sane and rational people, since, according to them, any self-inflicted death unaccompanied by insanity did not count as suicide at all.[7] But the scruples of Leadbeater and colleagues were apparently quite different. They seemed to want to soften the appearance of what they proposed by defining one of its most controversial aspects out of existence. In this respect, they perhaps more resembled probably the most notorious US-based advocate of assisted death, Dr Jack Kevorkian. In an interview with the *New York Times* in 1995, Kevorkian argued that the phrase 'assisted suicide' should be replaced with 'patholysis', meaning 'the destruction of suffering': 'We want to get away from all the negative connotations,' he declared at the time.[8]

Malthouse and Hopkins's technical objection to calling assisted suicide 'suicide' apparently related to the fact that the person involved would already be dying. They seemed to suggest that someone who is dying cannot be killed – you are merely 'shortening death'. But this is seriously confused; for if they were right, it would imply someone who was already dying could not be murdered either. Bad news for many an Agatha Christie plot, though perhaps good news for anyone contemplating getting rid of a seriously ill relative without much consequence.

In a piece for the Conservative Home website in November 2024, Malthouse also made a separate objection: those seeking assisted deaths because of terminal illness are not 'suicidal'.[9] By this, he presumably meant that people with terminal diagnoses could not possibly want to end their lives for reasons of chronic depression, intense anxiety, adverse social circumstances, or any other familiar aspect of suicidal ideation. But this just looks like wishful thinking. As we will see, there is plenty of evidence to suggest it is false.

Such nuances will become clearer in good time. The basic thing to grasp now is that even those with fatal illnesses are still alive. They are also potentially subject to all the various complicated circumstances and experiences that being alive can bring. What these politicians were ignoring in their desire to get the bill passed is that dying necessarily involves living. 'Dying' is simply a vague portion of life spent with a serious and escalating bodily disorder, immediately prior to its causing death. And wherever there is human life, including during the period of dying, there is always the possibility of artificially extinguishing life. Even in the last few hours, this remains true.

It is important, then, to say 'suicide' where the term applies. Equally, we must not lose sight of the fact that a suicide involves a *killing* – a self-killing, but a killing nonetheless. It is not a natural or a quasi-natural death, even in the context of severe illness. Not all self-killings are suicides, since some are accidental. But all intentional self-killings are suicides, including the assisted version. And I will also be referring to assisted deaths as 'early' or 'premature', relative to the natural endpoint: for that is also what they are.

The remarks of Malthouse and Hopkins reveal a tendency we will come across time and again. Namely: for those in favour of assisted death services, there is a temptation to treat the voluntary exits of terminally ill people as if they were wholly outside the bounds of ordinary discourse about acts of killing – whether self-killing, or death at another's hands. I will be arguing that a decent society cannot afford to accept this. For one thing, ordinary discourse about killing includes putting a spotlight on how to safeguard people from harm. Dying people deserve safeguarding just as much as those in the land of the well.

Perhaps spelling things out so baldly appears loaded with disapproval, but it is not. Words like 'suicide' and 'self-killing' carry a lot of emotional charge – understandably so, because we are talking about events that often bring devastation in their wake. But to use these terms does not prejudge the morality of suicide, assisted or otherwise. It is a neutral description of a distinctive kind of act, not intended to imply evaluation. It leaves open the possibility there might be reasonable, noble or other 'good' suicides as well as terribly destructive ones, and that some assisted deaths might be included among the former. The point here is only that being passed a lethal substance by a doctor at your own request, then intentionally and knowingly taking it, is still suicide. The fact that you are being helped by a doctor to complete the process makes no difference to the act's essential nature.

Over the last decade, in line with the global push for assisted death services, there have been lots of books, articles, and ad campaigns in favour. Many take a highly emotive tone. The process of supplying an early death is presented as a kind of much-needed medical treatment. The doctors who dispense death are implicitly brave moral champions. The people who receive it are described as intensely grateful for the opportunity. There is a lot of talk about 'control', 'autonomy', 'choice', and 'dignity'. Final deathbed scenes have a rosy glow, involving stories, music, hugging, and laughing through tears. After some time, the 'patient' floats peacefully away and everybody goes home, sad but also relieved that their loved one's suffering is over.

People without access to an assisted death service, in contrast, are presented by campaigning organisations as dying in pain, misery, fear, and loneliness. If they are desperate enough to want an assisted suicide on the basis of such suffering, they are terrified of the prospect of prosecution for the participant. If they can't face exposing family members to criminal risk, they are forced into the expense and stress of travelling to Switzerland. And indeed, the application of force is a general theme in such narratives. People are either forced to travel abroad to die at great expense; or forced to choose a brutal and lonely suicide on home soil; or forced into a painful, undignified natural death without any help. These are the only possibilities without a local assisted death service to call upon.

These pro-assisted death stories collapse the many

different deaths into three main kinds: unassisted, painful, lonely, and undignified; assisted, foreign, expensive, and stressful; assisted, homegrown, free, and peaceful. In their over-simplification, the stories act more like propaganda than argument. Each vision is designed to trigger strong emotional responses in favour of the cause, without further thought about relevant alternatives or wider social consequences. Sentiment is laid on with a trowel.

But when thinking about assisted death services, as well as zooming in on selected experiences or sets of feelings, we also need to zoom out to see their effects on society as a whole. We need to avoid semantic tricks, and try to see through the fog of personal emotion. This is not just a question about how your own death will be, or indeed mine. There is a lot more at stake. Whether to introduce an assisted death service is a moral question for the whole of society.

Talking of morality may seem a bit old-fashioned. (Though philosophers sometimes make fine-grained distinctions between 'ethics' and 'morality', I'm using them interchangeably.) Yet in my experience, even those modern-minded people nervous of using such Victorian-sounding concepts are willing to make judgements about right and wrong. Some shy away from the idea they are doing so, only because they associate moral judgement with a kind of Christian past from which they wish to be detached. But we should make no mistake: those who argue vociferously in favour of assisted death services are taking a moral stance on the matter. They think it is *right* we have such services. Indeed, they present this outcome as morally urgent. I disagree.

A personal ethic can get its energy from a live religious faith or from atheist sources. In this book I will be offering only secular arguments. But for the purposes of transparency, here are my religious affiliations, such as they are. I was raised as a Roman Catholic then lapsed for decades.

Recently I have found myself attending church services from time to time, looking for something that secular values can't seem to bring. I don't take communion. But I do sometimes go to church.

Judging from public discussion of Leadbeater's bill, there are several who would seize upon this as an admission of something sinister. In May 2025, Dame Esther Rantzen – one of the bill's most high-profile defenders – sent a letter to every MP, accusing critics of having 'undeclared religious beliefs which mean no precaution would satisfy them'.[10] It is a common complaint that arguments against assisted death services must be secretly religious if they aren't so explicitly, and that this discredits them. I don't see why we should accept either point, and especially since nearly every Western secular morality system, however ostentatiously rationalist, has roots in the history of Christian thought. Indeed, as we will see, grand-sounding ideas about the desirability of freedom, mercy, dignity, and equality, harnessed by champions of assisted death, are all deeply influenced by the Christian tradition. These ideas didn't come out of nowhere.

But in any case, there are plenty of Christians who think assisting in someone else's death is morally permissible. Dignity in Dying was actually *founded* by Christians. A more recent example is the theologian and Anglican priest Nigel Biggar (now Lord Biggar), who has written an interesting book arguing the case from a theistic perspective, albeit with heavy caveats.[11] And if I count as a religious believer, then I am another one who thinks participating in assisted death may occasionally be the right thing to do. But in any case, no argument in this book will depend on a background belief in God, or in the truth of Christian or biblical teaching. The whole thing will be thoroughly secular. Concerned atheists can be reassured on this point.

*

Some readers may by now be wondering: why the fuss? Practising modern medicine in the age of advanced technology requires wisdom and restraint. Doctors should not be in the business of keeping incurably ill and suffering people alive for as long as possible, no matter what. They already sometimes hasten death by withdrawing treatment where it seems it is no longer doing any good. Indeed, in modern healthcare there are protocols for doing so. So then: as long as the person agrees, what is the difference with offering an assisted death?

Equally, though, there is an important distinction between the passive withdrawal of medical treatment towards the end of natural life and the active administering of lethal substances. Letting a natural process – death – happen without further intervention is a different kind of action from deliberately bringing it about. Despite the impulse towards euphemism in this area, we have to keep remembering that our topic involves doctors helping people take poison to end their own lives, or administering it directly themselves. It isn't just a matter of doing nothing. (I also use the word 'poison' deliberately, because that is exactly what it is – a substance intended to be lethal.)

Still, the objector might reply: let's agree that a) positively doing something to get a particular outcome (e.g. administering poison in order to kill someone) and b) passively letting that very same outcome happen (withdrawing treatment and so letting someone die) are two different kinds of action. Even so, there is no interesting *moral* difference between the two. This was the influential argument of a philosopher called James Rachels writing in the 1980s, who thought that both actions were sometimes permissible in the context of medicine. To make the point, he called the latter 'active euthanasia' and the former 'passive euthanasia'.[12]

As already indicated, I grant that actively helping someone to die may be the right thing to do in some particular contexts;

though in other scenarios, it will be very wrong. And I also agree with Rachels that in some scenarios, letting someone die is just as bad as killing a person outright. Rachels has a compelling non-medical example of such a case: killing a child by deliberately drowning him in order to get an inheritance; as opposed to finding the child already drowning in the bath and choosing not to save him, for exactly the same reason.

But to be clear: comparing acts of assisted death with instances of withdrawal of treatment is not the right comparison. This book, to repeat, is about the ethical status of an *assisted death service* – an organised system, formally oriented to the active provision of early death by doctors at scale. This, I will be arguing, is much worse than a health system in which managed withdrawal of treatment sometimes happens. It has far more unacceptable consequences.

Another distinction ethicists like to invoke is between actions that are directly intended versus outcomes that are merely foreseen. Occasionally doctors give terminally ill patients deep palliative sedation if other methods of pain relief have failed. There is a belief (albeit contested) that this practice can artificially hasten death. Even so, it is thought permissible as long as the doctor's direct intention is to relieve bodily pain and suffering, and not to kill. The doctor is not deliberately ending life but deliberately stopping pain, with an earlier death a foreseeable but unintended consequence.

Understandably perhaps, some people encountering this line of argument think it pure sophistry. Working in the other direction, they may then protest: if it is occasionally OK to deeply sedate someone who is terminally ill in order to relieve them of pain, foreseeing as you do so that death is hastened, why can't you deliberately and intentionally help them die in order to stop terrible pain as well?

Luckily we can bypass tortuous philosophical discussions of the distinction between intending and foreseeing. For one thing, existing assisted death services permit doctors to deliberately help end life in a much wider range of circumstances than the presence of terrible pain – including where no pain is present at all. And for another, bringing the provision of deliberate killing into the medical world is a very bad idea, for reasons that go well beyond the practice of occasionally using palliative sedation.

There is one other terminological preliminary to tackle before we get going. Unlike early legalisers in Switzerland, most champions of assisted death services insist they offer a 'medical' procedure, but we should resist that description. Again, this is not to prejudge the ethics of the issue but only to make an important definitional point. For similar reasons I won't be calling the applicants for an assisted death 'patients', even though they count as such during other moments of contact with the medical profession.

This is partly because the bar for what counts as success in assisted death is by definition quite low. It's far easier to help kill an ill person than to keep them enjoying life. Getting the dosage exactly 'right' only means stopping the heart, not carefully adjusting a drug dose in order to maximise well-being and minimise harm. Handing over toxic chemicals to a patient to take, or setting up an IV to deliver them, are not skilled tasks requiring a medical degree. Indeed, in jurisdictions such as Oregon, lethal substances are simply given to the patient to take later with no medic present.

But there is also a more foundational issue. Discussion of whether assisted death is medical or not arose during the committee stage of Leadbeater's bill. According to the wording of the National Health Service Act 1946 as updated in 2006, the purpose of the NHS is (my italics) *'to secure improvement in the physical and mental health* of the people of England and in *the prevention, diagnosis and treatment of physical and mental illness'*. Leadbeater recognised that this definition, tightly focused on improving health, would exclude assisted death from its purview. So she moved an amendment: the stated foundational aim of the NHS would be altered to include mention of 'arrangements ... for the provision of voluntary assisted dying services'.[13] With the addition of just a few words, the rationale of the health service becomes fundamentally confused.

As the wording of the original Act indicates, medicine is fruitfully understood as a practice aimed at the treatment and prevention of disease or injury, for the purposes of improving human health. A shorter way of saying this is that medicine's purpose is 'life-sustaining'. Supporters of doctor-assisted death want us to view it as a sort of medical treatment for advanced disease and/or incapacity. But in the standard account, medical treatment is confined to relieving illness in a live patient and does not include deliberately producing a dead one.

Muddling the original conception is a very bad idea, bound to undermine effective prosecution of medicine's still crucial purpose. By the very nature of what we want from healthcare professionals, they should have a very low tolerance for bringing about death. Redefining medicine to bring the act of deliberate killing into the foundational aims of healthcare cannot fail to muddy the waters for both practitioners and their patients, resulting at the very least in a reduction of public trust. It is also likely to produce a host of ungovernable negative effects upon genuinely medical operations, downstream of this radical change. In its official response to the Leadbeater bill, the Royal College of Psychiatrists agreed: assisted death 'does not aim to improve a person's health and its intended consequence is death ... Should this Bill proceed, it should be explicit that [it] is not a treatment option.'[14]

The fact that it is doctors who are assisting with their patients' deaths does not change the situation. Doctors do lots of things in their daily lives which are not medical per se. And we should also remember that, despite their expertise in dealing with illness and disability, doctors are not experts in whether choosing death over life is the right thing for a particular individual. They can advise about likely disease progression, treatment options and their side effects, symptom management, and palliative alternatives. But nothing in their training or experience makes them especially suited to advising people about whether, or at what moment exactly, it is time to take their own lives.

To be or not to be, as Hamlet famously put it, is not actually a medical decision at all, but an existential one. It involves weighing up what one wants more – continuing life or self-annihilation – and examining the particular reasons for and against. It is intensely personal, about deep issues of meaning and value. It is philosophical, not scientific.

In arguing against assisted death services, I know I'm swimming against the tide. As one critic of the Canadian system puts it, 'there is a global push for legalizing ... organized ending of life, in whatever form it takes', in which advocates 'coordinate efforts, share experiences, write joined publications, and adjust tactics depending on local sensitivities'.[15] And it's all presented in the name of progress. In terms of popularity and the appearance of benevolence, this is a difficult narrative to stand against. The more assisted death is normalised, the more that places without it look like anachronistic holdouts – even cruel.

Even so, I think we should strongly object. On the face of it, defenders of organised assisted death are often highly compelling, and it can be hard to see what they are getting wrong. But one of the hidden reasons why they are difficult to pin down is that they are drawing on two different arguments, in tension with one another. One is the argument for pure personal freedom (my body, my choice) and the other is for mercy in the face of unbearable suffering (we should put this person out of their misery). As I will show, these two strands have their own conceptual problems, and are often in conflict.

The title of this book refers to the first stanza of 'Do Not Go Gentle Into That Good Night', a poem by Dylan Thomas written for his dying father in 1951. Thomas urges him to resist death in old age and to 'rage, rage against the dying of the light'. This book is not about resisting death when it finally finds you as the result of natural, inevitable processes of senescence and decay. It is about resisting assisted death services. They are presented by their supporters as a progressive, freeing, compassionate option for a more enlightened society, but quite the opposite is true. In officially approving such arrangements, societies cross over into moral darkness. Together we need to properly scrutinise the arguments for organised assisted death – before it is too late to turn back.

1

Give Me Liberty and Give Me Death

Let freedom ring

Was there ever such a rousing modern idea as finding freedom? Breaking loose from chafing constraints, whether literal or metaphorical, has been eulogised by a thousand political leaders, film directors, and advertising gurus. Sometimes it can seem that freedom is something tangible – grabbable, even – and you should be permanently interested in increasing your share.

In a certain frame of mind, the idea of exercising freedom is the main attraction of an assisted death. Let's call this intellectual archetype – a set of clustering ideas, rather than a real, breathing person – the 'Freedom Lover'. The Freedom Lover wishes to be able to choose when exactly to make an exit. Indeed, they say they have a right to do so, sometimes described as the 'right to die'. They frame a failure of authorities to provide assisted death as an active fettering of this freedom. And they tend to look askance at the suggestion that once assisted death is permitted, negative social changes might cascade uncontrollably afterwards. If they do, we can sort these things out later. Advancing freedom and respecting rights should come first.

If the Freedom Lover had a motto, it would be a twist on the famous Revolutionary War cry: 'Give me liberty *and* give me death!' On the face of it, Dame Esther Rantzen seems a prominent member of this independent-minded club. In 2023 she complained that 'I will probably not be given the chance to die in my favourite place, my New Forest cottage.' She continued: 'It is our life. It will be our death. It should be our choice.'[1]

In reality, though, most people in favour of assisted death services are not pure examples of the Freedom Loving type. Dame Esther herself sometimes cites the value of 'mercy' for people who are gravely suffering, a consideration which is quite different from freedom. Campaigners tend to shuttle between arguments for freedom and other concerns: mercy, compassion, dignity, and sometimes general utility too. Still, it is useful to separate out the strands.

Would-be Freedom Lovers are encouraged in their enthusiasms by a centuries-old paradigm. Liberalism, the political framework still definitive of Western nations, prioritises personal freedom above much else (even if the existence of CCTV cameras, planning laws, and cancelling mobs might suggest otherwise in practice). A famous liberal ideal says that each of us should be granted a private sphere in which to observe our own values and pursue our own goals, as long as we aren't infringing upon other people's capacity to do the same. 'It's not hurting anyone else' is, if not exactly the rallying cry of the age, then at least its polite shrug.

Certainly, it would be hubristic to get casual about the value of personal liberty. The history of absolute monarchs, totalitarian regimes, and cults starkly spells out what can be lost when others make decisions for us. Recognising this fact, our forebears formulated the notion of a 'right', understood roughly (for now) as an important freedom the individual should be able to exercise. And the idea took off. These days, rights – or their more magisterial-sounding version, 'human rights' – are treated with reverence, at least on paper.

Unsurprising, then, that during public discussion of Kim Leadbeater's Terminally Ill Adults Bill, language redolent of the Freedom Lover was a staple. An editorial in *The Economist* began: 'This newspaper believes in the liberal principle that people should have the right to choose the manner of their own death.'[2] Writing in the *Guardian*, columnist Polly Toynbee talked of 'the right to escape the last stages of dying if suffering is unbearable', also referring to it as a 'freedom'.[3] In an op-ed in the *Evening Standard* Andrew Copson, chief executive of the British Humanist Society, wrote: 'It's about freedom of choice – allowing competent adults who experience intolerable pain in ways unimaginable the ultimate freedom: control over our own selves.'[4] Other headlines referred simply to the 'right to die'.[5]

So it seems that freedom, rights, and choices are at the heart of defences of assisted death for many – albeit that references to mercy and compassion are also in the mix. And notice that the lines I just quoted invoke another important idea: that your body, your life, your death, your 'self', are all ultimately your own to decide what to do with. To put this in context, we need to consider a brief history of previous owners.

Self, take the wheel

> Turn your nose up at fortune. I have given it no weapon with which it can strike your mind. Above all beware that nothing hold you back against your will. The door lies open. If you don't want to fight, you can flee. Thus, of all

the things that I wanted to be required of you, I made nothing easier than death. I have placed your soul on a slanted slope: it is being dragged down. Only pay attention and you will see how short and how quick a road leads to freedom.[6]

So the Roman philosopher Seneca enthusiastically imagined a pre-Christian God talking to humans about the act of suicide. Around 450 years earlier, Socrates – on the point of being forced to take his own life by the state – had told his followers that 'as the chattels of the gods' it was not up to humans to decide when to die.[7] But the ancient philosophical cohort known as the Stoics, which included Seneca, famously approved of the act in some circumstances: to fulfil obligations towards your friends or country, or to avoid bringing shame on your family. They also thought it was sometimes appropriate in the context of serious illness.

Things changed with the arrival of the Christian God. We find St Paul at the beginning of what will be a gradual paradigm shift. Warning the Corinthians off sexual immorality, he implies that human bodies are both the property and the residence of God, and that our choices should be constrained by this: 'Do you not know that your bodies are temples of the Holy Spirit, who is in you, whom you have received from God? You are not your own; you were bought at a price.' Writing later from a Roman prison to the Philippians, St Paul seems to contemplate suicide but pulls back: 'Yet what shall I choose? I do not know! I am torn between the two: I desire to depart and be with Christ, which is better by far; but it is more necessary for you that I remain in the body.'[8]

Though no explicit injunction against suicide can be found in either Old or New Testaments, around AD 400 St Augustine made an important doctrinal intervention, based on the Sixth Commandment's general injunction against killing. Breaking from Graeco-Roman tradition, he proposed a

Christian argument against it – or at least, against suicides not commanded by God, since he thought some were divinely ordered.

Still, the prohibition didn't become firmly established until the medieval period. In the thirteenth century St Thomas Aquinas took up the theme, declaring that suicide is always 'unlawful'. He gave three reasons: first, because it is contrary to the natural law of self-preservation; second, because 'by killing himself' a man 'injures the community'; and third, because 'life is God's gift to man' and 'it belongs to God alone to pronounce sentence of death and life'.[9] The last one particularly stuck. What evolved into a strong injunction against suicide rested heavily on the idea that humans ultimately belong to God, as expressed via various metaphors. Life is given as a gift by Him or is on temporary loan; human bodies are made in His image or act as His temple.

Four centuries later Christianity began its slow retreat, while liberalism started to pick up steam as the dominant Western belief system. Now that God was vacating the premises, a different story was needed about who was ultimately in charge. A new model started to picture the body as belonging to the self. Or as the Enlightenment philosopher John Locke put it, 'every Man has a Property in his own Person. This no Body has any Right to but himself.'[10]

Locke still insisted suicide was not permitted, though, believing that human bodies were also the property of God in some kind of confusing co-ownership deal. But by the nineteenth century John Stuart Mill was stating that 'Over himself, over his own body and mind, the individual is sovereign' – and there was no mention of an embarrassing second proprietor. Modern liberal discourse was developing a God-shaped hole, to be filled with explicitly secular values. 'Freedom' (or 'liberty') was foremost among these.

This conception of the physical body as a self-owned asset,

over which its owner has special and important freedoms and powers of decision-making, still looms large in contemporary ethical deliberation. The feminist mantra 'my body my choice' pithily sums it up. And if it really is my body and my choice, I should be free to dispose of my body and my life as I see fit. After all, I am the one in charge.

The right to die alone

To better understand the Freedom Lover, let's continue to focus on solo suicide – the kind carried out alone, and with no accompanying terminal illnesses to complicate matters. This will help us make sense of arguments offered for assisted death.

Think of Cato the Younger stabbing himself in the stomach after learning of the victory of Julius Caesar, who then 'pushed the physician away, tore his bowels with his hands, rent the wound still more, and so died'.[11] Or Major General Sir William Erskine, veteran of the Napoleonic Wars, reportedly jumping out of a Lisbon window in 1813 with the words 'Now why did I do that?' Or what about author Virginia Woolf walking into a Sussex river in 1941 with stones in her pockets; or rock star Kurt Cobain turning a shotgun on himself in Seattle in 1994. We might ask: were these self-extinctions the exercise of freedom? Was there a 'right to die' here too?

To answer these questions, we need to know what they mean. In one obvious sense, having the 'freedom to die' just means that there are no obstacles to killing oneself. Cato, Erskine, Woolf, and Cobain were each free to die and the proof is they managed it. Plutarch tells us that Cato's friends and his doctor tried to save him, but couldn't. Woolf and Cobain had each been thwarted in previous attempts, but this time were alone and succeeded. It is not controversial that each of these people were free to end their lives in this sense. Saying so implies nothing about whether this was good or bad.

But the Freedom Lover wants more than this banal observation. Broadly speaking, they think it is a *good thing* that some people have this freedom. They have a *right* to it.

Talk of 'rights' has various meanings, not always easy to tell apart. If someone claims there's a 'right to die', the topic might be a legal right, assumed to flow from some law or treaty or other: the UK Human Rights Act, say, or the European Convention on Human Rights. But Freedom Lovers aren't (just) talking about legal rights, they are talking about ethics; about the shape of moral reality as they see it. Specifically, in talking of a right to die, the Freedom Lover is saying there is a *moral obligation upon others not to interfere in your suicide attempt*. They think there is a right to die in the precise sense that other people should not hinder you, if you wish to go.

This presumed right to die takes the form of what theorists call a 'claim right' – the sort of right that places obligations, aka 'claims', upon others. And it is known as a 'negative' right, in that the obligation it supposedly imposes is one of *noninterference*. Think of negative moral rights as imaginary fences marking the boundaries around you, which ought to be controlled by you alone. The imaginary fence has a gate you can choose to open – in which case you 'waive your right' to noninterference – but otherwise it is kept shut to exclude other people's actions. Either way, the power and control should be yours and not someone else's. Such rights are often described as 'inalienable': derived from general facts about human nature, meaning nobody can take them away.

The liberal framework says that you own your body; you, rather than others, should get to decide what to do with it. Many human rights can be pictured on this model: claim rights that are supposed to apply to humans universally, demarcating territories that ideally ought to be under individual control. Classically, these include rights to privacy, family life, freedom of association, and religious belief. (Another one is the right to refuse medical treatment.)

Arguably the most pre-eminent human right of all is also a negative right, at least in part. This is the 'right to life', associated with protections from life-threatening interference, but also bound up with living the kind of life you choose. Locke wrote that 'being all equal and independent, no one ought to harm another in his life, health, liberty, or possessions', while in the US Declaration of Independence, Thomas Jefferson famously talked of rights to 'life, liberty, and the pursuit of happiness'. And according to some Freedom Lovers, the right to life is what indirectly generates a right to die. Assuming you have an imaginary fence around your life – marking a territory that should be yours alone to govern – then you also have the power to open the gate voluntarily and let death in. If that's what you decide, no one else ought to stop you.

Against Big Suicide Prohibition

Inspired by the Stoics, the sixteenth-century French philosopher Michel de Montaigne was a proto-Freedom Lover about solo suicide – though not an open one, for the consequences from the Church would have been severe. In his essay 'A Custom of the Isle of Cea', he rehearsed various considerations for and against the permissibility of suicide, making sure to apply suitable ironic distance and presenting them only as deniable musings. But reading between the lines, it seems clear where his own sympathies lay.

One of Montaigne's arguments sounds distinctly modern: 'Living is slavery if the liberty of dying be wanting ... As I do not offend the law against thieves when I embezzle my own money and cut my own purse; nor that against incendiaries when I burn my own wood; so am I not under the lash of those made against murderers for having deprived myself of my own life.'[12] Here again, then, we meet the metaphor of your life or body as a piece of property you own and can do with what you wish.

But Montaigne didn't just toy with the idea that suicide in some cases is morally permissible. He also suggested it might be admirable: '[t]he most voluntary death is the finest'. A few decades later, the English metaphysical poet John Donne wrote a book defending suicide against the charge of Christian impiety – *Biothanatos: A Declaration of that Paradoxe, Or Thesis, that Self-homicide is not so naturally Sin, that it may never be otherwise* – in which he too connected certain kinds of suicide with a valuable expression of agency. Written in a period of melancholy, the poet had intended his text only to be circulated among friends, though his son published it after his death. In later life, Donne professed profound ambivalence about the work's content.

Unlike Montaigne, Donne's explicitly Christian framework presupposed a firm belief in the afterlife, and the continuing existence of the self after bodily death. In that context, he argued, suicide – like some acts of deliberate martyrdom – might be a means of positively transforming yourself in order to reach a higher plane of being. (Indeed, according to Jorge Luis Borges, writing in provocative mode in 1954, the poet's underlying aim was to 'indicate that Christ committed suicide'.[13]) At the time of writing, the attractions of exercising agency in choosing death were not just hypothetical for Donne. In a private letter to a friend he wrote:

> I would not that death should take me asleep. I would not have him merely seize me and only declare me to be dead, but win me and overcome me. When I must shipwreck, I would do it in a sea where my impotency might have some

excuse, not in a sullen, weedy lake where I could not have so much exercise for my swimming.[14]

Taking up a similar theme, some eighteenth-century Romantics believed suicide could positively express a person's freedom in a way that was a kind of noble achievement. Unlike those who sat back and waited for death, you were demonstrating commendable independence: perhaps even the ultimate form of self-possession. Literary German had an archaic word for this kind of death: a *Freitod* ('free death'), as opposed to the more negatively connoted *Selbstmord* ('self-murder') or *Selbsttötung* ('self-killing').[15]

But by the 1870s, Dostoevsky was satirising this vision in the character of Kirillov the engineer in his novel *Demons*, obsessed with killing himself in order to demonstrate the total self-directive power of his own will. In choosing his own exit, Kirillov is – or thinks he is – kicking against God, nature, social pressures, and superstitious traditions. In a pivotal speech he declares: 'If God exists, then all will is his, and I can't escape his will. If he does not exist, then all will is mine ... I am killing myself in order to show my independence and my new terrible freedom.' In fact, when the time comes, Kirillov's suicide is an awful mess of accident, confusion, and horror.

During the twentieth century the suicidal act came to be viewed as more passive, stemming from some preventable affliction: mental illness, poverty, or loneliness, for instance. On the cusp of the new century, Durkheim had published *Suicide: A Study in Sociology* – twelve years after the suicide of his close friend Victor Hommay. In this seminal work, he presented suicide as the product of four main kinds of social condition. One of these in particular would have great significance for the century to follow. The 'egoistic suicide' was described as taking place in societies in which 'excessive individualism' was on the rise as a social force, dissolving communal bonds and eroding a sense of personal identity as tied to the fortunes of wider groups. Durkheim was watching from the sidelines as the self, not religion or community, was gradually becoming the central source of meaning.

There were other historical developments, of course. In the wake of two world wars in which millions of people were helplessly caught up, the idea of radically free agency struggled to survive as a credible ideal. And among the intelligentsia, existentialist philosophers like Albert Camus began to undermine the idea of suicide as a meaningful expression of autonomy – for in an already absurd universe, choosing to die must be meaningless too.

But what seems to philosophers to be the product of faulty ideology – or to sociologists, the result of social forces, or to psychologists, the outcome of mental illness – might still appear to the individual as entirely self-directed behaviour. And in the second half of the twentieth century, we find possibly the most hardcore modern Freedom Lover there has ever been. The eminent Hungarian-American psychiatrist Thomas Szasz kept the flame alive, arguing bullishly that humans have a 'right to freedom from suicide prevention'.

According to the logic of Szasz's position, suicidal people like Cato, Erskine, Woolf and Cobain acted freely and responsibly in ending their lives, and their choices must be respected. In one of several books on the subject, he wrote: 'there is no objectively "good death" or "bad death"; there is only dying – or living – deemed "good" or "bad", according to the values of the person doing the judging'. Szasz was particularly critical of attempts to stop psychiatric patients killing themselves, believing that whereas 'the treatment of medical patients requires their consent . . . the prevention of suicide entails their coercion'. Noting the popularity of the critical term 'Big Pharma', Szasz offered the label 'Big Suicide Prohibition', though for perhaps understandable reasons it didn't take off.[16]

Shortly before the end of his life, Szasz fell and broke his spine. As a friend wrote afterwards: 'The hospital physician wanted to admit him and put him on what would likely have been a morphine drip, and proposed surgery to help heal the break – there was talk about inserting a piece of plastic to hold the vertebral fracture together so it could heal, but Tom would have none of that.'[17] Two days later, he killed himself.

Freedom and autonomy

So far I've talked a lot about freedom, but I haven't mentioned a close relation that often comes up in defences of assisted death: autonomy. Szasz's insistence that any kind of suicide prevention must count as coercion gives us an opportunity to explore the issue now.

If you know something of their histories, you might baulk at Szasz's generally approving conclusion as applied to Woolf, Erskine, and Cobain. Mental illness and drug addiction were significant background factors in all three cases. Erskine had been declared insane shortly before jumping. Woolf's suicide note to her husband starts 'I fear I am going mad again' and divulges she is hearing voices, as she had done once before, when the birds outside her window seemed to speak Greek. Cobain was helplessly addicted to heroin, had been suffering from agonising stomach pain, and was chronically depressed.

Yet according to Szasz's logic, in ending their own lives these people acted freely even so. Indeed, in the 1980s he wrote a book about Woolf, arguing that despite some apparently severe symptoms of mental illness at times, she was in control both of her life and death.[18] Szasz's model of personal freedom was pretty simple: it was just the absence of external obstacle. If you decide to do something and successfully manage it, unfettered by outside forces or agencies (by other people, laws, electric fences, natural events, or whatever), then you are free to do it. If you are stopped by some external force or agency, then you are not free. Equally, where you are positively forced into an action by someone else – as when someone has a gun to your head – you are (obviously) not free either.

But other versions of the Freedom Lover are available, for whom things are not so black-and-white. On occasion you can decide to do something, complete your action, and meet no external obstacle, nor be subject to any outside coercion. Yet both you and your action can still count as unfree in one important sense: namely, if you were 'of unsound mind' as you acted. If this applies, your action still won't count as properly autonomous.

What 'autonomous' means here is not easy to pin down in a sentence. Essentially, it refers to the idea of being self-governing. Your decisions are your own. They represent your true will, and are not constrained by illicit forces. Illicit forces can include external people or events, as Szasz would agree. But crucially, they can also consist in so-called 'internal' obstacles: impediments to genuinely free action coming from within your own mind or brain.

A classic example is someone who acts under the influence of a powerful addiction to drugs, alcohol, or gambling. Although nobody else is directly forcing your hand, there is still a sense in which you are not in charge of some of your actions. The cravings are at the helm, hijacking your decision-making, even as a deeper part of you perhaps recognises you are acting self-destructively. In that case, the story goes, you are not wholly self-governing. Your mind is divided against itself.

A second example is the presence of mental disorder or illness. If you are under the influence of depression, psychosis, or mania, some of the things you do are not really 'your' actions. Executive agency is diminished; alien mental states have taken over. Metaphorically speaking, the threat is coming from inside the house. This framing seems borne out by the way people can sincerely disavow depressive, psychotic, or manic actions afterwards, looking back with confusion or horror once things have stabilised. 'That wasn't me; that was a different person' is a typical thing to hear. Perhaps it isn't literally true, but it has a ring of truth about it.

If allowing for internal threats to autonomy is right, then Szasz is wrong: there is a legitimate role for suicide prevention sometimes, compatible with the goal of protecting freedom in this wider sense. It can stop people from carrying out an act that seems attractive in the mentally hijacked, destabilised moment, but which doesn't properly represent the decisions of the more permanent, more stable, deeper self. In contrast to a radical Freedom Lover like Szasz, the archetype I'll be calling a 'moderate' Freedom Lover approves of interfering in an attempted suicide in certain circumstances. Generally, an adult person's suicidal intentions are not to be hindered by others – *except when they are the result of internal obstacles to freedom like mental illness or addiction.* We should at least check for such things before giving the green light. And if we do detect their presence in someone with suicidal plans, we are obliged to try to stop them. We can still do this in the name of preserving freedom; it's just a different conception from the simplistic Szaszian idea that freedom means only a lack of external force or impediment.

Moderate Freedom Lovers don't think every suicide is the result of destabilising factors such as addiction or madness. They would object, for instance, to the old coroner's practice of recording 'the balance of mind was disturbed' as the norm. Equally, though, they concede that this description sometimes applies. For Szasz, on the other hand, the idea that the mind can be divided between the true self and other aspects – aspects just passing through, as it were – allows the possibility of an unacceptable paternalism. It allows authorities to think of minds as clouded by delusions, unable to accurately determine what lies in their owners' interests – at which point, a gap opens up for the authorities to take charge. And in this matter, Szasz was nothing if not consistent. He thought that those with diagnoses of schizophrenia and the like are 'always responsible for their conduct'.[19] Aside from his views on suicide, he was well-known for another stance, relatively unusual for a psychiatrist: declaring the whole concept of mental illness a myth.[20]

Despite Szasz's misgivings, I assume most people will be more attracted to the moderate Freedom Lover archetype than to the radical one. They will want to take concerns about the complex nature of autonomy seriously. Suicide prevention – for the purpose of checking whether someone is of sound mind – is not always paternalistic but sometimes happens in the services of true freedom's preservation.

No suicidal man is an island

I would go further than the moderate Freedom Lover. Sticking to the topic of solo suicide for now, it's important to recognise that there is no general moral obligation upon other people to stay out of it. This is not just because a suicidal person's perspective might be temporarily confused. It is also because staying out of someone's suicide is not like turning a blind eye to their hobbies or who they are friends with. Suicide is not an essentially private matter.

Readers who are Freedom Lovers may protest: am I seriously suggesting that intervening in someone's decision to end their own life is morally *required*? Absolutely not: I agree that this would look like unacceptably sweeping deference to the interests of other people over those of the self. Saying that there is *no general obligation of noninterference* does not mean there *is* a positive general duty of *interference.* Sometimes – even most of the time – intervention in another's suicide attempt will be the right thing to do; but also, very occasionally, perhaps not. As with so many ethical questions, it will depend on the case.

This is a distinction worth pausing over. Asserting there is no general right of noninterference in a particular kind of action does not mean that the action is always wrong. It depends on circumstance. Here is an analogy, not meant to trivialise suicide but only to illuminate my general point. Young teenagers have no general right of noninterference from adults in their attempts to consume alcohol. Still, sometimes allowing a young teen a drink will be the right thing to do – or, at least, not the wrong thing.

Societies such as ours still go to great lengths to stop solo suicides. That is a very good thing. Vulnerable groups are identified, safeguarding policies devised, and emergency phonelines manned. Penal institutions have suicide watches; volunteers monitor geographical hot spots; bystanders try to talk people down from bridges or buildings. People bravely risk their own lives to save those of others in despair. One historian of suicide tells us that when a particular swing bridge was built in London's East End in 1830, 'the police were constantly rescuing the local prostitutes from the deep water below'. In 1879, four constables were permanently put on suicide watch at the new bridges at the London docks.[21]

Szasz would have viewed these efforts as essentially coercive. But most of the time, the desire to stop someone else's suicidal act comes from feelings of love, friendship, care, or solidarity. An action born of such motives cannot generally be off-limits, and especially when it concerns preventing early death. It is true that there is a trend to frame motives like love and friendship as potentially pressurising to the recipient – as bonds to be shrugged off, if unwanted – but the impulse to see things this way should surely be resisted.

In the aftermath of a suicide, loved ones are often tormented by thoughts about what they might have done differently. In an interview in 2021, TV presenter Dan Walker remembered his friend Gary Speed, the former footballer and manager who killed himself very suddenly ten years earlier, at the age of forty-two. Walker had been filming with Speed on the day he died. Voice choking with emotion, Walker said: 'I do go over it in my mind quite a bit ... you go back over absolutely everything. You can't help asking yourself whether you could have done something ... or whether there were some signs there you could have helped.'[22]

And this points to a consideration which the Freedom Lover ignores: the often terrible effects of solo suicide upon loved ones left behind. A suicidal person might comfort himself with Epicurus' dictum that 'when we are, death is not come, and when death is come, we are not.'[23] But even if your death is not part of your own life, strictly speaking, it will certainly be part of the life of others. Grief and emotional devastation, financial destitution, and even housing upheaval can follow. Such consequences cannot be morally detached from the act itself. This is (emphatically) not to say that a person should be blamed for trying to take their own life; but only that where loved ones and dependents are bound to suffer, there could not possibly be a general moral obligation upon everyone else to stay out of it.

Spouses, parents, children, and siblings have significant moral interests. Not being particularly known for their empathic skills, intellectual types sometimes seem to forget this point. Writing his famous essay 'On Suicide' in the 1750s, Scottish philosopher David Hume took issue with Aquinas on the alleged impermissibility of suicide. On the question of potential injury to the community, this unmarried and childless man wondered whether suicide may be a 'breach to one's neighbour', and cheerfully concluded in the negative: 'A man who retires from life does no harm to society: he only ceases to do good, which, if it is an injury, is of the lowest kind.' But presumably he wasn't thinking of those who have to pick up the pieces afterwards.

The self as gated community

To deprioritise the effects of suicide on other people is, I suggest, to fail to grasp the lie of the moral land. Why do people get this wrong? One possibility is that the background metaphysics of the self is faulty. Consciously or not, many people attracted to the Freedom Lover archetype conceive of the self as a gated community of one – an atom trying hard not to collide with other atoms. Their inner landscape seems like the lone subject of Caspar David Friedrich's famous painting *Wanderer above the Sea of Fog*: someone perched on a rocky crag, miles and miles from other human beings. (As a colleague and friend of Szasz admitted in his obituary: 'If anyone could value autonomy too much, perhaps Tom did. He did not like to admit that he needed people.'[24])

Rights, understood as imaginary fences, surround this imagined self to protect it from the unwanted interference of others. Rational choices or preferences form its core. Relationships with those on the outside are contractual. If a person decides to open a gate because it suits him in some way, other people may come in – but their presence is always provisional. If you don't like your friend, ghost him. If you don't enjoy your spouse, get a better one. If you think your parents have been inadequate, cut them out of your life.

The person who thinks of himself as a Freedom Lover didn't invent this picture of the self. He got it from the zeitgeist: the kind of excessively individualistic society that Durkheim describes. It is a reductive mash-up of some of liberalism's greatest hits, set to a catchy beat that readily turns into an earworm; the product of three centuries of picturing the self as bound up with rational decision-making, much of it self-interested, and of other people as potential impediments to that process. This is certainly not the whole of liberalism's legacy, but it is a popular, bastardised version of it. In the words of the philosopher Alasdair MacIntyre, talking about liberal opponent John Rawls, we are encouraged to think of ourselves 'as though we had been shipwrecked on an uninhabited island with a group of other individuals, each of whom is a stranger to ... all the others', trying to work out 'rules which will safeguard each one of us maximally in such a situation'.[25]

To see the self this way involves what I will be calling a 'hyperliberal' outlook. There are hyperliberals in every political party; it is a perspective that cuts across left and right. Still, other pictures of the self are available. Rather than an atom avoiding other atoms, a different metaphor is of a node on a wider network. We are connected to one another in ways that have nothing to do with making contracts first. We come into the world dependent on others, and stay that way. Some bonds between humans may be intrinsically coercive but those forged by love, friendship, and solidarity are not.

Humanity is an essentially social species for whom close associations are vital: whose minds can understand and empathise with one another, whose language can underpin shared meaning and joint plans, and whose bodies can joyfully intertwine. Equally we can misunderstand, hate, abandon, and destroy each other; all of it is human. But we are not just, or essentially, islands made out of flesh, each with an imaginary fence around us. Even if it is sometimes useful for a state to picture its citizens this way in order to avoid illiberal overstepping, it is not the sum total of who we are.

Two puzzles

We have emerged from this discussion accompanied by two versions of the Freedom Lover. One of these is pretty radical. It does not recognise so-called 'internal' obstacles to freedom and autonomy like addiction and mental illness. It thinks that if someone wants to end their life, for pretty much any reason, no one else should interfere. As long as there is no external coercion, there is a negative right to noninterference in the suicidal project, no matter what.

The moderate version of the Freedom Lover, in contrast, can allow some beneficial interference from others, but only for the limited purposes of allowing a person to come to a more genuinely autonomous position: to get treatment for mental illness, or to overcome addiction. In the absence of such factors, there is still a negative right to go ahead – meaning everyone else should stay away.

Let's now turn back to our main topic, assisted death – both suicide and voluntary euthanasia. It's worth noting that there is likely to be significant tension between these two versions of the Freedom Lover when it comes to what assisted death services should look like in practice. The radical Freedom Lover won't want the applicant for an assisted death to be held up for very long. Indeed, although very much against suicide prohibition, Thomas Szasz opposed the assisted kind, apparently on the grounds that organising the process at scale would limit personal autonomy to end your life at exactly the moment you wanted.[26] In contrast, the moderate Freedom Lover is likely to tolerate – indeed, if consistent, should require – some safeguards within a system, in order for professionals to check for soundness of mind in applicants. So what look like useful safeguards to the moderate Freedom Lover will look like authoritarian hold-ups to the radical Freedom Lover. This is a point to keep for later.

There are also two puzzling things to bookmark. The first concerns the much cited 'right to die', a favourite with campaigners for assisted death services. So far, we have found nothing in our investigation of the Freedom Lover, either radical or moderate, to justify the idea that there is a right to *assistance* in death, specifically: to being helped by someone else (a doctor, in fact) to kill yourself. All we have found is the argument that there is a right to *noninterference* in your own private suicidal intentions; to being left alone to get on with it.

The radical Freedom Lover thinks the latter is an unrestricted right. The moderate Freedom Lover restricts it to people who aren't mentally destabilised in an autonomy-threatening way. But either way, it is still unclear why being helped to die is a right. We can perhaps anticipate why, in some contexts, it might be a good thing to have. But lots of things are good-to-haves without counting as rights or fundamental freedoms. Another way of putting this point is: yes, assisted death services offer people a choice they did not have before. But so do new breakfast cereals on supermarket shelves. Why is this choice, in particular, the recognition of a *right*?

When thinking about this, there is an uncomfortable fact we need to acknowledge. Most people are already free to end their own lives if they so choose, including when terminally ill or suffering dreadfully. The door lies open, to use Seneca's euphemistic phrase – though one may well prefer an easier route to passing through.

There is no legislative barrier in the case of suicide – attempted suicide hasn't been a criminal offence in the UK since 1961, and we are far from the days when failed attempts were punishable by imprisonment.[27] Many of us are lucky enough to have loved ones who would do their best to try to prevent us from going down this path; but it is still usually possible for the determined and desperate to find a way. Campaigners for assisted death services will say they don't want only this option, perhaps understandably so. But nothing in the basic logic of the Freedom Lover position justifies the demand. There is perhaps room to argue that an assisted death service should be supplied only for those who are severely physically incapacitated, and so literally unfree to choose suicide on their own – say, because they are substantially paralysed. But equally, very few assisted dying campaigners suggest that a suicide service should be reserved *only* for paralysed people.

So there is an argumentative gap here. Meanwhile the second puzzle concerns the scope of Freedom Lovers' arguments, when compared to the workings of assisted death services as actually found in the world. Existing services seem interested in allowing that there is a 'right to die' only under limited conditions: the presence of terminal or incurable illness, or of unbearable suffering, depending on who you are talking to. For instance, in 2024 Kim Leadbeater went on record to insist about her bill: 'I'm really clear. This is about people who are terminally ill.'[28] The 'only' was implied. Other countries' systems are more expansive but still limit eligibility in a substantial way. But for the Freedom Lover, such limitations should look arbitrary. On their behalf we might ask: don't non-terminally ill people deserve freedom too?

The philosopher A. C. Grayling – a patron of Dignity in Dying and himself a member of Dignitas – initially seems more clear-sighted. In a letter to the *Observer* in 2025, he wrote that he supported 'an individual's freely chosen right to die if the circumstances of their life are overwhelmingly compelling to them as a reason for preferring its quality to its quantity'.[29] Elsewhere he has said that he backs assisted death 'for any reason'.[30] Here, then, it might seem we have found a true Freedom Lover in the wild, placing few limits on who exactly may be permitted an assisted exit. Taken at face value, he seems to be saying that if and when you decide it is time to go, then it *is* time – with no further qualification needed.

On closer inspection, though, things look more hedged. In evidence submitted to Parliament in 2023, Grayling implied that simply judging that your time is up should not mean you qualify for an assisted death.[31] You only have this right if you can make 'what is rationally recognizable as a considered case for ending [your] life which fully engages our sympathy and understanding', and is distinct from 'merely transient depression or emotional upset'. In other words: in order to justify an assisted death, the reasons you give for wanting to die must at least make sense to sympathetic hearers, and your suicidal state of mind must be relatively deep and long-lasting. This last point makes Grayling sound more like a moderate Freedom Lover than a radical one, concerned to eliminate temporary mental disturbances. And it also appears he would limit eligibility for assisted death to people with motives that seem reasonable to an outsider. That seems like quite a big restriction.

Though it is easy to forget, historically people have wanted to kill themselves for lots of different reasons, not all of them easy to sympathise with or condone. As the poet and critic Al Alvarez, himself a survivor of a failed suicide attempt, observed:

> there is a whole class of suicides ... who take their own lives not in order to die but to escape confusion, to clear their own heads. They deliberately use suicide to create an unencumbered reality for themselves or to break through the patterns of obsession and necessity which they have unwittingly imposed upon their lives.[32]

A study of attempted suicide in Iranian women found suicides 'characterised by flight from grief, loss of honour, shame, infamy or memories of failure incidents'.[33] Alvarez also described a suicide note found in a house in Hampstead that said only: 'Why Suicide? Why not?'

So to return to our second puzzle, and assuming that there are a variety of suicidal motives: with so much talk of freedom in the air, why is it so difficult for campaigners for assisted death services to endorse the cause in a full-throated fashion? Why does the 'right to die' extend only to people with certain serious bodily disorders or certain approved reasons?

It doesn't have to be this way, as we can see when we look again at Switzerland. Since assisted suicide is legal there wherever it is pursued for motives that are not 'selfish', in practice this means there are few restrictions on the reasons for which someone can be helped to die. Though now ruled out by medical bodies, in the past doctors were able to assist in the suicides of people in good health without facing professional cost.[34] So at least originally, the process seemed to fit the stated goals of Freedom Lovers far better than in other jurisdictions. Why don't the legislators creating new assisted death services follow suit?

In 2023, a bill was submitted to the Dutch parliament, aimed at making euthanasia available for those who feel they have 'completed life'.[35] The only other proposed condition was that recipients be over seventy. The true Freedom Lover would surely approve – though perhaps quibble at the arbitrary age limit.

2

Better Off Dead

A new character enters the scene

To answer our two puzzles, I need to introduce another philosophical character. Supporters of assisted death services, I suggest, are not only moved by the ethical vision of the Freedom Lover. There are many who tend towards a different ideal, which I'll call the 'Merciful Helper'. Simply put, Merciful Helpers want to instigate assisted death services in order to alleviate pain and suffering. They are explicitly altruistic. Their buzzwords are not freedom and autonomy, but mercy, compassion, sympathy, and pity.

To get a grip on this new character, here are four basic features, contrasted with those of the Freedom Lover:

- Whereas Freedom Lovers are *permitters*, Merciful Helpers are *enablers*. Freedom Lovers think that – once soundness of mind has been determined – everyone has the right to be left alone to arrange their own lives and deaths as they see fit. In contrast, Merciful Helpers prioritise positive intervention. They think intervening to help bring about an early, non-natural death is a good thing in certain specific circumstances: when, and only when, a person's pain and suffering is bad enough. They attach significance to that person's consent to dying, but autonomy is not the main justification for the act. Alleviation of the underlying suffering is the real concern.

- As this suggests, the Merciful Helper thinks only certain defined circumstances are good ones in which to end your life: those that involve terrible illness and/or suffering. The Freedom Lover, on the other hand, thinks (at least, for someone of sound mind) that any reason for ending your own life is a good one, as long as it is yours.
- Being concerned with agency and autonomy, Freedom Lovers are most interested in legalising assisted *suicide*. If they want to legalise voluntary euthanasia as well, it is because they are thinking of a situation in which someone might be so physically incapacitated they cannot complete the act on their own. But Merciful Helpers are much less likely to make a principled difference between assisted suicide and voluntary euthanasia. Since both lead to the main goal, as far as they are concerned – to alleviate suffering – it doesn't make much difference which is used.
- Finally – in the ideal case, anyway – Merciful Helpers have an implicit model of the self as essentially connected to others, and particularly to those the self cares for. They approve of certain positive acts of intervention in other people's lives – including when they are dying – because that is what emotions like love or compassion require.

Like the Freedom Lover, the archetype of the Merciful Helper is another abstract sketch, simplified for the sake of better understanding more complicated thought patterns, and is not supposed to represent the whole of anyone's actual mind. In terms of background ideology, it is this archetype that sets many of the terms of the assisted death discourse, not the Freedom Lover. For instance, it is the Merciful Helper's formative influence which explains why *help* or *assistance* is positively justified, not just noninterference. Helping people to die – as opposed to simply leaving them alone to end their own lives – is a positively good thing to do, on the assumption that the people in question are suffering greatly.

And it is also the presence of the Merciful Helper which explains the placing of restrictions upon who, exactly, is allowed to die. Terminally ill cohorts should be allowed to end their lives *because they are suffering badly*. That is the justification for offering them – and not other people – access to assisted death. Though they mean it kindly, Merciful Helpers believe that certain kinds of lives are so very terrible, their owners are better off dead.

There's no pain like burning

In an episode of *Yellowstone*, the TV drama series set in Montana, one of the show's main characters Kayce witnesses an explosion in a meth lab, as he drives along a deserted country road with his wife Monica. In the aftermath they discover a man on the ground, hideously burned and with his lower legs blown off. 'Kill me,' the man quietly groans.

Kayce runs to his truck to get his gun. Monica tells him she has called an ambulance and asks: 'Are there people back there?' 'Not any more,' says Kayce. The couple return to the man. 'Please kill me,' he moans again. Kayce asks his wife how long the ambulance will take. 'Forty-five minutes.' 'He ain't got forty-five minutes,' he mutters. 'There's no pain like burning.' He unholsters his gun, cocks it, and looks at Monica, who nods resignedly: 'Do it.' Kayce does.

In dramatic form, this fictional case encapsulates a dilemma whose urgency should be understandable to anyone in possession of a modicum of empathy. Another person is in terrible, terminal agony. You long for the suffering to stop. More: you want it on *their* behalf. You think it is important that they die now. What should you do?

The desire to help end someone's extreme suffering is moved by a human impulse that has appeared throughout history, albeit patchily and under different names. Aristotle talked of 'pity', though the word has since gone out of fashion: 'a feeling of pain caused by the sight of something evil, destructive or painful, which befalls one who does not deserve it, and which we might expect to befall ourselves or some friend of ours, and moreover to befall us soon'.[1] Related terms, perhaps less condescending to modern ears, are 'compassion' and 'sympathy'.

Another old-fashioned word is 'mercy'. Its connotations are often judicial, where it means something like 'leniency that goes beyond justice'. Think of a Roman emperor magnanimously allowing a favoured gladiator to live, or a judge lifting a prisoner's sentence. In Portia's famous speech from *The Merchant of Venice*, mercy – the thing whose quality 'is not strained' and 'droppeth as the gentle rain from heaven' from the sceptres of kings – 'becomes the throned monarch better than his crown'.

In the Christian tradition, mercy appears a lot, understood as magnanimous leniency from on high. God shows mercy to sinners by saving them from the fires of hell. But we have also inherited from our Christian forebears a more personal sense of the term. We can show mercy to each other by engaging in 'charitable actions by which we come to the aid of our neighbour in his spiritual and bodily necessities' including 'feeding the hungry, sheltering the homeless, clothing the naked, visiting the sick and imprisoned, and burying the dead'.[2]

What connects the two uses of 'mercy' – judicial and personal – is the presence of *alleviation*. You are helping to lift a terrible burden from someone else. From the perspective of the person receiving mercy, there is a sense of deliverance – something awful was about to happen that they were thankfully spared.

Again, Aquinas is an important influence here. He defines mercy 'as heartfelt sympathy for another's distress, impelling us to succour him if we can'. That is, he connects an internal feeling of pity or compassion to the outward action of helping. Aquinas thinks of mercy as part of the wider virtue of 'charity', understood as love of God.[3] Loving God includes loving what He loves, and that includes other people. 'Succouring' (helping) others during times of trouble is part of this.

In medieval times, acts of mercy were wildly popular. Monastics and laypeople alike founded hospitals for lepers and the syphilitic, ran houses of refuge for prostitutes, and engaged in elaborate acts of hospitality for wayfarers and pilgrims. Not surprising, then, that to end someone's life to relieve them of intractable suffering came to be known as 'mercy killing'. This term too has fallen from fashion, partly because of the unpalatably bald use of 'killing', but also because of de-Christianisation. Still, I think mercy continues to be a useful word in the context of secular discussions of assisted death, capturing one of the main sources of justification offered for its accomplishment.

Mercy is a social attitude: directed towards other people, and manifested via the action of helping them. The background conception of the self is far from the Freedom Lover's island or atom, metaphorically stuck behind fences, diligently policing boundaries to keep others out. Each self is seen as naturally – optimally, even – morally intertwined with other selves, standing in relations of care not mutually agreed beforehand. And this touches on something easy to miss in the *Yellowstone* example. Kayce shows mercy to a stranger. Yet the most familiar cases of 'mercy killing' in the original sense are preceded by the especially intense mental agony of witnessing someone you love in painful extremity.

Aquinas writes that when it comes to the suffering of those 'who are so closely united to us, as to be part of ourselves, such as our children or our parents', what we experience is more like our own suffering than simply witnessing and pitying theirs at a distance. He adds: 'we do not pity their distress, but *suffer as for our own sores*'[4] (my emphasis). This is perhaps a version of the emotion you might feel for a stranger in torment, but intensified as a function of the depth of love. The word 'compassion' – from the Latin 'to suffer with' or 'to suffer together' – conveys roughly the same idea. You are feeling something of your beloved one's pain.

In this respect, the much-publicised case of Kay Gilderdale seems more germane than that of Kayce's stranger. In 2010, she was acquitted of the attempted murder of her daughter Lynn, then aged thirty-one. Paralysed, bedridden, and tube-fed from the age of fourteen as a result of ME, Lynn had publicly expressed a wish to die on several occasions. She was unable to swallow, had microfractures in her bones, major organ damage, multiple other serious complications, and was in considerable pain.

One day in 2008, Kay discovered Lynn in the middle of administering morphine directly into her own vein. Though Kay pleaded with her to stop, Lynn insisted she wanted to die and asked her mother to get more. After an hour of discussion, Kay eventually brought further syringes, which Lynn used and then fell unconscious. Later, fearing her daughter was in distress and wishing to end things quickly, Kay administered more sedative and three syringes of air intravenously.

Lynn died some hours later of morphine toxicity. After being cleared of attempted murder, Kay told the BBC: 'I didn't want to cause her any harm, I wanted to ease her passing or her suffering ... I was worried that she was suffering and that she wasn't able to tell me.'[5]

'To put quietly and undemonstrably out to sea'

Despite his sympathetic understanding of some of the feelings involved, Aquinas did not agree with the practice of so-called mercy killing, either in the form of an assisted suicide or of euthanasia – literally meaning bringing about an 'easy death'. Just as the medieval Church outlawed suicide partly due to his influence, all the more firmly did it outlaw acts of assisted death.

In 1516 Thomas More, later Henry VIII's Lord High Chancellor and an eventual Catholic saint, appeared to toy with the idea of a compassionate assisted death service in *Utopia*, his satire of a supposedly perfect society. He pictured a service available to those whose diseases were 'not onelye uncurable, but also full of contynuall payne and anguyshe', assuming they had the permission of magistrates and priests. Given his fervent Catholicism, it seems unlikely More approved of what he was imaginatively conjuring for readers – and even if he had done, he couldn't have said so outright.[6] (Interpretive ambiguity here has not deterred supporters of assisted death services from claiming More as an ally. In 2004, Dignitas submitted evidence to the UK Parliament that quoted More extensively.[7])

Yet by the early twentieth century, some Christians – specifically, Nonconformists – were less conflicted. They found the confidence to argue that, when circumstances were grave enough and someone was pleading for it, voluntary euthanasia was not only permitted but admirable. Many of these were Unitarian clergymen and laypeople.[8] Unitarianism, already placed outside mainstream Christianity because of its denial of the divinity of Jesus, places great emphasis on freedom of conscience, good works, and socially improving campaigns, so the connection is perhaps unsurprising.

In its present incarnation, Dignity in Dying – the organisation heavily involved in rallying support for Kim Leadbeater's Terminally Ill Adults Bill – is firmly associated with secularism. But when founded in Leicester in 1935, it was called the Voluntary Euthanasia Legalisation Society (VELS), and its main architect was a Unitarian public health doctor called Charles Killick Millard.

There were various strains of ideology behind Millard's views about assisted death, partly connected to his religious faith and partly connected to the time in which he lived. Back then, there was a general worry among the intelligentsia about future populations outstripping available resources, and birth control was a hot topic. Prior to setting up VELS, Millard had been a member of the Malthusian League – a family planning organisation – and had also founded Leicester's first birth control clinic. He had a more than passing interest in eugenics.[9] It therefore seems fair to say his motives for advocating voluntary euthanasia were not solely grounded in compassion for the suffering. Nevertheless, this does seem to have been one concern of his, and he certainly understood the rhetorical power of compassion when it came to persuading others. Millard – at least some of the time – resembled a Merciful Helper.

In 1936, under Millard's guidance, the newly formed VELS proposed a bill to Parliament: the Voluntary Euthanasia (Legalisation) Bill. Its aim was to allow voluntary euthanasia for people who were twenty-one or over, of sound mind, and suffering from an incurable and fatal illness accompanied by severe pain. Millard told reporters: 'We are asking that sufferers shall be allowed to choose between a quick, painless death and a lingering one.' A *Guardian* editorial, entitled 'Merciful death', was tentatively supportive: 'Nobody who knows of the terrible suffering which incurable illness may bring in its train can doubt that this proposal deserves the most searching consideration from every citizen.'[10] Proposed safeguards included the involvement of at least one official 'euthanasia referee' appointed by the Minister of Health, who would interview the prospective candidate and, if satisfied that all conditions were met, issue a licence.

Debate of the bill in the House of Lords was framed by the understanding that euthanasia was being proposed only as a possibility for those in extreme pain, and thus was dominated by discussion of the practical meaning of emotions like mercy, compassion, and pity. Twenty-first-century notions of 'choice' and 'control' were entirely absent. One supporter, the Earl of Listowel, urged sceptical Christian hearers to note that '[a]ny Bill that would extend [the] principle of charity, of pity and compassion is surely one that is in harmony with the main body of the Christian tradition.'[11] The well-read peer charged with introducing the bill, Lord Ponsonby, attempted to claim Thomas More as an ally, along with David Hume and John Donne. Ponsonby concluded his speech in a crescendo of emotion:

> [M]ay we not spare some part of our attention to help the relief, and the humane termination of the acute anguish, of those who themselves ask to be released from continued agonies from which there is no hope of recovery? May we not unlock the door of compassion and allow the cord to be cut which tethers them to a lingering agony of hopeless and helpless suffering?

But despite such stirring sentiment, the bill was eventually defeated. An instrumental intervention had come from the King's physician, Lord Horder, and another from Lord Dawson – a man who, according to one source, 'earlier the same year had allegedly performed euthanasia on King George V, then dying painfully from cancer'.[12] Talking through euphemisms, neither of these medical men seemed particularly against euthanasia for terminal cases, but didn't want the doctor–patient relationship to be hampered by officialdom and red tape. Clumsy proceduralism could be no substitute for fine-grained judgement about when exactly to do the deed. That, under the proposed measures, officials would have to issue licences in order to permit voluntary euthanasia would turn 'the sick room into a bureau', as Dawson put it, and 'deter those who are, as I think, carrying out their mission of mercy'. Horder also talked of the interference of 'the bureau' as undermining that 'complete confidence and understanding which is one of the most satisfactory of all human relationships'; 'this relationship with the patient ... [which] enables him to put quietly and undemonstrably out to sea'.[13]

Freedom gets tempered by mercy

Back in the present day, assisted death campaigns are influenced by Freedom Lovers as well as Merciful Helpers. In a 2024 parliamentary debate of the Terminally Ill Adults Bill, 'mercy' appeared only once, but its close relative 'compassion', or 'compassionate', made an appearance 29 times. 'Choice' was mentioned 104 times, 'control' 27, and 'freedom' 11. Quite often the same MP appeared moved by both sets of considerations at once.

Dignity in Dying also sends out strategically mixed messages in this respect. Its principal activities listed at

Companies House include securing 'choice for persons at the end of life' – so far, so Freedom Lover – but it also names the goal of relieving suffering.[14] As I write, the website homepage states that: 'No one should be forced to suffer as they die. That's why we campaign to change the law to allow terminally ill people control over their death.'[15] This phrasing is as much in the idiom of the Freedom Lover as of the Merciful Helper, with its implication of suffering being 'forced' upon a person, and of taking back control.

This move towards the interests of Freedom Lovers is partly a reflection of a change in cultural priorities more broadly. As presciently anticipated by Durkheim, there was a decline in organised Christianity and a rise in Western hyperliberalism during the second half of the twentieth century. Free market economics and liberation from restrictive cultural traditions are the twin obsessions of the new creed; and there is great emphasis on autonomy, control, and choice. For this style of thinker, picturing terminally or incurably ill people actively seizing their own destinies is probably more palatable than focusing on dependence upon others.

And there is a related concern that also makes mercy look somewhat undesirable to modern thinking – or at least when cited as the only grounds for offering an assisted death service, unleavened by aspects of the Freedom Lover's viewpoint. Essentially, Merciful Helpers are making a negative value judgement about the quality of someone else's life. In our hyperliberal times, this is quite an unfashionable way of thinking. Secular, relativist sensibilities are uncomfortable with strong opinions about the value of particular kinds of life. Such reservations are a better fit with the perspective of the Freedom Lover, constitutionally unwilling to move past subjective perceptions and private decisions to so-called objective moral facts. Freedom Lovers hold that – at least, once soundness of mind has been ascertained – any reason is a good reason for you to seek an early death, as long as it's yours. And they are not particularly inclined to grant powerful people the right to make paternalistic value judgements about the value of a life, which might turn out to differ from its owner's personal assessment.

But despite all this, the Merciful Helper remains a powerful ethical archetype in assisted death discourse – not as visible as it used to be, perhaps, but still very much around. And a very good bit of evidence is that in existing legislation, limits are placed upon the kinds of people eligible for assisted death services. Whereas the arguments of the Freedom Lover would seem to include everyone in their scope, the influence of the Merciful Helper explains why in practice only certain groups get the benefits of assisted death services. Merciful Helpers think only certain kinds of lives are bearable. They want to help lives that are unbearable to end.

A difference between archetypes

Let's pause briefly here to further develop the contrast between the Freedom Lover and Merciful Helper archetypes. In particular I want to emphasise a difference between their respective aims that will have big implications for what is to come.

As we know, the Freedom Lover comes from an angle of non-intervention (at least, where an individual contemplating suicide is of sound mind) – protecting the supposed right to end your own life if you see fit. The Freedom Lover is not especially concerned with approved reasons to end a life. They don't want to spend much time second-guessing a suicidal person's reasons, and they don't want anyone else to do so either. The owner of that particular life and that particular body should be in charge, for better or worse.

The Merciful Helper, in contrast, wants to give an account of the limited circumstances in which it is a good thing to help end someone else's life. Though likely to agree consent is important, they are not particularly interested in protecting autonomy for its own sake. Instead they want to invoke a certain kind of severe suffering as the main ethical justification.

But this means they cannot agree with the Freedom Lover that any individual who asks for help to die should just be given it. In other words, unlike the Freedom Lover, they are *absolutely committed* to second-guessing the reasons of suicidal people – or at least they should be, if they are scrupulous. They should insist upon checking that whatever suffering is present is grave and irremediable enough to morally justify a very definitive, lethal form of help.

Suffering changes

The Merciful Helper archetype has changed over time. The old-fashioned ideal of the family doctor, getting to know his patients well and treating them throughout their lives, is now largely unknown or only dimly remembered. This was the upper-class medical model presupposed by Lords Horder and Dawson when they worried about bureaucrats disrupting the essential personal relationship between doctor and patient, threatening his ability to mercifully release the patient at what seemed to him exactly the right time. In contemporary healthcare systems such as the UK's, you are lucky if you meet the same doctor twice.

Another change is in the way suffering is pictured. In Charles Killick Millard's day, the thing to be relieved by assisted death was, unambiguously, pain and other forms of severe bodily discomfort, and the suffering that these directly caused. These days though, the burden to be lifted is conceptualised more widely to include 'psychological' or 'mental' suffering too.

Not all bodily pain causes suffering – some people say they enjoy a bit of deliberate pain, and I see no reason to argue. Others can ignore moderate amounts of it. But most pain, and especially unsought pain, causes suffering; and severe pain perhaps always does. In this book, whenever I talk about treating or relieving 'pain' or 'bodily pain', I am assuming it is pain that causes suffering to the person who has it (that is: they aren't indifferent or even enjoying it). And I find it is useful to make a distinction between, on the one hand, the sort of suffering directly caused by bodily pain and discomfort (which I'll mostly just refer to as 'pain' or 'bodily pain'), and, on the other, psychological suffering. Of course, great psychological suffering is often caused by bodily pain, either in its presence or the anticipation of it. But they are not exactly the same in conceptual terms.

Psychological suffering includes familiar negative affective states like depression, fear, anxiety, worry, and grief. We all know what these feelings are – it is impossible to go through life without meeting at least some of them. The term 'psychological' is not meant to denote scepticism that such forms of suffering are any less real than bodily pain, but only that they are intimately tied up with the conscious mind and what goes on there. On the whole, they are more emotional than sensory, and can happen in someone's life without bodily pain being present at all.

Equally, and perhaps confusingly for our purposes, psychological suffering can sometimes cause pain experienced somewhere in the body. Intense grief can make your chest hurt, and in rare cases can even cause heart damage. Still, not all psychological suffering causes bodily pain. And a further complication is that, in one sense at least, psychological suffering is 'physical' in origin – for the brain and nervous system are centrally implicated in all of it. But – to repeat – this sort of suffering is not inevitably experienced as located somewhere in the body. (To try to make this contrast clearer, I use the term 'bodily pain' rather than the more usual 'physical pain'.)

Many assisted death services aim to relieve *both* bodily pain and psychological suffering under the catch-all description of 'suffering'. Canada's law mentions an experience of 'enduring physical or psychological suffering that is intolerable'. In the Netherlands, the concern is suffering that is 'unbearable with no prospect of improvement'. In the Australian state of Victoria, a disease must be 'causing suffering to the person that cannot be relieved in a manner that the person finds tolerable'. Leadbeater's proposed UK legislation makes no formal mention of suffering at all; but still, it is clear that a diagnosis of terminal illness is being used as shorthand for the likelihood of it. Presenting early death as a morally urgent option for this particular cohort – and only this particular cohort – would look incomprehensible otherwise.

It is an interesting question why psychological suffering became prominent in the assisted death discourse, rather than cleaving strictly to the object of relieving bodily pain. It is perhaps partly because, as we will be seeing later, advances in scientific understanding of pain have made treatments for it much more sophisticated and widely available. At the same time there has been a widespread 'medicalisation' of concepts of psychological suffering, approaching states like anxiety and depression as pathologies to be treated rather than inevitable aspects of life to be patiently endured. But whatever its origins, the consequences of this discursive shift – from death as a proposed solution to intense bodily pain, to death as a proposed solution to the kinds of psychological suffering caused more generally by serious illness and disability – are legion, and we will explore many of them in chapters to come.

For now, we can simply note how this widens the scope of

arguments for assisted death services in practice. One argument frequently made is that a certain kind of impoverished 'quality of life' during terminal or incurable illness is too dreadful to be borne. Shape-shifting from the Freedom Lover we met in the last chapter, A. C. Grayling makes this sort of Merciful Helper-style point when he argues that:

> A 'right to life' cannot mean a right to merely bare existence. It must at least mean a right to a certain minimum experienced quality of life. For example: if someone were confined in a small cage and provided with nothing more than bread and water in perpetuity, this would scarcely be to accord him a life in any acceptable sense ... [W]hen a life of suffering or disability has come to be experienced as below that [minimally acceptable] level of quality ... then in the light of the individual's right to terminate his life, he should be accorded assistance if he cannot himself implement the means of doing so.[16]

Basically, this argument says: if your life is one of terrible suffering, and you request help to end it, it is morally appropriate for another person to step in, assuming you can't. (Grayling is unusual in confining the scope of his argument only to those who are too incapacitated to end their own lives.) This is appropriate, he thinks, not just because you asked for it but also – and crucially – because your 'quality of life' has fallen below a minimum acceptable standard.

The trouble is, though, that if the suffering in question meant only 'intense bodily pain', then with the invention of good pain relief, the argument would become less persuasive. Generally speaking, if your quality of life falls below a certain minimum standard there are usually a number of things which can be done to make things better, rather than to help you end your life altogether. The starving man in Grayling's cage example might be released and given food, for instance, which is surely a more merciful option than helping to kill him. Equally, these days it is often possible to manage severe pain. The general moral is one that will recur throughout this book: wherever there are less drastic approaches available than administering an early death, for the sake of true mercy those options should be pursued first.

The modern-day Merciful Helper can avoid this sort of objection by claiming that what should be alleviated is not just bodily agony specifically but suffering more generally. Suffering is taken to encompass feelings like depression, hopelessness, and intense anxiety about future states of bodily deterioration. Even without the immediate presence of physical torment, you can still feel that your life is one of 'bare existence'. Thus the ethical rationale for Merciful Helping appears – for now – to survive unscathed.

'My family won't have to see me suffer'

When you think about the ethics of assisted death services, perhaps your mind goes first to cases involving an urgent crisis of bodily pain. But this is not in fact the only, or even the most frequent, kind of modern case. When researchers in Oregon and Canada asked applicants about their reasons for seeking an assisted death, the presence of pain came surprisingly far down the list of commonly given answers.[17] Respondents were often more concerned with what would happen in the future than what was physically happening to them now.

This is a change worth pausing over. Effectively it moves us far from examples of so-called 'mercy killing': Kayce shooting the burns victim in Yellowstone, or even Kay Gilderdale injecting her distressed daughter. Both mercy and its motivating emotion, compassion, are classically supposed to involve the helper suffering with another person in the moment of their agony. In an assisted death service, death is often supplied before any agony kicks in.

This change has a strange and rather unnerving consequence. In 2024, posters sponsored by Dignity in Dying appeared in London Underground stations, depicting a glamorous young woman dancing energetically and happily round her kitchen. Her image was overlaid with the words 'My dying wish is my family won't see me suffer. And I won't have to.' Clearly, viewers were not supposed to think of this woman suffering in any way at all at the moment the photograph was taken. The logic of the poster changed the familiar locus of moral pressure: not calling for compassion or mercy towards someone suffering badly because of their own terminal or incurable illness, but rather nudging anticipatory compassion from the ill person herself towards the psychological suffering of loved ones looking on. If you are terminally ill, the poster seemed to chide, deciding to opt for assisted death can be an act of compassionate concern for your family and friends – mercifully sparing *them* the eventual burden of watching you suffer.

This subtle shift of emphasis often goes unnoticed. Arguments for assisted death services imply they are beneficial, not only for what they can do for terminally ill people directly, but because they can relieve the psychological suffering of relatives and friends. Here is Sarah Wootton, chief executive of Dignity in Dying, commenting in a press release during the committee stage of the Terminally Ill Adults Bill:

> As the Committee's detailed, technical discussions continue, it's people like Nat, Elise and Jenny who remind us who and what this Bill is for. They have watched the proceedings from the public gallery this week. Each of them has terminal cancer and is currently denied a safe, legal

choice to die on their own terms here at home. Each has seen loved ones suffer agonising deaths.[18]

Such examples are chosen for the amount of meaning they can pack in. One message for terminally ill people says: assisted death will be good for you; it will spare you terrible suffering and offer you a choice. And there is an implication for loved ones: assisted death will be good for you too; it will relieve you of the mental agony of watching the person you love suffering. But this latter message can then be aimed back at the ill person, reframed in terms of a call to compassion rather than self-interest. It says: choosing an assisted death will be a mercy for those who love you, as well as for yourself.

Better than the alternative?

We have just seen that an assisted death service can be spun as merciful in a number of directions. Here is one more. It is often suggested that an assisted death service mercifully spares terminally ill and suffering people the burden of having to kill themselves alone. Solo suicide is lonely, messy, potentially painful in its own right, and might not work. It is also horrific for whoever comes across your body or has to retrieve it. In his book against assisted death services, Kevin Yuill quotes Compassion and Choices, a US lobbying group, who said on their website at the time (my italics): 'Too many suffer needlessly. Too many endure unrelenting pain. *Too many turn to violent means at the end of life.*'[19] Put like this, the state-managed version of an early death looks better. It is less violent, not as lonely, and it is easier to deal with your remains afterwards.

In fact, though, claiming assisted death services count as merciful rests on a questionable assumption: that most users of an assisted death service would have chosen solo suicide, had the assisted version not been available. This is undoubtedly false. What *is* true is that a diagnosis of terminal illness increases the risk of suicide somewhat. A 2022 study found that for 'low-survival' cancer patients, one year after diagnosis the rate of suicide had doubled, from 9.5 to 21.6 people in 100,000. People with degenerative neurological conditions had the highest rise in risk, to 114.5 per 100,000 patients; though this was an extrapolation from a database finding of 11 suicides in total, and it was noted that 'the estimate was imprecise due to the low number of suicides'. This study also found that the 'increase in risk was more pronounced in the first six months after diagnosis or first treatment', after which it started to drop.[20]

Important as these findings are, they don't establish that, out of all the people with a terminal diagnosis who also wish for an assisted death, most or many will try to take their own lives alone if not offered one first. For the still relatively few who do, based on this evidence it might be argued that the presence of an 'easy' assisted death service would have been a merciful option, relative to the much harder unassisted kind. But this argument needs to be weighed up against the fact that, with an assisted death service in the vicinity, many who would never have contemplated the hard route will end up taking the easy one.

This point is backed up by research into solo suicide. In his book *Why People Die by Suicide* clinical psychologist Thomas Joiner – whose own father died in a violent suicide – meticulously documents the way that people with suicidal thinking usually have to 'work up' to the 'ability to enact lethal self-injury' in order to overcome the basic fear of pain nearly all of us have. A person can acquire high tolerance for self-injury through more minor acts of deliberate self-harm; or through accidental bodily injuries acquired in the course of risk-taking behaviour; or through having been exposed to dangerous and abusive situations in the past. As Al Alvarez wrote of his own failed attempt: 'I built up to the act carefully and for a long time, with a kind of blank pertinacity.'[21] And we might also consider Kurt Cobain, of whom Joiner writes:

> Through repeated exposure and practice, a person initially afraid of needles, heights, and guns later became a daily self-injecting drug user, someone who climbed and dangled from thirty-foot scaffolding during concerts ... and someone who enjoyed shooting guns. Regarding guns, Cobain initially felt that they were barbaric and wanted nothing to do with them; later he agreed to go with his friend to shoot guns but would not get out of the car; on later excursions, he got out of the car but would not touch the guns; and on still later trips, he agreed to let his friend show him how to aim and fire. Cobain died by self-inflicted gunshot wound in 1994 at the age of twenty-seven.[22]

Most people are like Cobain at the beginning of this desensitisation process, not the end. They cannot bring themselves to radically self-injure, even if in the grip of suicidal thinking. On the other hand, once an assisted death service is offering the option of an easy death managed by medics, the psychological requirement of a high tolerance for self-injury becomes much less relevant. For many applicants, suicide only becomes viable at all given provision of a service. These individuals are not in fact being mercifully spared a violent, lonely death, because that sort of death was not otherwise on the cards.

Perhaps you wonder whether, in pointing this out, I have inadvertently provided a separate justification for assisted death. If a person who really wants to end his life cannot bring himself to self-harm, isn't this a justification for an institution stepping in to help him complete the task? But the state is not there to help us do everything we cannot do ourselves. And if we return for a moment to the Freedom Lover archetype, there is no obvious source of support here. Even a Freedom Lover willing to admit that obstacles to true autonomy can come from within the mind is unlikely to treat the aversion to self-destruction as one such case. Meanwhile, Merciful Helpers are likely to say that we need to look at the nature of the suffering involved – is it so awful that granting an early death looks like a good solution? If it is, they will think help is justified, whether the individual in question feels able to complete the task himself or not. If it isn't, they won't.

A second questionable aspect of the idea that an easy assisted death is more 'merciful' than a violent solo one is the implication that there are only two relevant alternatives for a terminally ill, severely suffering person: a) solo suicide, which is lonely, painful, messy; and b) supported, painless, 'clean' assisted death. In fact, there is a very important alternative to add here: a scenario where the terminally ill person's remaining life is made qualitatively better, in ways that don't involve provision of an early death, whether solo or assisted. Decent palliative care from doctors, good social and financial support, love and solace from friends and family are just some of the ways in which both suffering and suicidal thinking in the terminally ill can be lessened. I will explore these aspects in depth later; but it is important to mention them here too.

A right to life, resurrected?

I return now to a puzzle we identified in the last chapter. What justifies the Freedom Lover's insistence on a 'right' to be helped to die by others, as opposed to a simple right to noninterference in your own private decisions? And especially when – unfortunately – most people already have access to the means and the opportunity, assuming they can eventually overcome their own natural fear of self-destruction?

The logic of mercy might seem to help paper over the gap. As we now know, the Merciful Helper thinks it is a good thing to help other people who are suffering terribly – whether or not they are physically immobilised or can already find the 'open door' for themselves. Merciful Helpers believe that this is what showing mercy requires. But still: ideally the Freedom Lover wouldn't use the Merciful Helper as argumentative cover here, given the differences in their philosophical motivations.

I think at least two answers are available. The first of these, conducive to the original terms of the Freedom Lover, would say that the individual has a negative right – understood as a protected permission, described in Chapter One – to enter into a voluntary arrangement with another person who will help them die. As long as the assistance is offered willingly, they each have the right to see their joint project protected from interference – in other words, a 'right to die' understood as a right to kill oneself without intervention, but scaled up a bit. The imaginary fence beloved of the Freedom Lover goes round the pair of them together, keeping interfering busybodies at bay.

But if this indeed is the background thinking, it is hard to see why people are arguing for a whole assisted death *service*, when they could have just argued for the simple decriminalisation of private acts of assistance – as indeed was the case in Switzerland, before outfits like Dignitas came along. A doctor wouldn't need to be involved, nor any medical institutions. So perhaps simple decriminalisation is not what is wanted after all.

The second answer – and a better fit with what supporters of assisted death services actually say – is that whether or not they know it, they have effectively switched discourses and are no longer talking about freedom or negative rights of noninterference at all. Instead they are invoking what is sometimes called a 'positive' right – a different ball game. They share the concerns of the Merciful Helper about alleviating terrible suffering but have folded these concerns into a view which says that each person is owed a basic quality of life, free of terrible suffering, by 'right'.

Early liberal thinkers tended to be minimalist about rights, sticking to only a few core obligations. As we have seen, rights during this period were thought of more like fences keeping other people out than things which gave other people positive moral obligations to do things for you. But by the twentieth century, lists of rights had got longer, and they had been officially rebranded as the more glamorous 'human rights': universal claim rights, supposed to apply to all of us, cross-culturally and pan-historically. Documents such as the Universal Declaration of Human Rights added a new kind of right to the familiar list, not just to do with noninterference but aimed at positively providing basic goods and services from the state – things it was presumed everybody needs, such as food, housing, education, and meaningful work.

Earlier in this chapter, we heard A. C. Grayling saying that a 'right to life' implied 'a right to a certain minimum experienced quality of life'. Here, I think, he was not rehearsing the old point about a right to noninterference. He was saying that, alongside basic needs for food and shelter and so forth, the (universal) need for a minimally acceptable quality of life generates a (universal) need for an easy death at the appropriate time. And this need supposedly generates a moral obligation upon medical institutions to offer assisted death, if the circumstances are bad enough. A positive right to a minimal standard of life means you have a positive right to an assisted death, if your own life fails to meet that standard.

Some will find this approach strangely defeatist in the face of social injustice – and I would agree – but let's ignore that for now. We can accept there is a universal need for a basic quality of life, and this includes having food, shelter, education, meaningful work, etc. Let's also accept that this basic quality of life includes being free of illness-related pain so severe it impairs normal function. Still, for every need, there is usually more than one way to meet it, and here is no different. As intimated earlier – and to be explored in detail later – these days the medical specialty known as palliative care can supply substantial relief from many of the physical challenges of advanced disease and dying. This means that the case for meeting the need by supplying an assisted death, rather than by providing adequate palliative care during life, is not yet made. (It is true that adequate palliative care is not actually available to all who need it. But this doesn't affect this part of our discussion, which is about what should happen, not what does happen.)

There are universal needs and perceived good-to-haves. These are not the same, though an anxious, acquisitive society like ours often confuses the two. Let's agree for the sake of argument that universal needs give rise to positive rights, with knock-on obligations placed upon state-backed institutions. There is a universal need for, and so a positive right to, food, let's say – but not to your favourite kind of meal. There's a universal need for, and so a positive right to, adequate shelter, but not to a three-storey house located exactly where you want to live; a universal need for, and so a positive right to, meaningful work, but not to the job of your dreams. Equally, if we allow there is a positive right to a basic quality of life, including freedom from severe pain, this doesn't mean there is a positive right to an assisted death, as long as there are other ways to reach the same goal.

I imagine someone objecting at this point: what if my goal is just to die the way I wish? Why shouldn't I be allowed to decide to shun pain relief, and to take death instead? This will sound a compelling response to some Freedom Lovers, but only because it superficially resembles the assertion of a right to noninterference in private suicidal projects. But that is not the issue here; we are talking about a joint project, and a demand that someone else help you. The presence of great pain and suffering is being offered as the pretext for *assisted* death from another person: a quality of life which falls below the minimum thanks to terrible pain, and to which assisted death is being proposed as the only real merciful solution. If in fact there are other approaches which get rid of pain, then an early death is no longer the only game in town – and from the perspective of careful mercy would seem to fall quickly down the rankings.

But what about if we move to the wider and now more popular conception of suffering already noted, including psychological suffering? Can the presence of things like depression and anxiety also make for a quality of life that falls below an acceptable standard? And if so, does this generate a universal need for – in other words, a positive right to – relief in the form of assisted death from medical institutions?

One quick but reasonable answer is that there are remedies for things like depression and anxiety too. But this reply, though true, doesn't get to the heart of the problem with the proposal. In a nutshell, it is this: once deeper causes of suffering are addressed, a positive human right to a life free of even terrible psychological suffering (about the near prospect of death, or anything else) does not exist. Humans may have a positive right to life free of many of the traditional causes of terrible psychological suffering – but that is a different point.

To be clear: we aren't discussing whether it is a morally good or admirable thing to relieve the terrible psychological suffering of others. It most certainly is a good thing; and much of the rest of this book presupposes this point. We are discussing the much narrower question of whether each of us is owed the relief of terrible psychological suffering by *right*, in a way that imposes a moral obligation upon relevant state-backed institutions to provide such relief, meaning that they fail in their obligation if they don't. There is lots of ethically admirable behaviour which has nothing to do with responding to a person's fundamental rights.

In the manner of Thomas More, let us imagine a highly unrealistic Utopia: a place where basic material needs for food, water, housing, meaningful work, etc. are already being met for everybody on the planet, and where rights to bodily noninterference and safety are respected too. And let's also imagine that proper medical care is available for everybody when they need it, including palliative care. In this sort of imaginary place, and with those needs cleared up, there would be no further obligation upon institutions to supply citizens with lives free of terrible psychological suffering more generally – and perhaps especially not psychological suffering about the prospect of death, the fact of which is outside human control.

One sign of this is that heavy suffering is often detached from material needs altogether. Classically, people who seem to have everything sometimes suffer enormously too; a point well made in the Bible and by many thinkers before and since. Durkheim developed this idea, describing a second kind of suicide brought on by prevailing social forces alongside the 'egoistic' suicide described in the last chapter – what he called the 'anomic suicide'. Human desire does not have a natural limit, he says, but is socially determined; it rushes to fill whatever vacuum is provided. Stable standards of living act as a container for, and a regulator of, desire: you tend to want only what you are likely to be able to get. But where economic conditions are rapidly deteriorating or (perhaps surprisingly) improving, desires become unregulated, and what is longed for gets out of sync with what is available. Suffering and increased suicide rates are the result, he writes, but not because there is something objectively wrong. Anomie is a 'disease of the infinite'; there is no limit to the superfluities you might desperately long for as a result of social determinants, nor the suffering you might feel when you don't get them.[23]

For this sort of reason, there would be little sense in interpreting the prevention of great suffering, detached from material causes, as itself a 'human right'. And another indicator is that cultural attitudes radically differ on the value of such suffering, in a way they don't tend to differ on the value of minimally life-sustaining amounts of food, water, or shelter. Buddhism sees it as a means of spiritual awakening. Some Christian traditions view it as bringing you closer to God. Jung and his psychoanalytic followers thought deep depression could be creative and self-transformative. And many different philosophical traditions think of death-anxiety, in particular, as a crucial and enlightening part of the human condition, usefully forcing us to reflect upon our finite natures. If the absence of psychological suffering really was a universal need, there would not be such plenitude of diverging views about its value.

No right to die

This is a good moment to gather up thoughts about the idea of a general 'right to die', parts of which appeared in the previous chapter too. The uncomfortable truth is that most people are already free to end their lives, if they are really determined to. The refusal to provide an assisted death service in the vicinity does not affect this fact. Equally, I have argued, there is no 'right to die' in the sense of any general negative right to non-interference from others in an act of self-destruction. This is true of assisted suicides just as much as solo projects. It is not just the fact that you might be in the grip of an internal threat to true autonomy such as mental illness or addiction. It is also that you might be gravely harming the interests of close family members who depend upon and love you. It might be right to end your own life sometimes, in some particular contexts; but there is no general 'right to die' in this sense.

Meanwhile, as I have just argued, there is no positive human right to an *assisted* death, understood as placing a moral obligation upon medical or other institutions to help you do it. Where life is being made dreadful in terms of pain and psychological suffering, we can agree that there is a right to receive proper relief to address some root causes – including during terminal illness and disability – but there are other less drastic and effective ways to solve the problem than for doctors to offer an early death.

Still, despite these large flaws in the background reasoning, the Freedom Lover archetype remains a powerful force in campaigns for assisted death, and we cannot see it off so easily. For the next two chapters, I will continue with my focus on the Merciful Helper; but the Freedom Lover lingers in the background, making it much harder for critics of assisted death services to fight a battle on two fronts. We will run into this apparently irresistible set of ideas again in due time.

3

Suffering What You Fear

Uncharted seas

When someone receives an assisted death, they don't just die. They are being killed. Either it is by suicide, with the help of other people; or – as in the case of voluntary euthanasia – another person kills them outright. Life is deliberately ended, unnaturally and earlier than otherwise would have occurred. Death is the intentionally produced outcome.

During parliamentary scrutiny of Kim Leadbeater's Terminally Ill Adults Bill, there was heated discussion about who should oversee the process of accepting and denying requests for assistance in death. In the end Leadbeater opted for two doctors, followed by a panel composed of a social worker, a psychiatrist, and a legal professional. The whole system would be overseen by a judge. But a more fundamental question remained unanswered. Namely: assuming that not everyone who asks for an assisted death gets one, how should professionals in medicine, social care, or the law decide which suicides will be legitimate and which won't be?

Our current approach to suicide is to try to prevent it happening, no matter what. There is never a question of working out on a suicidal person's behalf whether their proposed course of action is a fitting one. This includes in healthcare settings. Where there is a proven link between certain medical conditions and increased suicide risk – as in illnesses such as Parkinson's, which raise the likelihood of depression – doctors are alert for signs of suicidal thinking. If signs are discovered, this is treated as an urgent problem. Yet when it comes to assisted deaths, professionals are suddenly supposed to be nuanced about who may receive an early death and who may not. The question is: how?

Though assisted death is not a medical procedure, it is widely treated as such. The gold standard for medical decisions is something called 'informed consent'. The broad idea is that patients be equipped, as far as possible, to make decisions in their own best interests. Doctors are not deciding for the patient, though they may advise. Patients contemplating a procedure are supposed to be made aware of all known or suspected relevant information: what is likely to happen; what are common or serious possible complications; what alternatives there are, either in terms of other forms of treatment or doing nothing; and what the consequences of choosing those alternatives might be. And doctors are also supposed to be clear about what they themselves don't know.

Unfortunately, you can't apply the model of informed consent to assisted death. One troubling issue – albeit ultimately solvable – is a lack of information about the lethal drugs used, and whether they make for a genuinely painless end. There have been reported cases of nausea, vomiting, gastritis, regurgitation, and seizures. In Oregon, annual complication rates have been as high as 14.8% – probably a conservative number, given that most deaths take place without a physician present. As one 2022 study put it: 'The prevalence of reported and suspected complications suggest there stands a risk of subjecting patients to a less than peaceful death and their loved ones to a traumatic bereavement.'[1] This is obviously worrying. Most people seeking an assisted death would be much less likely to apply if they suspected this was the case.

But there's a deeper philosophical problem too. Informed consent requires something called 'mental capacity' (also known as 'mental competence'). In the proposed UK system, what counts as mental capacity for the purposes of deciding to have an assisted death looks likely to be defined by the Mental Capacity Act 2005. This Act says that a person must be able to 'understand the information relevant to the decision', 'to retain that information', 'to use or weigh that information as part of the process of making the decision', and 'to communicate' that decision to the doctor. But how do doctors themselves get a handle on what relevant information to give the patient?

The basic issue here is that medical treatments are designed to be life-sustaining, not life-destroying. This is so deeply presupposed by the practice of medicine, it barely needs to be said. Patients usually want to get better, even if they sometimes differ with doctors about methods. Doctors assume that patients want to get better, and also want that outcome for patients too. This is the shared basis upon which discussions of capacity take place. Doctors have a reasonable grasp of the benefits and risks of life-sustaining treatment, and about what decision might be in a patient's interests. Once this is explained, it is up to the patient whether or not to go ahead with a particular procedure. And if the patient is judged to lack the capacity to make a decision (something which is relatively unusual), doctors will know at least vaguely what a good outcome looks like, so that they can work towards that on the patient's behalf.

But once doctors move out of this familiar territory, they are understandably at sea. A person actively choosing immediate death by taking poison, when they could have gone on living – at least for a few days, weeks, or months, and perhaps longer – is not like choosing to have a life-sustaining operation with known benefits and costs. If a person asks a clinician what will happen after a self-chosen death, most will not know how to reply. The clinician is not equipped to get into a discussion of the existence or otherwise of an afterlife; weigh the loss of what is being left behind against the benefit of any suffering avoided; or discuss the moral consequences of your own death for your family. Some doctors may fill in the gaps with strong personal opinions; but in doing so they will have moved well beyond the normal boundaries of medical expertise.

In practice, this affects informed consent in two ways. First, the doctor doesn't know what information to communicate to help patients judge whether self-extinction is in their best interests. All a doctor can offer is information about how the physical process of ending life works (as far as they know, given the lack of evidence about methods just mentioned); and about what therapeutic alternatives might be chosen instead. Second, because of the first problem, the doctor doesn't know how to judge whether the patient has the mental capacity to understand, let alone 'weigh', all the information relevant to the decision. For it is unclear to everyone, including the clinicians, what such information even amounts to.

It is partly for these reasons that the Royal College of Psychiatrists responded critically to Leadbeater's bill by declaring that '[t]he Mental Capacity Act does not provide a framework for assessing decisions about ending one's own life'.[2] Or as King's College London's Complex Life and Death Decisions research group put the point in written evidence: whether to choose an assisted death 'is essentially an existential matter'.[3] Unlike with standard tests of mental capacity, there are no agreed-upon protocols for deciding whether someone is existentially competent or not to take their own life.

Critics may object that doctors know how to assess mental capacity in decisions about whether to *withdraw* treatment towards the end of life; and that it is scarcely a stretch to extend such expertise to providing assisted death as well. Actually, in practice many clinicians will confess that this too is a difficult matter. But in additional evidence to the committee, the Complex Life and Death Decisions group noted important differences between these two situations.[4]

While refusing treatment may lead to the patient's natural death, it is unlikely to do so immediately (although it sometimes does). Both accepting treatment and refusing it are events that happen during the patient's life. Equally, whatever happens as a result of the patient's decision over the following days, weeks, or months will also be events that happen during the patient's life. Based on expertise, the doctor will usually be able to offer informed comment about what may happen in physical terms, and so about what might be in the patient's interests – reasonably attributing to them a wish to live comfortably during that period. But this is not the case with assisted death. Here the alternatives supposedly to be explored in an informed discussion are not 'living with treatment' versus 'living with no treatment', but the passive continuation of life versus an actively supplied, immediate extinction of life.

And there is also the fact of the doctor's own responsibility. When a patient refuses treatment after being given all relevant medical information, by definition the doctor does nothing much further. In contrast, where someone chooses an assisted death, the doctor who will carry it out is made an active participant in a killing. You may protest that, at least in the prospective UK system, it is 'only' a suicide; but the whole rationale of the elaborate set-up is that help from a medic is required. It is not solo suicide but *assisted* suicide. This makes it even more vital that the doctor is able to advise the patient correctly beforehand. The question remains: how? You can't just default to the patient's perspective; you wouldn't do that in any other medical context. As a doctor, you are not just a blind instrument of your patient's will.

So assisted death puts medical professionals in new ethical territory. Deliberately participating in the practice means that death would not otherwise have happened at that precise moment. It might not have happened for weeks, months, or even years. That is a heavy burden for anyone to bear, and all the more so for those who entered their profession intent on saving life, not taking it. Most will surely take the responsibility seriously, but have scant information upon which to draw.

On the other hand, some are very confident they have all the answers.

'The most compassionate individual I have ever met'

By the time he became famous, Dr Jack Kevorkian was a sprightly sixty-something on a mission. He wanted to get both assisted suicide and voluntary euthanasia legalised in the US, and was prepared to do whatever it took. By all accounts a child prodigy, he had become obsessed with death early on in life. His parents had each lost nearly every living relative in the Armenian genocide of 1915, meeting in Michigan as refugees and making a new life there together.

A brilliantly clever man with a cold disregard for ordinary mortals' feelings, Kevorkian's specialism was inventing Heath Robinson contraptions to solve medical challenges. 'We would take anything that was taboo [or] untouchable because of religion ... or emotions,' he later recalled about these enthusiasms.[5] These included photographing the eyes of dying patients to study the earliest post-mortem changes as blood vessels in the retina fragmented. It is said he would sometimes jokily arrive at the bed of a dying person wearing a black armband.[6] Keen to find a means of carrying out transfusions on the battlefield, he experimented on himself with the blood of cadavers, catching hepatitis C in the process. He also argued that convicts should be allowed to volunteer for painless medical experiments, and that those on death row should have their organs harvested after execution.

Unsurprisingly, none of these ideas took off. But eventually Kevorkian found his métier. After watching his mother die painfully from cancer, he became interested in assisted death. He built a 'suicide machine' out of household tools and toy parts, which he called the Thanatron. It would inject painkillers and poisons intravenously when its user pulled a trigger. In 1990 he drove a volunteer suffering from Alzheimer's, Janet Adkins, to a beauty spot in his van and then hooked her up to his machine. After it was over, he called the police. He was arrested, tried, and acquitted by a sympathetic jury, something that would happen a further three times.

During the next eight years, as his lawyer told it, Kevorkian participated in the deaths of 130 people. All the while, his appetite for publicity grew. At one point he announced to the world he had harvested a kidney from an assisted suicide case, despite knowing that no legal donation service could take it. In 1998 he took things further, euthanising a patient on camera without the intermediary help of the Thanatron. Here he found the limits of judicial toleration and was convicted of second-degree murder. Eight years later he got out of prison and then tried to run for Congress. He became a regular on chat shows and was the subject of a TV biopic, where he was played by Al Pacino. He died – apparently of natural causes – in 2011.

For some, Kevorkian was a pioneering medical hero and 'the most compassionate individual I have ever met', as an admiring colleague put it in an obituary.[7] Others disagreed.

He was not in fact a clinician but a pathologist, with little experience of dealing with living patients. A 1997 investigation by the *Detroit Free Press* found that 60% of those Kevorkian helped to die were not terminally ill. In some cases autopsies revealed 'no anatomical evidence of disease' and others had not complained of any pain beforehand.[8]

For those who were in pain, Kevorkian had a patchy record of working with specialists to explore palliative alternatives; and he did not always consult psychiatric colleagues, including about people with a history of depression. He also tended to build in minimal time for reflection, sometimes bestowing death on a first encounter. And he could be negligent in seeking information about background issues that might be motivating someone's desire to die. In one instance, he reportedly 'failed to uncover multiple allegations of spousal abuse and debts of more than $320,000'.[9]

Viewing the pattern of his decision-making as a whole, nobody could claim that Kevorkian was reliably merciful (and nor for that matter did he care much about real autonomy). In fact, he was reckless and sometimes cruel. He did not confine himself to genuinely severe suffering nor even to bodily illness; and there were other forms of help he could have offered that would have been more appropriate and proportionate, and less horribly final. Like some other brilliant people of a scientific mindset, he was arrogant, cavalier, and missing an empathy chip.

The lure of the 'simple' solution

Most people on both sides of the assisted death debate now agree that lone operators like Kevorkian should not be allowed to make up the rules as they go along. Legal assisted death services have since emerged, with supposedly strict protocols to try to avoid the sorts of outcomes he produced. Yet some of these seem no better than loose-cannon individuals.

Many systems have disquieting aspects. In Belgium and the Netherlands, a growing number of people in good bodily health but with diagnoses of personality disorders and depression are euthanised on request. Death rates are rising each year, including for applicants in their twenties. Also in the Netherlands, there is evidence that several people with learning disabilities and autism have chosen an assisted death, citing reasons exclusively or mainly to do with their condition: 'feeling unable to cope with the world', 'changes around them', or 'a struggle to form friendships'.[10] In Oregon, meanwhile, early deaths have been granted for treatable conditions including diabetes, anorexia, and complications from a hernia.[11] In Australia, there are reports of hospital patients opting for assisted death because they don't wish to enter a care home; or because they are under pressure from family and confused under the influence of pain medication.[12]

But of all the systems in which things seem to be going wrong, Canada's is the most notorious. In 2023, 4.7% of all Canadian deaths were due to 'medical assistance in dying', or 'MAID' for short. There are reports of people being granted an assisted death because of non-terminal conditions such as chemical sensitivity to cigarette smoke, the effects of long Covid, or blindness.[13] Poverty, homelessness, a lack of daily support, and feeling like a burden mean that many are choosing early death as an alternative to struggling on.

One applicant for an assisted death told a reporter she had no income and was unable to access food banks. 'An increase [in income support] is the only thing that could save my life. I have no other reason to want to apply for assisted suicide, other than I simply cannot afford to keep on living.'[14] A woman with motor neurone disease opted for assisted death because she wasn't offered enough carer hours at home.

'Ultimately it was not a genetic disease that took me out, it was a system,' her farewell note read.[15]

As is the case in Belgium and the Netherlands, plans to extend the Canadian service to physically healthy people with severe psychological suffering have been formally approved, though implementation is postponed until 2027. Many health professionals feel out of their depth. One worried doctor told colleagues on a private forum that he doesn't want assisted death 'to become the solution to every kind of suffering out there'.[16]

Various problems with the Canadian system will be considered in due course, but for now it is enough to describe one further case. Alan Nichols, sixty-one, had some mobility issues and partial deafness from childhood, and had recently had a stroke, but he could live independently and was otherwise in reasonable health. He was, however, subject to recurrent spells of depression. As his brother said: 'He would go through stages where life was good and then he'd hit a stage for a while, for a month or two, where he didn't feel like living.'[17]

In 2019 elements of Alan's support network had recently fallen away, and he lapsed into a major depressive episode. Paramedics found him lying malnourished on the floor of his apartment. He was taken to hospital, admitted involuntarily under the provisions of the Canadian Mental Health Act, and put on suicide watch. While recovering, Alan applied for assisted death, citing hearing loss as the supposedly qualifying illness. Somehow his application was accepted by the system, and his status officially changed from someone for whom suicide was a risk to be avoided, to someone for whom it was tacitly agreed to be a good thing.

He began to refuse visits from family. The hospital did not tell them about his request to die, citing patient confidentiality. Loved ones found out only a few days before his death and were powerless to stop it. As his sister-in-law later recounted, in the days beforehand Alan was agitated, confused, and refusing to wear the cochlear implant that enabled him to hear. 'Alan did not have a valid diagnosis for MAID,' the BBC reports her as saying. 'Would you feel safe now, bringing your suicidal loved one to seek medical care for recovery when there are no oversight or stringent safeguards surrounding a procedure that kills people?'[18] I think most of us would agree that we would not. Jack Kevorkian could not have done much worse with his Thanatron. Whatever mercy looks like in the medical system, it is surely not this.

Examples like this give rise to a suspicion. In face of the messiness of humans – sometimes emotionally disordered, socially challenging, and physically compromised, in a way that undercuts any latent aesthetic fantasies of perfection or neatness – there is a temptation to think of death as a pleasingly simple solution. It can seem so much cleaner and quicker than complex, uncertain, resource-heavy alternatives. By granting death, a problem is definitively taken off busy hands.

Kevorkian seems to have sometimes thought this way. Recalling the death of Janet Adkins, the volunteer with Alzheimer's, in a 2010 documentary, he laughingly said that the police 'made a big deal investigation of it ... to me, it was just a medical procedure, that's all'. The 'just' gives the game away. Whatever the rights or wrongs of assisted death, insofar as it involves deliberately causing premature death, it is never 'just' a procedure (and nor, for that matter, is it medical). I mark this temptingly detached and oversimplified approach here, so that we can guard against it.

Two kinds of Merciful Helper

Imagine that you are a doctor, faced with someone who is asking you for help to die. Don't just think of a stereotypically urgent case: someone in bodily agony with only hours of natural life remaining, like the man Kayce met in *Yellowstone*. These are actually pretty rare. Think of the sort of complex situation that is much more common. Someone has terminal cancer but can move around freely, is experiencing little pain currently, and – it seems – has at least several months to live. He is homeless, experiencing a lot of fear about the future, and relying upon alcohol. When he is drunk he becomes nihilistic and depressive, though is less so when he is sober. He is eligible for social housing, but is also dyslexic, stressed, and feels unable to negotiate the attendant bureaucracy. Even if he did manage to, there would be a long wait. He has no family and feels very alone. He qualifies for an assisted death, at least in terms of his physical condition, and is now asking for one. Should he get it?

The Freedom Lover is likely to say that it is nobody else's business. This attitude might conceivably work, were we talking about a decision to take matters into one's own hands – and even here I would disagree, for reasons I've described – but we are not. We are considering on what grounds a doctor (or lawyer, or social worker, etc.) should participate in the process of helping to kill someone else. As we now know, there is no good reason why the average individual's 'freedom' or 'choice' should place a moral demand upon other people to help. So, to justify the doctor's involvement, it seems we have to talk in detail about the nature of the suffering involved. Is it so genuinely awful that putting this person 'out of their misery' is the right thing to do? This dilemma moves us out of the territory of the Freedom Lover and into that of the Merciful Helper, compassionately concerned to facilitate an early death only where, objectively speaking, a person's suffering is too horrible to be borne.

You might still insist: why can't a Merciful Helper just default to the suffering person's point of view? If someone says things are bad enough to warrant an early death, aren't they the authority, not you? But to repeat the basic point, completely obvious in other contexts: suffering individuals don't always know how best to help themselves, and sometimes do things which are positively counterproductive. We are looking for a moral justification for a doctor to help end somebody else's life. With an outcome that final, it had better be a robust one. It can't just be 'because he said he wanted it'. Mercy (or its modern counterpart, compassion) is aimed at the provision of genuine help and relief to others, not just its superficial appearance.

This, at least, is the ideal. In practice, there are two versions of the Merciful Helper in the world, one much more conscientious than the other. The less ideal kind, which I'll call the 'simplistic Merciful Helper', is attracted to the idea of being merciful, kind, compassionate, and so on, in the face of what they assume to be extreme suffering. In practice, however, they have little interest in finding out the details of such suffering, or properly scrutinising whether granting an early death really is a merciful response. Where someone who seems sufficiently ill and suffering is asking for an assisted death, the simplistic Merciful Helper is happy to take appearances at face value. They are also uninterested in thinking about less drastic alternatives to death, preferring to label attempts to thwart the provision of it as 'cruel'.

In contrast, what I'll be calling the 'careful Merciful Helper' is concerned to get things right. They want to find out what is really going on, in some detail, for a person seeking an assisted death, and to set a high bar for the sort of suffering which counts as a good reason to grant one. They don't just assume that denying an assisted death to an ill and suffering person must be unacceptably cruel. They recognise that there are ways to alleviate even serious suffering that don't involve dispensing irreversible death. And they grasp that, in virtue of death's habit of definitively foreclosing all future possibilities, the option of ending someone's life should be a last resort. It is an extremely serious matter, and we have to get it right.

In the previous chapter, we learnt that – at least, in its most archetypal guise, where agonising bodily pain is at issue – the Merciful Helper is concerned to relieve people in the following type of case. First, the person must have severe pain or other discomfort – the kind that completely impedes normal function. Second, the pain must be (broadly speaking) unrelenting: meaning, if it ever remits or abates, it doesn't do so for very long. Third, the pain must be irremediable, in the sense that there is good reason to think it cannot be alleviated by medical treatment or palliation. Kayce's burns victim in *Yellowstone* definitely satisfied this description. Perhaps long-term ME sufferer Lynn Gilderdale, with all her multiple bodily complications, did too. Certainly, her mother reasonably believed she did.

Over time, it has become accepted that a Merciful Helper is concerned with alleviating psychological suffering as well as bodily pain and discomfort. But still, the careful version should surely demand that the suffering caused by an illness must be of the same sort of magnitude and urgency as these more classic sorts of case. Death is the proposed solution; it's not like trying a new treatment which you can ditch if it doesn't work out. So let's insist that for the act of bringing about someone's early death to count as *truly* merciful and helpful, it must at least be a response to pain *or* psychological suffering which is:

a) severe, to the point of impeding all normal function
b) unrelenting – if it does remit or abate, it does not do so for very long
c) otherwise irremediable – it can't be remedied through any other method of treatment or approach

Anything less than this, I suggest, will make the facilitation of early death an unmerciful response, no matter how keen the suffering person is to obtain one at the time.

I can imagine someone dragging their heels at this point. Why should a person who is terminally ill have to wait until suffering is severe and unrelenting before being granted an early death? Would it not be more merciful to do this *before* such suffering starts? As philosopher Iain Brassington puts it, 'a law that will allow people to seek assistance to end suffering but will not allow them to seek assistance never to begin suffering is perplexing'. In fact, he goes further: such a law would be 'brutal'.[19]

Applied to assisted death services, the line of thought seems to be that doctors should be able to help kill consenting terminally ill people before their predicted suffering even begins. But if so, I urge readers to think this through. (Remember, mercy is our focus now, not personal freedom.) Anticipating the progression of an illness is hard enough. Predicting how that individual will respond psychologically to symptoms is even harder. And doctors have a range of sophisticated methods available to palliate pain and suffering if and when they arrive. Where someone has the potential for many months or even years of comfortable living in front of them, then helping them carry out their own suicide now is not merciful in the slightest.

For assisted death to count as genuinely merciful, it must be a response to severe, unrelenting, and irremediable suffering in the moment. So our question now becomes: how well do existing assisted death services prioritise a carefully merciful approach of this nature over a simplistic one? In the case of the Canadian system, I think we can already see the beginnings of an answer.

How long is terminal?

The careful Merciful Helper should be attentive to the issue of accurate diagnosis and prognosis. For there is a very basic way in which someone's suffering at the prospect of imminent death might not be unrelenting or irremediable after all – namely, where doctors have got things wrong. (Immediately we see a major problem with offering death as the solution, before anticipated suffering even starts.)

One of the many shocking things about the treatment of Alan Nichols was that he was euthanised under a system which – at the time, anyway – purported to reserve assisted death only for those who were terminally ill. In the Canadian system, a terminal diagnosis is defined as one in which natural death is 'reasonably foreseeable'. As far as we know, Nichols had no condition which made this clearly true. But equally, given the looseness of this criterion it is hard to say of a person like Nichols (or indeed, of anyone) that his death was definitely *not* reasonably foreseeable. We are finite creatures. In a broad sense, death is reasonably foreseeable for all of us. But the Merciful Helper should surely hope for more clarity than this.

Part of the problem is that saying something is 'reasonably foreseeable' is inherently vague. The Canadian Association of MAID Assessors and Providers makes this clear in its guidelines, stating that the requirement does not mean that a person must be 'expected to die within a set period such as six or twelve months'.[20] And what seems reasonably foreseeable to one doctor may not be to another. The first might cheerfully sign you off, while the second is doubtful. Also worryingly, the less a doctor knows, the more liberal they may be prepared to be in their predictions. A non-specialist clinician who knows relatively little about a disease, other than that it does eventually cause death, is perhaps more likely to grant that death is 'reasonably foreseeable' than a specialist who has a lot more concrete information about how things tend to play out. Yet most assessments for assisted death are made by non-experts in the disease in question.

In contrast, Leadbeater's bill requires that a person qualifying for an assisted death be given a prognosis of six months to live or less. This is better; but it should not be assumed that more specificity clears up all difficulties. UK government benefit data suggests that one in five people given six months to live by their doctors are still alive after three years.[21] Indeed, one of the bill's most prominent supporters, Dame Esther Rantzen, who has stage 4 lung cancer, was told in 2023 that she had weeks to live. At the time of writing, she is still alive.

Predicting whether someone has only six months to live is particularly tricky, it turns out. A review of prognostic tools for life expectancy with primary cancer has found several limitations, including that the tools are more accurate when trying to predict 'shorter prognoses, such as weeks to months, rather than six months'. Disturbingly, given the present discussion, the tools also tended to weigh 'functionality' – i.e. the capacity to function independently in daily life – heavily in making a prognosis, which meant that predictions for people disabled due to some other non-life-threatening condition were often inaccurately shortened.[22]

And there is also over-simplification in thinking about life expectancies. Since outcomes often vary significantly even for a single disease, talking about the midpoint in the range won't be much help in predicting an individual outcome. Yet this time frame is often treated as a likelihood. As one senior medic put it in a letter to *The Times* in 2025:

> [T]he mean (average) assumes that the range is normally distributed, a symmetric curve with equal numbers on each side of the peak, whereas the median is the middle

value if the dataset is arranged in ascending order. A good example is carcinoma of the pancreas, where the median expectation of life is ten months. Sadly, this has been so since I qualified in 1960. You can't tell the patient to come back in four months to qualify for assisted dying, because I've known patients who have lived in reasonable comfort for four years.[23]

So, even for the most highly qualified specialist, predicting the time someone has left can be hit and miss. And the risk is worsened in any assisted death service which puts the burden of prognosis on only two doctors. As the Royal College of Physicians noted in their critical response to Leadbeater's bill, the two doctors framed as responsible for signing off assisted deaths would each be working alone, yet jointly responsible for prognosis and other vital checks. They observed: 'These decisions would not be made by doctors alone in any other aspect of clinical practice.'[24] Instead, the norm is a multidisciplinary team. The absence of this collegial support makes mistakes more likely.

In my own circle, I am close to three people who have received terminal diagnoses and yet delighted everybody with their subsequent longevity. One is my friend Amanda, diagnosed with triple negative breast cancer ten years ago, which then spread to her brain. Alongside the surgery and chemotherapy for her primary cancer – bad enough on their own – she later had neurological surgery twice, alongside stereotactic radiosurgery. Eventually she was given three months to live and started to receive hospice outpatient care. At that point she held what she called her own living 'funeral', where we celebrated her life in her presence with a meal, speeches, a memory board, and many tears.

Completely unexpectedly, Amanda has now been cancer-free for years. A committed Christian, she tells me she would not have contemplated assisted death had it been available, though she fully understands why some are tempted. If assisted death had been available and had she wanted one, there is no question that she would have got it. She satisfied every possible condition. And in that case, quite simply, she would not be here now.

Every kind of suffering out there

The Canadian law is aimed at alleviating 'enduring and intolerable physical or psychological suffering that cannot be alleviated under conditions the person considers acceptable', for people with 'serious and incurable illness, disease or disability' who are in an 'advanced state of irreversible decline in capability that cannot be reversed'. Since Alan Nichols's time, the system has withdrawn even the nominal requirement of a terminal diagnosis. Now people who appear to have this degree of suffering, and whose deaths are also classified as reasonably foreseeable, are eligible for an assisted death on a fast-track route which has become known as 'Track 1'. Meanwhile, disabled people with the required level of suffering but whose natural deaths are not thought to be reasonably foreseeable – so not terminally ill, though they may be incurably so – can also be eligible for an assisted death on the slower route known as 'Track 2'.

One way to try to get some order back into this situation would be to put much tighter controls on what counts as 'serious and incurable illness', 'advanced' and 'irreversible' decline, and indeed 'reasonably foreseeable death'. Cases like those of Alan Nichols and many others show us these already vague terms are being applied in the most perfunctory of ways. But important as this would be, it would not solve what strikes many people as a more fundamental problem. Experiences such as poverty, homelessness, a lack of available medical treatment or social care, a dislike of feeling burdensome to relatives, and so on are motivating seriously ill and disabled people to opt for early deaths. And they are getting them from the state.

In 2022, there were 13,241 assisted deaths in Canada. Researchers recorded the most commonly offered personal motives, describing these as capturing the 'nature of suffering'. Some respondents' answers referred, relatively strictly, to bodily symptoms and the effects of illness and disability: for instance 'loss of ability to perform activities of daily living', 'loss of control of bodily functions', and 'inadequate pain control'. But the most popular reason appeared to refer, at least potentially, to more than this. It cited a felt lack of meaning, one of depression's core features: namely, a 'loss of ability to engage in *meaningful* activities' (my italics). Other reasons also referred to negative states of mind, and became less specifically focused on illness as they went along: 'concern' about future pain or other symptoms; a 'loss of dignity'; being a 'perceived burden on family, friends or caregivers'; 'isolation or loneliness'; and 'emotional distress/existential suffering/fear/anxiety'. The last group of feelings was specified so vaguely that, for all we know, they might have been about aspects of the ill person's life that had very little to do with their disease.

Let's call the collective set of reasons for which a person is seeking an early death from doctors their 'suicidal mindset'. Some assisted death services don't even try to sort through the potentially anarchic sprawl of suicidal mindsets in gravely ill people – they just give in. This includes Kim Leadbeater's prospective system for the UK, and the one in Oregon on which it was modelled. Once the establishment of mental capacity and other formalities are out the way, these systems make a diagnosis of terminal illness the only real criterion of eligibility for an early assisted death, with nothing further mentioned about background thinking. In fact, the word 'suffering' does not appear in Leadbeater's bill at all. In plain terms, applicants will not have to be questioned about their desire to die, or why they have it. The diagnosis of terminal illness will be presumed to speak for itself.

In practice, this means that once you have a terminal diagnosis, your suicidal mindset can be of practically any form and you can still get an assisted death. It doesn't need to have very much, or indeed anything at all, to do with your illness. You might want to die because you are preoccupied by grief brought on by a recent bereavement; or from the boredom of your everyday life; or from wishing to avoid tax obligations. Here, it really does seem as if an assisted death at the hands of doctors is potentially the answer to 'every kind of suffering out there'.

Careful Merciful Helpers might wish to do better. Along with beleaguered Canadian doctors, we might wonder: is there any easy way to remove from the pool of candidates for assisted death those who wish to die because of reasons that aren't mainly about serious illness or disability, but (also) about wider psychosocial aspects? Is there a simple way to stop the system attempting to address 'every kind of suffering out there', as long as a diagnosis of terminal illness or incurable disability is also attached?

I'm afraid the answer is no. As soon as assisted dying services became aimed at relieving the psychological suffering caused by illness, and not just associated severe bodily pain, the sprawl of reasons became inevitable. Charles Killick Millard insisted that euthanasia could not, for instance, be an 'easy way out of difficulties, financial or otherwise'.[25] But he could afford to say this, because he and his fellow advocates for euthanasia were mainly focused on alleviating agonising pain. Once the emphasis shifted to psychological suffering, things got more complicated.

To understand this, let's look at some important differences between severe bodily pain caused by terminal illness (the kinds of case in which Millard and co. were primarily interested) and severe psychological suffering caused by terminal illness. These differences explain why reasons for opting for assisted death in the modern context tend to sprawl uncontrollably.

First, bodily pain is caused by illness in a relatively direct way. Even if the sufferer knew nothing much about the nature of their illness – perhaps even did not know they were terminally ill – they would still be in pain. Bodily pain has a way of muscling its way to the forefront of your consciousness, even when you have no idea of its origin.

Second, severe or agonising pain as a result of terminal or incurable illness is what might be called relatively 'one-dimensional', meaning it has a brute kind of mental presence. This is not to say it does not have emotional consequences; but rather that, unlike most of our thoughts, pain is not a representation of something in the world. As cultural philosopher Elaine Scarry has put it, pain 'has no referential content. It is not of or for anything.'[26] It just is. And this means it is not easily modified – lessened or aggravated – by accompanying thoughts and feelings. (Actually, this is an oversimplification. Sometimes the experience of pain can indeed be modified by the presence of other thoughts. Still, flexibility in one's pain experience is relatively limited, at least compared to the contrast I am about to make.)

Psychological suffering as a result of terminal or incurable illness is not like pain in these respects. The suffering is caused differently. Unlike for bodily pain, it is not true that your psychological suffering would be largely unchanged even if you didn't know much about the nature of your illness, or that you were ill at all. Much of your suffering in this case will be significantly influenced by your *beliefs about* your illness, and not just by the illness directly. These include beliefs about how serious your illness is, how much pain is likely to ensue, where it is located in your body, what remedies are available, and so on. If you didn't have those beliefs, you wouldn't be suffering as much – or at least not in that particular way.

Unlike our sketch of bodily pain above, psychological suffering is profoundly multidimensional. It is essentially tied up with other beliefs and feelings: not even just about your illness, but about your situation as a whole. That is simply how beliefs and feelings are – they roam around in your mind, as it were, meeting up with other beliefs and feelings and forming new inferences. And any psychological suffering you are experiencing, caused by having certain thoughts about your illness or disability, normally cannot help but be affected by other thoughts: for instance, about the future, how much money you have to live on, whether you are likely to get adequate treatment, or how your family will react. It is the multidimensionality of psychological suffering that Montaigne gets at in his witty warning against pointless rumination: 'He who fears he shall suffer, already suffers what he fears.'[27]

What all this means is that – perhaps unlike with bodily pain, or at least not to the same extent – it is impossible to narrow down the story of psychological suffering associated with grave illness or disability to a simple tale about a one-dimensional experience, caused only by the illness itself and not broader factors too. And there is also the fact that such suffering – how much of it you feel, and how severely – is strongly modified by prior personality traits and habits of mind. A person already prone to depression or anxiety suffers more from the diagnosis of serious illness than someone constitutionally cheerful. Those who have strong religious beliefs may suffer less. Some will care more about a loss of independence than they do about pain. Others will prioritise not feeling lonely or burdensome over not feeling nauseous.

Such facts point to the essential difficulty of stopping the unwieldy spread of suicidal mindsets, including in the severely ill. Media guidelines from the Samaritans, the UK charity dedicated to general suicide prevention, underline this point: 'Suicide is extremely complex and most of the time there is no single event or factor that leads someone to take their own life.'[28] From their owner's perspective, mental states like depression, anxiety, and fear colour the world alike, making everything look worse, not just some things in particular. In the grip of such widely dispersed feelings, the business of rationally sorting your problems into mental boxes respectively marked 'illness' and 'not-illness' feels impossible.

In short: psychological suffering is disorderly and often hard to untangle conceptually. Once assisted death services officially became available for the psychological suffering caused by serious illness and disability, I am not sure what legal wording could have prevented ill or disabled people from seeking an early death because they were depressed, lonely, or cash-strapped, and only secondarily because they were ill.

Unbearable loads

We have identified one reasonable requirement of genuinely careful, merciful help: that it should target only pain or suffering which is severe, to the point of impeding normal function. From the perspective of mercy, people should not be helped to die in response to anything less.

There is no doubt that the suffering caused by illness can be severe: a mix of many negative emotions all at once, exacerbated by exhaustion and pain. At the beginning of his essay 'The Nature of Suffering and the Goals of Medicine', the doctor and bioethicist Eric Cassell memorably described the plight of one young woman, a sculptor, with breast cancer that had metastasised:

> [S]he lost strength in the hand that she had used in sculpturing, and she became profoundly depressed. She had a pathologic fracture of the femur, and treatment was delayed while her physicians openly disagreed about pinning her hip ... [W]hen a new course of chemotherapy was started, she was torn between a desire to live and the fear that allowing hope to emerge again would merely expose her to misery if the treatment failed. The nausea and vomiting from the chemotherapy were distressing, but no more so than the anticipation of hair loss. She feared the future ... She felt isolated because she was no longer like other people and could not do what other people did. She feared that her friends would stop visiting her. She was sure that she would die.[29]

With severe bodily pain and a conscious patient, a person may be able to point to different pain sites on their body; count the number of recent episodes and describe how long they lasted; describe the distinct character of the pain or discomfort (burning, stabbing, throbbing, tingling, sharp, dull); rate pain severity by using a scale; and report effects on sleep and appetite. And though the patient's self-report forms an important part of the story, there are also often other signs for a clinician to notice – tenderness on examination, involuntary sounds and grimacing, hypersensitivity to touch, restricted movement, clamminess, a quickened pulse, and so on.

But things are more difficult with psychological suffering. Clinical dependence upon self-report in this area is much heavier. The assessor can examine a person's facial appearance, behaviour, and their tone of voice, but these will provide limited information. And though sometimes there will be accompanying signs – for instance, sleeplessness, loss of interest in food or sex, over-reliance on alcohol, poor memory – there is rarely a question of clinicians observing these things in the moment. For these reasons, psychologists and psychiatrists tend to use structured questionnaires and interviews to measure the severity of depression, anxiety, and other forms of distress. In the context of palliative care, dedicated tools have also been developed to assess severity of psychological suffering for terminally or incurably ill people.[30]

But assisted death laws that define eligible thresholds of suffering don't just require that a person's suffering be deemed severe. They go further: the suffering in question, to which an assisted death is supposed to be the answer, must be 'unbearable', or its synonym, 'intolerable'. Legislators seem to think this adds a helpful note of seriousness and objectivity; but in fact it just muddies the waters. Whether suffering is experienced as unbearable is a wholly subjective matter, adding nothing except further rhetorical emphasis that the patient is feeling awful.

The intensity of suffering is connected to personal meaning-making.[31] Some pain seems to its owner to have no meaning and suffuses the mind with despair. In *The Rack* by A. E. Ellis – a pseudonym for the playwright Derek Lindsay – Ellis figuratively describes his own tortuous experience of tuberculosis treatments in an Alpine sanatorium. Subjected to interminable-seeming painful tests and interventions, at one point the protagonist feels that:

> ... his existence was purely physical; an agglomeration of aching, burning flesh. He felt that there was nothing more; that life, engaged in his progressive humiliation, had overborne itself, for his spirit was now dead and he could be tormented no further.[32]

Equally there is bodily suffering that can be rationalised as in the service of a higher purpose and so more easily borne: the suffering of religious martyrs, for example, or that of a soldier full of patriotic feeling, agonisingly wounded for his country. A palliative care doctor tells me that he has twice experienced, in his words, 'devoutly Buddhist and Hindu patients who declined analgesia while dying because they saw pain as a way of effacing the karmic debt accrued in life'.[33] Cultures have various ways of assenting to the meaning of particular kinds of suffering – a soldier's sacrifice is often thought of as 'noble', for instance – and this can help cement the individual's positive orientation towards their own situation.

In other cases, severe suffering might just be downplayed in the mind because some other valuable goal is more important. Single-minded personal projects – house-building, work plans, parenthood – have been pursued in the presence even of severe illness, pain, or grief. Henry James wrote his novels through the chronic pain of a mystery injury acquired in his teens when trying to put out a fire – sometimes speculated to be a genital injury – which, he wrote, gave him a 'horrid even if an obscure hurt; and what was interesting from the first was my not doubting in the least its duration – though what seemed equally clear was that I needn't as a matter of course adopt and appropriate it, so to speak, or place it for increase of interest on exhibition'.[34] Translated into a non-Jamesian idiom: there were more important things in life to focus upon.

Some seem to want to take the request for death from a patient as a sign in itself that suffering is 'unbearable' and so meets the required threshold. But suicidal thinking absolutely cannot be reliable evidence on its own, and the contrast with suicide outside the context of illness makes that clear. Those who focus on general suicide prevention don't take an expressed desire to die from a person as showing that the person's suffering is so unbearable that they should be allowed to go through with it – quite the opposite, in fact. They understand that suicidal thinking is an aspect of depression, and may recede as that issue is addressed and treated. Desires for death that are linked to stressful life circumstances may also disappear once the circumstances start to resolve. Many who have drawn back from the brink will later say that they hadn't got their priorities straight, and are glad they didn't go through with it. Hard as it seems to be for some onlookers to believe, this can also be true after a terminal diagnosis.

Wishing perhaps to find something more scientific to help in this area, in 2009 some Dutch clinicians proposed a standardised metric for gauging 'unbearable' suffering in terminal or incurable illness.[35] First, respondents were asked about the intensity of a particular element of their experience, then given a question about how bearable it was. Aspects covered in the questionnaire included bodily symptoms; limitations on daily activities; interpersonal relationships with friends, family, and sexual partners; feelings of guilt, shame, loneliness, and hopelessness; and fears about the future. The authors noted that for some, the conclusion that suffering is unbearable 'may occur at the level of individual dimensions' while for others it 'may occur when the sum of suffering of diverse dimensions exceeds the bearing capacity'.

'Bearing capacity' here sounds reassuringly scientific – as if an engineer is measuring the load-bearing capacity of a bridge. However, it turns out that how the researchers assessed this 'bearing capacity' was just by asking respondents whether their suffering felt bearable, whatever standard that denoted for them personally. In other words, they were still in the realm of subjectivity, though it is easy to see how any clinicians using the questionnaire might not realise it.

The unbearable heaviness of disability

Expecting health professionals to discern when a person's suffering is truly unbearable has its dangers. A clinician might discount the suffering of one group, relatively speaking, while overplaying the severity of that of another. For instance, it is easy to imagine a situation where a doctor tends to assent to assisted death more commonly for one sex than the other, partly due to assumptions about the different levels of suffering each sex can 'bear'. The point extrapolates for other groups too.

And we don't have to look too far to find some evidence of this possibility: namely, the fact that systems such as Canada's allow for assisted death for those with severe physical disability who don't have terminal illness. This inclusion *in itself* seems to reflect a value judgement on the part of legislators: namely, that long lives spent with severe physical disability are more likely than other lives to be unbearable. And it's a viewpoint that seems to be shared by some clinicians involved in assisted death decisions. That severe bodily disability, on its own, doesn't just make life *much more difficult* than for able-bodied people, but – much more strongly – is likely to make life *unbearable*, is an assumption strenuously disputed by disability activist groups objecting to assisted death laws. As the campaigning group Not Dead Yet UK say on their website: 'we're worried this debate is tied to the value our society places on disabled people's lives'.

I will return to this important question in Chapter Six. In the meantime, we should note the following alarming prospect, concerning a case where a severely disabled patient applies to die. If the clinician in charge of decision-making is trying to exert some objective judgement about whether this person's life is unbearable or not, it seems likely the decision will be affected, not just by how that clinician sees the individual patient's circumstances, but also by general judgements they make about the quality of life involved in similarly severe disability. And they might well be getting this wrong.

Though this issue emerges starkly in the case of those with

disabilities, in fact the issue is a general one. There is always the danger of clinicians projecting their own negative feelings about an applicant's situation onto that applicant and concluding that their suffering is 'unbearable', when really it is not. In order to count as merciful, assessors should surely stick to trying to work out whether suffering is sufficiently severe (something which is hard enough). The addition of 'unbearable' does nothing much, except colourfully express the severity of the felt distress of the sufferer. Attempts to objectively gauge whether a particular mental burden is really unbearable or not are bound to fail.

4

Worse Than the Disease

The hour of lead

When you are afflicted by severe bodily pain, every second can seem unending. Writers have long tried to capture the quality that crushes both future and past into the present moment like a black hole. Emily Dickinson talked of 'the Hour of Lead'; Sylvia Plath of 'that long, blind, doorless and windowless corridor'. In another poem, Dickinson wrote:

> Pain—has an Element of Blank—
> It cannot recollect
> When it began—or if there were
> A time when it was not— [1]

While you are well and not in pain, the future prospect of it can seem monolithic and overwhelming – how will you possibly manage? Many traditional arguments for assisted death services rely on the idea that great pain at the end of life is likely or even inevitable, and that death at the hands of doctors is the only solution. But there is good news – this is simply not true. There are sophisticated and effective medical tools for alleviating pain. Applied sensitively, they unambiguously offer a form of mercy.

While some basic pain-relieving treatments are as old as medicine itself, specialist palliative care is quite new. Even relatively recently, doctors were mainly focused on staving off death in life-threatening situations without paying huge attention to the feelings of the patient. As the American doctor and author Jennifer Nutik Zitter writes of her early training in intensive care medicine, doctors sometimes held off from treating pain until after senior colleagues had done their rounds, for fear of losing useful diagnostic information:

> In addition, treating pain almost felt as though we were accepting that it might be here to stay. That felt like failure. It took the palliative care movement to teach me that treating pain early on was one of the most important things I could do for my patients – almost as important as maintaining blood pressure or treating infection.[2]

The word 'palliative' comes from the Latin *palliare* – to cloak. In 1967 Cicely Saunders (later Dame Cicely) founded the world's first modern hospice in England, St Christopher's. There she pioneered a number of principles for caring for terminally ill people and 'cloaking' their pain. Her 2005 obituary in the *British Medical Journal* credits her with being 'more than anybody else ... responsible for establishing the discipline and the culture of palliative care'. First trained as a nurse, then a medical social worker, then a doctor, Dame Cicely came to theorise bodily pain as a 'total' experience which had physical, emotional, social, and spiritual aspects. And she proposed new ways of dealing with it.

One of her most important insights was that 'constant pain needs constant control'; so she did away with protocols that insisted pain-relieving drugs could only be given after the last dose had worn off and the pain had returned. This meant there was much less anxiety for patients, a factor which in itself lessened the intensity of their pain if it did return. Drugs were not the only solution, though. In a letter to the *British Medical Journal* published in 1963, she wrote: 'Listening ... has a therapeutic effect on many symptoms ... Anxiety and depression can be helped by drugs, but it is the true listener who helps most of all.'[3] Relatives and friends were encouraged to visit throughout the day at St Christopher's, rather than only during visiting hours. Her compassionate attitude to the dying was beautifully summarised by a statement quoted at her memorial service: 'You matter because you are you, and you matter to the last moment of your life. We will do all that we can not only to help you die peacefully, but also to live until you die.'[4]

At the same time as the hospice movement was forming in Britain, greater understanding of pain was emerging. In 1965 Canadian psychologist Ronald Melzack and British neuroscientist Patrick Wall proposed what became known as the 'gate control' theory of pain – modified in various respects since, but still forming a central plank in understanding how pain works. Put simply, this theory says that pain signals, transmitted to your brain via small-fibre neurons from the local pain site on your body, can be interrupted at the level of the spinal cord by stimulating other neurons to exert a blocking effect. The classical example of this is rubbing your shin to dull pain after banging it. The same blocking effect can be modulated by your mental state and patterns of attention, which is why distraction can make pain better and low mood make it worse.

This insight has given rise to a host of drug developments and other pain management techniques, including spinal cord and peripheral nerve stimulation devices (think of the TENs machine in labour, for instance). And it has also produced psychological interventions that can modify attention to, and perception of, pain. An example of the latter is the distracting effect of using immersive video games during extremely painful medical processes, such as wound dressing in burns victims.[5]

Research shows that, quite apart from bodily injury and degeneration, things that can 'open the gate' to more pain in an already suffering person include: depression and anxiety; fear, rumination, and hopelessness about pain; too much physical activity or too little; muscle tension; a lack of social support; and friends and family who constantly focus on your pain, so it is made harder for you to ignore it. (As Seneca presciently wrote to Lucilius: 'We take our cue from people's thinking even in the way we feel pain.'[6]) Things that can 'close the gate', besides drugs and medical devices, include: mental distraction and turning your attention outwards; a belief that you have some control over pain, and can predict and manage it; relaxation and calm; pacing yourself properly in activity; and having strong social support networks around you.[7]

Still, the efficacy of some of these things probably shouldn't be overplayed. For most people facing bodily torment, the most reliable kind of pain relief will still be pharmaceutical. If you've ever had an epidural, morphine after a major operation, or strong painkillers for toothache, you will probably know the sweet, melting glow of the release.

The sophisticated drugs now used to address pain have advanced even since Dame Cicely Saunders's day, and if in adequate supply can deal with many challenging bodily circumstances. Opioids can be delivered orally, in patches or injections, or directly into a vein or into the spine. If someone is allergic to morphine – something that is fairly rare – alternative options are usually tolerated, and there are also non-opioid forms of relief. Steroids, non-steroidal anti-inflammatories, neuropathic agents, and muscle relaxants all have their place, as well as local and regional nerve blocks. There are also medicines to address persistent side effects of pain relief medicine – anti-emetics for feelings of nausea, for instance. At the very end of life, deep palliative sedation is an option to control symptoms that cannot be alleviated otherwise.

What such facts points towards is that bodily pain, even in terminal illness, need not be unrelenting, nor is it irremediable. No one should minimise the weight of it but, together with dedicated professionals and new technological developments, there are ways at chipping away at the edifice. This fact on its own is a blow to the cause of the simplistic Merciful Helper, talking as if an early death was automatically appropriate for pain during terminal illness.

Unfortunately, it is clear that too few people get access to adequate pain relief. Research from King's College London estimates that 'every year, more than 100,000 people die in the UK with unmet palliative care needs' and that due to an ageing population, 'by 2040, palliative care needs in England and Wales will be 25–40% higher than in 2020'. Among other lacks, there are gaps in training, staffing, funding, evidence-gathering about effectiveness, and proper integration into primary care. The hospice movement is also facing a funding crisis, with many places reducing beds, cutting staff, or facing closure. Taxpayer contributions have dropped significantly and now stand at only around a third of total costs. The rest comes from donations, which are also falling. Meanwhile, there is a general lack of understanding of palliative care and hospices in the population at large, exacerbated by the taboo around talking about dying.

It is sometimes claimed by supporters that palliative care provision tends to improve with the introduction of assisted death services. In fact, it turns out the relationship between palliation and assisted death is more complicated. According to Dr Sarah Cox of the Association for Palliative Medicine:

[R]ecent evidence shows that although palliative care services have improved in those countries where assisted dying has been implemented, they have improved three times more in countries where assisted dying has not been implemented. The evidence from that study shows that the implementation of assisted dying is impeding the development of palliative care services.[8]

In other words: in places where assisted death is being offered as an alternative, palliative care provision is improving much more slowly than the norm. Dr Cox gave a possible explanation for this:

There are finite numbers of doctors, nurses and side rooms in hospitals. If palliative care and assisted dying were funded from the same pot, I think there would be a massive detrimental effect on palliative care because we would be in competition for a limited resource.

Certainly, in any health system with straitened means, confronted by a choice between offering relatively cheap death on the one hand and palliative treatment on the other, you would not expect both of these paths to be pursued with equal vigour.

Such depressing facts make it understandable why seriously ill people, devoid of proper palliation, might demand help to die early. But this is not a book about whether a person is ever right to ask for an assisted death, nor about whether it is ever right for an individual to grant them one. It is about whether governments, law-makers, and the medical profession are right to provide this option to large cohorts, systematically. And the fact remains that the state has a choice. Rather than offering assisted death, it could focus on improving palliative care and properly supporting the hospice movement instead.

The scarcity of palliative care provision also has an impact on public discourse. If you have watched a close relative or friend die with uncontrolled pain, that may well influence your thoughts. Equally, for those who have no idea that palliative care even exists as a specialty – as, it seems, many don't – it is understandable that, faced with the prospect of pain during terminal illness, an early death may look like the only desirable way out. If more people realised it lay within the government's power to see that most pain is managed during terminal illness, perhaps the popularity of assisted death would not be as high as it is.

'Avoid a remedy that is worse than the disease,' Aesop tells us in one of his fables.[9] Wherever there are less drastic solutions than an early death, these should be pursued first. And we must continue to remember that opting for death is the ultimate drastic solution.

Opiates as 'psychological euthanasia'?

Some people positively don't want pain relief, even in heavy agony. They might try to give their natural pain a valuable meaning, in the vein of Khalil Gibran's poetic line: 'your pain is the breaking of the shell that encloses your understanding' – as with the patients mentioned in the last chapter, who rejected pain relief for religious reasons.[10]

A. C. Grayling uses the fact some don't want pain relief to mount a further argument for assisted death. Opiates, he thinks, cause debilitating cognitive side effects such as confusion. For some people, strong pain relief is experienced as 'a deprivation of the chance to take rational farewell of loved ones and of life itself'. He goes further: it can even be a form of 'psychological euthanasia'. In this case, he argues, the suffering patient should be offered assisted death instead, to escape pain by a more palatable, clear-headed means.[11]

We should note that even if this particular argument worked, it would be limited in scope: only justifying assisted death for those people who were dying in bad pain (which is far from a given, even in terminal illness) and who also refuse pain relief for the reasons he cites. And if he takes himself to be offering an argument based on the value of personal freedom/autonomy for such people, it is no more successful than other versions we have looked at: for while you (of course) have the right to refuse pain relief, you can't get a justification of assistance in your own suicide from a right to noninterference alone.

In terms of a desire to offer merciful help, meanwhile, the argument doesn't seem persuasive either; mainly because it is out of touch with the facts of modern medicine. As a palliative care doctor told me:

> There's a widespread misconception that doctors just slosh opioids around, but in end of life care they are selected and titrated very carefully. You 'start low and go slow', increasing doses gradually to ensure they are tolerated. If there are significant side effects, you would regard that as treatment failure and change tack. Cognitive symptoms are rare and probably a sign you're using the wrong drug or too much of it. There's a wide array of opioid and non-opioid analgesics, with different side effect profiles – and many patients who struggle with one are then absolutely fine with another. Of course nothing in medicine is guaranteed but most of the time we're able to control pain with minimal side effects.[12]

This surely changes things. If a patient is refusing pain relief for fear of side effects that are in fact unlikely to happen, the most merciful thing for the doctor to do is to try to explain the real situation, rather than offer death as an alternative. And if the patient still declines, it is not the responsibility of the doctor, having offered a proportionate and reasonable solution, to address the problem with a much more drastic one. Generally, a patient doesn't get to choose exactly the treatment they want.

So pain-relieving drugs, properly managed, are not a major threat to rationality. But perhaps severe pain itself is. In Chapter One, we looked at arguments that mental illness or addiction can be 'internal' obstacles to autonomous decision-making, coming from within the mind and hijacking rational thought processes. It has seemed credible to many writers that severe and all-consuming pain is another such obstacle. Elaine Scarry, discussing the subject of torture, notes the way pain 'annihilates... the objects of complex thought and emotion... [It] begins by being "not oneself" and ends by having eliminated all that is "not itself".'[13] And the philosopher J. David Velleman agrees:

> Pain that tyrannizes the patient ... undermines his rational agency, by preventing him from choosing any ends for himself other than relief. It reduces the patient to the psychological hedonist's image of a person – a pleasure-seeking, pain-fleeing animal.[14]

I can certainly relate: when I was in labour with my second child, an extremely intense experience without any pain relief, I kept trying to leave the hospital room, as if that might put a stop to it.

This point has implications for the provision of assisted death under conditions of severe pain, impinging upon autonomy and consent. When a person in terrible pain asks for an assisted death, and with palliation also available as a remedy, then – at least, if the patient consents to pain relief, which most will – medical efforts should be made to manage pain for a while, in order to allow space to think through the decision properly.

Crystallised

What about psychological suffering during terminal illness? Is it always unrelenting and irremediable? As you have possibly already guessed – no, of course not.

For one thing, drugs are available here too: anti-anxiety medications and anti-depressants. Evidence from their use in terminally ill cohorts suggests that effectiveness does not change, and that they can make a big difference to some.[15] Still, as Dame Cicely Saunders recognised, offering pharmaceuticals is not the only approach to alleviating psychological suffering caused by illness, and not always the best way.

When in suffering's grip, everything can feel hopelessly connected and stuck. Pull at one or two central threads, and the knot may be unpicked. In this sense, the multidimensionality of psychological suffering, discussed in the previous chapter, can be helpful. The suffering of a very ill person is not ever 'just' about illness, but also about fear of the future, worry about loved ones, loneliness, anxiety about being a burden, and so on. This might make it disorderly and sprawling, but equally, it can make it easier to tackle. Address one or two of the key components and you might make a big difference to the overall state of mind.

Anxiety about symptoms is often high after diagnosis, but speaking with medical professionals can ease unrealistic fears. Talking therapy may also be useful for those with a terminal diagnosis, or who are feeling hopeless because of the onset of disability. If there is time – and there often is, despite initial panicky feelings of urgency – anxieties can be aired and sense-tested; grief felt and expressed; guilt, shame, and regret about the past addressed.

For, quite obviously, these very human concerns are often uppermost in a person's mind when they contemplate their own mortality, just as much as worrying about bodily pain or decline. And not every form of alleviation has to come from professionals. Overall, suffering people are probably helped by family, friends, and community just as much, if not more, than by someone paid to do it. Being around caring loved ones can shift your perspective. Fear of being a burden can be lessened by getting reassurance from family. Reaching out to others or allowing oneself to be reached might reduce loneliness. For some, trusted religious figures will help.

Distress induced by a new diagnosis can also reduce once you get used to the idea. For those still in the land of the well, imagining what it is like to believe you will die soon is difficult. Many leap straight to the worst possible picture. Yet it's worth noticing it isn't always like this. Suicidal thinking tends to peak in the months after diagnosis of a severe physical health condition, but then tails off.[16] Lost in desperation, it may be hard to imagine feeling any different; but feelings can change over time.

Of course it doesn't always go this way. One hospice chaplain writes of a patient called Charlie, 'presented as a problem because he was constantly "miserable" and uncooperative. When told, "You know, you don't have to be happy about dying, Charlie," his face lit up for the first time. "Thank God," he said, "I'm sick and tired of people trying to cheer me up."'[17] But for some people things do get brighter. The careful Merciful Helper has to take in the full range of possibilities.

Working in a university, I was once visited in my office by a student I had never met before. A middle-aged man who had just enrolled onto a philosophy degree, he told me he was unable to continue his course because he had just learnt he had only a few months to live. Unsure of what to say, I clumsily asked him how he was feeling. He said it was awful for his family, but that strictly for himself, he was enjoying the newfound intensity of everyday experiences. And he seemed to mean it. His demeanour was calm and he had the look of someone who was happy. Others report similar feelings. 'Suddenly pink roses are much pinker than they used to be, and the blue sky is bluer than it used to be,' one woman told a researcher, while another reported that:

> Everything is in focus. Uh, I call it crystal. What this crystal means, it's like after a snow, on a real cold night when there's fog in the air and every tree branch is covered with ice the next morning, and the sun shines, and it's just a different world – beautiful. That is as close as I could come to describing crystal. My world is in focus. It's crystallized ... Every moment has meaning to me.[18]

And here's dramatist Dennis Potter in his final television interview in 1994, living with terminal pancreatic and liver cancer:

> Below my window ... the blossom is out in full now, there in the west early. It's a plum tree, it looks like apple blossom but it's white, and looking at it, instead of saying 'Oh that's nice blossom', last week looking at it through the window when I'm writing, I see it is the whitest, frothiest, blossomest blossom that there ever could be, and I can see it. Things are both more trivial than they ever were, and more important than they ever were, and the difference between the trivial and the important doesn't seem to matter. But the nowness of everything is absolutely wondrous, and if people could see that, you know. There's no way of telling you; you have to experience it, but the glory of it, if you like, the comfort of it, the reassurance – not that I'm interested in reassuring people, bugger that. The fact is, if you see the present tense, boy do you see it. And boy can you celebrate it.[19]

The point is not that everyone will feel like this during terminal illness; far from it. The point is that, from the perspective of a careful Merciful Helper, the possibility of transcending the first shock of diagnosis to reach a better mental state has to be kept in mind.

The cloud of depression

People who support the existence of assisted death services often seem strangely untroubled by the fact that people with long histories of clinical depression are accessing them. We saw an example of this with Alan Nichols in Canada. In most areas of health, depression is recognised as a threat to good decision-making and the fostering of true self-interest. It is also recognised that it can be treated or just go away on its own. We know that this issue should be of interest to the moderate Freedom Lover, wanting to exclude the influence on decision-making of 'internal' threats to autonomy, such as destabilising mental disorders. But it should also be of concern to the careful Merciful Helper, wishing to offer death only as a response to genuinely irremediable suffering.

Bouts of depression can pass – indeed, psychiatry used to recognise a separate category of depression called 'reactive', in response to changing circumstances. There are also a number of therapeutic approaches to addressing depression which remain applicable in the context of terminal or incurable illness. And yet, in practice, assisted death services don't tend to recognise this fact. It is true that a judgement of 'mental capacity' by a professional is usually required in order for someone to access an assisted death; but this is a minimal bar which won't rule many depressed people out.

Mental capacity is typically framed as time-specific and situation-specific, meaning that a person can have it for one decision and not for another. The principles governing the UK's Mental Capacity Act insist both that 'a person must be assumed to have capacity unless it is established that he lacks capacity' and that 'a person is not to be treated as unable to make a decision merely because he makes an unwise decision'. This makes the test a relatively undemanding one.[20] These conditions might easily be met by someone in the grip of serious depression; and indeed, the vast majority of the millions of patients diagnosed with depression are not treated as lacking mental capacity for the life decisions they make.

Equally: some assisted death services, including the one proposed for the UK, make it nearly impossible to exclude depression as a motive for seeking assisted death because they never ask about it. As we know, once a diagnosis of terminal illness has been issued, the system will not even attempt to find out the thinking behind a personal decision to die. All that is required is a diagnosis of terminal illness, with no interrogation of the nature of any suffering attached.

Labour MP Rachel Hopkins, speaking in favour of Leadbeater's bill during its scrutiny period, approvingly summed up this attitude. Imagining herself as an applicant for an assisted death, she said, 'It is none of your business why I want to pursue this legal course of action.' It is hard to imagine politicians adopting such a deliberately incurious approach to would-be solo suicides (also a legal course of action). Here again we find the tendency to treat the voluntary deaths of terminally ill people as if they are outside the bounds of everyday discourse about premature death. It is the very opposite of the compassionate attitude urged by Dame Cicely Saunders: that you, the dying patient, 'matter to the last moment of your life'.

It is an interesting question why depression is often seen as unrelated to sound decision-making in terminal illness. The main reason, I think, is that depression is often conceived of as an *irrational* and *distorted* response to life. Clinicians don't necessarily think of it this way – that is, they don't view it in terms of rationality or irrationality at all, but just try to address symptoms – but I think plenty of other people do. Depression during ordinary life is assumed to be something that should not be given in to: life for the suffering person is not objectively as bad as they feel it to be, and there is always the potential for a change of mind.

On the other hand, as soon as someone has a terminal or incurable diagnosis, it is tacitly assumed by some, and especially those supportive of assisted death services, that life is now objectively terrible. The experience of depression is perceived as a perfectly rational response to your predicament and not a distortion of thinking at all. This is why some MPs and witnesses during bill scrutiny kept insisting that those requesting assisted death were not suicidal in their outlook. They assume that 'suicidal' thinking, including depression, is irrational; whereas the request for assisted death from a terminally ill person makes complete sense. And this is thought to hold, even for someone with a documented history of depression prior to their terminal diagnosis.

Again we see an outbreak of simplistic Merciful Helper thinking, based on the assumption that life with a terminal or incurable illness is inevitably unbearable. For a few terminally or incurably ill people, it may be true that to die an early death is in their best interests. Not being against assisted death in principle, I don't rule this out. But for others it will not be, even if they very much want to cease living right now. The distorting depression they feel is indeed temporary. Life can still be good again, even in the knowledge of encroaching mortality and serious suffering. In choosing to think of all applicants for an assisted death as members of the first group, legislators and campaigners radically over-simplify the range of cases.

Regulating for a change of mind

So how do drafters of assisted death legislation safeguard against the fact that the initial attractions of early death might decrease over time? This point bears on what counts as genuine mercy – our main focus at the moment – but also relates to the question of what counts as autonomy for the moderate Freedom Lover, wishing to protect the individual from destabilising mental disorders that undermine true self-government.

The short answer is: services hardly try. Here again, it is easy to get the sense that death – that simple and rational-looking solution – is unconsciously being preferred over the messiness and complication of ongoing lives.

In theory at least, existing assisted death services are supposed to ensure that a person's intention to die is 'settled' – meaning unlikely to change. Of course, it might change even at the last moment. No matter how often it has been rehearsed in imagination, new thoughts might suddenly emerge as fantasy meets reality. In Robert Burton's seventeenth-century treatise *The Anatomy of Melancholy*, the author memorably speculated that for a suicidal person suffering from 'melancholy', what he called 'God's mercy' in the form of repentance might come 'betwixt the bridge and the brook, the knife and the throat'. The point transfers to a secular context. A 2003 *New Yorker* article about suicide attempts from the Golden Gate Bridge reports one survivor saying: 'I instantly realized that everything in my life that I'd thought was unfixable was totally fixable – except for having just jumped.' According to another: 'My first thought was, What the hell did I just do? I don't want to die.'[21]

To avoid this problem, most assisted death services require a final statement of consent just before the act itself. But a system should obviously accommodate more substantial time for reflection. After all, the old-fashioned assumption that the applicant must be fighting urgent pain is no longer applicable for most. Yet for those on Track 1 in Canada, no reflection period is required at all: you can even sometimes get 'same day' assisted death. In other systems, waiting periods are longer but still alarmingly short. In Belgium, there is a minimum of one month between request and death. In Oregon, it's fifteen days; in the proposed UK system and in Switzerland, fourteen; in Australia, ten. Generally it is assumed that once suicidal thinking arrives, there is no need to wait for long to see if the perspective will shift.

Efforts to offer less drastic remedies for a suicidal person's situation are also desultory. Services tend to insist only that *information* about alternatives is given, not that they are actually tried. And even this is patchy: on Track 1 in Canada, the legal requirement to offer information about palliative alternatives was removed in 2021.

Oregon's system requires only that the attending doctor tell a terminally ill person about 'feasible alternatives, including, but not limited to, comfort care, hospice care and pain control'. The UK's prospective system says that the applicant must be informed about 'any available palliative, hospice or other care, including symptom management and psychological support'. A parliamentary amendment to ensure every applicant would actually meet a palliative specialist was rejected. Swiss Medical Association regulations, though not legally binding, initially sound as if other treatment options must have been exhausted first – surely better than simply getting information about them – but in the next clause they default to the suicidal person's potentially hopeless view of the world. A presiding doctor must ascertain – my italics – that 'other options have been unsuccessful or *are rejected by the patient as unreasonable*'.[22]

For those on Track 2 in Canada – that is, disabled people whose natural deaths are not deemed reasonably foreseeable – the official reflection period is longer, though the requisite ninety-day wait is not always observed. Legislation for this route also requires that the patient must be 'informed of available and appropriate means to relieve their suffering, including counselling services, mental health and disability support services, community services, and palliative care, and must be offered consultations with professionals who provide those services'. Obviously, though, being 'offered' is not the same as 'having'. The law also specifies that the patient must have 'seriously considered' these alternatives. But in practice, this seems only to amount to putting on a serious face as you tell a doctor you have thought hard about it.

Most assisted death services don't even insist that a severely ill person opting for assisted death should have tried potentially effective medical treatments *for the very condition that is making them ill*. Someone with a treatable condition might become eligible for an assisted death simply because they have stopped taking medication or because they don't have access to life-saving treatment. In Oregon, the list of conditions has now expanded to include virtually any serious medical condition; for instance, the 2017 Data Summary includes arthritis, HIV, and diabetes.[23] And in Canada, some have argued that the severely obese should also count as eligible, since obesity is 'a medical condition which is indeed grievous and irremediable'.[24] The UK's prospective system defines terminal illness as (my italics) 'an inevitably progressive illness or disease *which cannot be reversed by treatment*'; but not being able to be 'reversed' – as opposed to simply slowed down or controlled – is a pretty low bar. (Indeed, the bill committee positively rejected an amendment to exclude those illnesses whose progress can be significantly slowed or controlled by medical treatment.)

Disturbingly, researchers estimate that at least sixty patients with eating disorders have died by physician-assisted suicide or euthanasia in Belgium, the Netherlands, and the USA. Many of them were in their teens and twenties. Most were women, starving their bodies to the point at which, without a change in behaviour, natural death became likely. At this point they were diagnosed as terminally ill, or else as having irremediable suffering with no prospect of improvement, giving them access to assisted death either way. In some cases the suffering of a person experiencing anorexia was deemed irremediable because it had been going on for a long time.[25] The fact that even long-term patients have improved given access to new treatments and approaches appears not to have mattered.

Despite much concern expressed in the UK about this grim possibility, Leadbeater refused to alter her bill to formally exclude people experiencing anorexia from its purview. She was apparently unmoved by the very real prospect of a self-starved twenty-something receiving poison on request from the NHS. The wording of her bill stipulated that 'a person is not to be considered to be terminally ill only because they are a person with a disability or mental disorder (or both)', a clause which Leadbeater often suggested would mean those with eating disorders would be out of bounds, since they 'only' had a mental disorder. But the terrible thing about anorexia is that it is a mental disorder that often results in great bodily deterioration. Combined with the fact that there was nothing in Leadbeater's bill to stop doctors raising assisted death even with eighteen-year-old sufferers, this 'anorexia loophole' started to look bleak indeed.

The triumph of the simplistic

Why do assisted death services tend to end up being run by simplistic Merciful Helpers, not careful ones? *It is partly because the logic of its rival archetype the Freedom Lover keeps intervening.* Undercutting the attempts of careful Merciful

Helpers to detect severe and irremediable suffering, the subjective idiom of the Freedom Lover keeps getting inserted into the conversation: 'who are we to say?'; 'it is up to the individual'; 'it is none of our business'; 'the applicant knows best'; and so on.

The Freedom Lover wants you to default to the language of noninterference: my body, my choice; my life, my death. Paternalistic busybodies should stay out of it. We have seen that this outlook does not produce justification for *assisted* death, in particular, but – since many seem unaware – the Freedom Loving outlook persists as a big ideological player. Thanks to its influence, the concerns of a careful Merciful Helper – for instance, to build in suitable time delays, and make sure applicants explore other treatment options first – get elbowed aside. If an applicant who is technically ill enough thinks an early death is best, then they should have one – case closed. In practice, the idiom of the Freedom Lover ends up favouring the approach of the simplistic Merciful Helper, who doesn't mind the loss of checks and safeguards, lazily assuming that mercy will have been delivered either way.

Freedom Loving rhetoric also shapes the attitude towards patients who refuse treatment for treatable diseases like diabetes or anorexia but still want an assisted suicide. The underlying assumption of legislators seems to be that the patient is making a free, autonomous choice, with which no one else should interfere. But this still does not explain why a patient engaging in such self-destructive behaviour is morally owed an early death from doctors.

And it is also the unfortunate dynamic between Merciful Helper and Freedom Lover that explains the unsatisfactory shape of Leadbeater's proposed UK service. As we know, only a restricted group of people will get access to an assisted death: those who are diagnosed as having less than six months to live. The moral justification for focusing on this cohort can only be a desire to offer them Merciful Help during a time of serious suffering. For why else would they be offered assisted death in the first place? Yet once an applicant has a diagnosis of terminal illness, the system becomes completely uninterested in the nature of the accompanying suffering. Indeed there is no mention of suffering in Leadbeater's bill at all.

During discussion of her bill in Parliament, it was clear that this lack of interest was seen as a plus point by its supporters. Precisely why an applicant wished to die was, in Rachel Hopkins's words, 'none of your business'. Whether the applicant's suffering looked serious or fleeting, unrelenting or transitory, remediable or irremediable, would go unexplored by assessors. It is as if the Merciful Helper was allowed to select the cohort, but at that point the Freedom Lover took over, insisting that, once you were a member of this cohort, almost any reason to end your life would be good enough to ensure that a doctor helped you to do it.

Here too, then, we have the supposed goal of freedom working against that of real mercy. And things are made worse when the Freedom Lover in question is of the radical variety. Moderate Freedom Lovers, at least if they are being consistent, should approve of some safeguards in the assisted death process – checking that applicants are of sound mind and that the desire to die is relatively settled. But in practice many Freedom Lovers – and especially, it seems, when making assisted death legislation – are not like this. They tend to be far more attached to ensuring that people will not be held back by systems against their will than they are to imagining scenarios where slowing someone down might have been helpful.

'I have finished treatment'

Some assisted death services handle illness-related suffering not by acknowledging its complexities but by pathologising it. These services treat 'psychiatric' suffering – that is, psychological suffering – as a good reason to help end someone's life. No accompanying bodily illness is required, let alone a terminal one.

This is the case in the Netherlands, Belgium, and Luxembourg. Canada is also due to go down this route in 2027. Talk of 'psychiatric' rather than psychological suffering might sound reassuringly medico-scientific, but in practice adds no reassurance. The psychiatric professions, unlike merely psychological ones, have medical training and are licensed to prescribe psychopharmaceutical drugs. Killing people, however, is not a medical treatment.

In the Netherlands, one particular case in the 1990s seems to have galvanised professional and public acceptance of assisted death for psychological suffering. A woman depressed over the deaths of her two sons – one from cancer, one from suicide – wished to end her life. She 'was unable to accept her loss and lived every day wanting to die', as a newspaper later put it.[26] She declined both therapy and anti-depressants. Eventually, after two months of discussion with a psychiatrist called Dr Boudewijn Chabot, he helped her to kill herself. Chabot was arrested for assisting in suicide, but no criminal penalty was imposed and he was allowed to carry on practising. Not long afterwards, it was agreed by the Royal Dutch Medical Association that Chabot's approach could be merciful. Official guidelines were introduced sanctioning assisted death for this sort of case.[27]

Dutch laws state that an assisted death is available for those who have a 'voluntary and well-considered death wish' and who suffer from a condition – either 'medical' or 'psychiatric' – that is 'unbearable' and with 'no prospect of improvement'.[28] The doctor and the prospective candidate for an assisted death must 'discuss the situation ... and come to the joint conclusion that there is no other reasonable solution'.

Luxembourg's rules are roughly similar. Belgian laws require that the person's condition must be 'medically futile', and suffering must be 'constant and unbearable', as a result of 'a serious disorder with no reasonable treatment alternatives or therapeutic perspective'.

In these countries, doctors have a duty to prevent people suffering from mental illnesses from pursuing suicide, right up until the moment that a psychiatrist diagnoses a hopeless case. At that point, the patient in question can be helped by doctors to die. Acknowledging the concerns of moderate Freedom Lovers, serious mental disorders – particularly those seen as temporary – are still sometimes treated as a threat to genuinely autonomous decision-making. However, if your depression is judged 'unbearable' and long-lasting enough, it is assumed that it has become a core part of the self, and worries about threats to self-government apparently drop away.

According to one Dutch study from 2022, 95% of requests for assisted death via this route are turned down. Still, the numbers being accepted are rising. In the 1990s, when assisted death was first decriminalised, only a few such requests were granted each year. In 2023, 138 were accepted: twice as many as in 2019, and 20% more than the year before.[29] In 2024 there was a 60% increase, to 219 deaths. Thirty of these involved people under thirty years of age.[30] Among them was twenty-nine-year-old Zoraya ter Beek, who cited depression, autism, and borderline personality disorder as her qualifying conditions. 'I wanted to heal,' she told the press before her death. 'I have tried every conceivable treatment or medication. But nothing worked. According to the doctors, I have "finished treatment".'[31]

Like ter Beek, most of the successful applicants for early death via this route – if one can talk of 'success' – have multiple diagnoses, with depression as the most common one. Personality disorders, anxiety disorders, and PTSD are also well represented. One might wonder how psychiatrists can reliably ascertain whether such conditions have 'no prospect of improvement'. The short answer is they cannot. Whoever confidently told ter Beek that she had 'finished treatment' was technically correct, but only in the chilling sense that her ensuing death made sure this was true.

Psychiatric prognosis is generally difficult to establish. The causes of clinically salient suffering are not well understood, and treatment effects are difficult to predict.[32] As a Dutch psychiatrist – someone who had herself recently euthanised one of her own patients – commented to the newspapers in 2024: 'You can look at psychiatric problems in so many different ways that there is always another treatment option available. So is the suffering really hopeless?'[33] There are potentially decades of life ahead of patients in which their condition might remit or some new treatment might work. Even if someone is repeatedly making suicide attempts, this doesn't seem an adequate reason for medics to take over and make a more efficient job of it.

There is also an interesting question about how a mental health professional is supposed to judge whether something like depression or anxiety is 'long-term' or more transitory. It seems partly to depend on what you are counting. The medical consensus on how to think about the duration of depression has changed. In the 1960s and 70s it was seen as episodic, perhaps coming and going over a lifetime but with periods where no illness was present at all. These days depression is thought of more as a chronic long-term disorder, even during periods of remission.[34] It is salutary to consider how a difference in understanding the time frame of depression might have a big influence on who gets to live and who gets to die.

Other conceptual questions about mental health that previously looked relatively academic also get a sudden dramatic urgency when assisted death is on the table. Sex-related prevalence rates for borderline personality disorder (BPD) appear to differ according to country. Traditionally the diagnosis was thought more common in women than men, but recent studies suggest a more complicated picture. In the USA, the prevalence does not differ significantly by sex; in the UK it is more prevalent in men; and in Norway more prevalent in women.[35]

Since there can be many background causes for differing prevalence rates, including local approaches to diagnosis, this fact alone suggests the potential for a kind of macabre national lottery when it comes to assisted death being available for people with BPD. But there are further worrying issues. One recent review looked at two decades' worth of studies and concluded that, overall, men diagnosed with BPD were more likely to fit with diagnostic criteria of 'intense and inappropriate anger' and 'impulsivity', whereas women were more likely to fit 'chronic feelings of emptiness', 'affective instability', and 'suicidality/self-harm behaviors'. It also found that women with BPD had higher rates of comorbidity with 'depressive and anxiety disorders, eating disorders, and somatoform disorders' whereas men had 'antisocial personality disorder or substance use disorder'. Meanwhile, the study also found, women are more likely to seek medical or psychiatric help than men.[36]

Put together, this data seems to predict that women are more likely than men to be helped to die via the psychiatric route. Indeed, a 2023 Dutch study found that more women than men were both requesting and receiving assisted death via this route, something they took to fit with the fact that more women than men make use of mental healthcare services. The study's authors noted that this was apparently at odds with the fact that men are approximately twice as likely to die from solo suicide as women; but they regarded it as 'consistent with the finding that more women than men attempt suicide, suggesting that the availability of [euthanasia] in the Netherlands may render more effective the wish to die of women whose suffering from mental illness is unbearable'. They concluded: 'This raises an important question for future research, whether, and if so why, more women than men may have a non-treatable wish to die.'[37] One might have hoped this question could have been properly investigated before doctors started carrying out the wishes of suicidal women with mental illness.

A different question: can grief be part of depression? Some psychiatrists validate a category of 'complicated grief', estimating it to occur in about 10% of bereaved people and resulting in a 'failure to transition from acute to integrated grief'.[38] In such cases, grief is 'prolonged, perhaps indefinitely', and 'intense separation and traumatic distress may last well beyond six months'. 'Complicated grievers', we are told, 'may perceive their grief as frightening, shameful, and strange. They may believe that their life is over and that the intense pain they constantly endure will never cease.' Who could rule out some psychiatrists judging this situation as unbearable, with no prospect of improvement, especially if it goes on for years? Indeed, this seems to be exactly what happened in the case of the first Dutch woman helped to die by Chabot. The mind boggles: what might happen if you get an assisted death for your complicated grief, and then your loved ones go into complicated grief too, unable to fully accept your early exit? Might the death spiral eventually result in the termination of your entire family? This seems like a facetious question, but actually I'm not sure why.

In this psychiatric arena, again we meet the problem of people refusing treatment and tipping themselves into a category deemed 'irremediable' – and perhaps more often, since mental illness makes self-treatment more erratic. For example, people experiencing anorexia can become attached to being near death, seeing it as a sign they are starving themselves effectively. Indeed, women with anorexia have a relatively high rate of solo suicide attempts.

As the journalist Hadley Freeman, a former sufferer, has written, 'the more ill a person becomes, the more they resist treatment (eating, in other words) and the more they want to die'.[39] And there is no use hoping doctors will classify any such candidates as ineligible for an assisted death on the grounds of diminished mental capacity. Aside from the fact that assessors are already signing such candidates off, among themselves doctors disagree significantly about whether people experiencing severe anorexia are impaired in their decision-making.[40]

With mental illness, patterns of taking medication can easily fluctuate depending on current state of mind. A 2017 systematic review summarised some common reasons. These included, in descending order of popularity: 'poor insight', 'substance abuse', 'medication side effects', and 'cognitive impairments'.[41] Not taking your meds can make your psychological health worse, and sometimes death starts to look like an appealing release. In such cases it would seem very wrong for a doctor to accept the situation, rather than redoubling efforts to get the patient back on track. Yet some doctors apparently think it acceptable to help kill such a person. In one study of Dutch recipients of assisted death due to psychiatric suffering, 50% of them had refused some sort of treatment beforehand.[42]

If all this wasn't bad enough, there is also evidence that some people with autism and learning disabilities, and no other qualifying underlying condition, are being euthanised under the Dutch system. In 2023 a team from Kingston University in the UK searched a database of 927 Dutch case reports of assisted death and found that thirty-nine involved the early deaths of people with either learning disabilities or autism spectrum disorder (ASD), or both. In some cases these disabilities were described as the 'sole cause of suffering'; in others they were a 'major contributing factor'. Further reasons cited for these people wanting to die included 'social isolation and loneliness', 'lack of resilience or coping strategies', 'lack of flexibility (rigid thinking or difficulty adapting to change)', and 'oversensitivity to stimuli'.[43]

It seems that the judgement from a psychiatrist that learning disabilities and ASD are conditions with 'no prospect of improvement' played a role in a third of the cases. Yet this is a clear category error, applying terminology from the context of bodily diseases to the realm of psychological conditions which by their very nature are life-long, and need not even be especially dysfunctional. No 'recovery' from these conditions is possible, but this fact is not particularly dramatic. Assessing a condition like ASD or a learning disability in such terms carries with it the implication of being a hopeless case; yet it is compatible with someone living a contented life. The right sort of educational and community support can make a huge difference to happiness. To help kill people because they struggle to fit in with wider society seems about as defeatist a capitulation to the sorry status quo as you can get.

In modern life more generally, there is a growing temptation to treat personality types we formerly used to think of as 'quirky', 'eccentric', 'highly strung', 'gloomy' (and so on) as having psychological disabilities with medical-sounding names. Diagnoses, including self-diagnoses, of things like BPD, ASD, attention deficit hyperactivity disorder (ADHD), dyspraxia, and obsessive–compulsive disorder (OCD) are extremely commonplace. The more these behaviours and thought patterns are treated as indicating permanent and debilitating impairments, the more likely it is they will eventually come to feature in acceptable narratives for assisted death.

It is not hard to conclude that something has gone terribly wrong. If blame is to be assigned, the damage seems to be the fault of professionals tempted by the paradigm of the Merciful Helper, rather than that of the Freedom Lover. Focusing on providing early death for psychological suffering alone cannot easily be defended on grounds conducive to the prioritisation of freedom – especially not if the Freedom Lover is able to recognise that someone in the grip of mental illness is often not acting autonomously. So we seem to be in the territory of mercy, at least ostensibly. But it is the fruit of an overly simplistic, quasi-merciful impulse that has got wildly out of control.

Bureaucratic processes and professionally sanctioned guidelines have grown up around that merciful impulse and become calcified, giving individual decisions to kill suffering people a reassuring sense of solidity and gravitas. But at the heart of this sort of system is an unavoidable lack of information about what would have happened, had doctors not intervened with their lethal substances. Despite the apparent confidence shown by people like Dr Chabot, psychiatrists are not omniscient.

Worse, it is possible that doctors could be projecting onto the patient's future what they themselves unconsciously wish to see there – a possibility any mental health professional versed in the psychoanalytic tradition should recognise. And a very few might be enjoying the unusual degree of power and control they have over someone else's fate.

5

A Few Grannies

Big fences

Freedom Lovers in their purest incarnation want people to be free to end their lives when, where, and how they want. Yet the way in which most say they wish to exercise this freedom depends upon the involvement of lots of other people – not an obvious route to getting something done precisely to one's liking.

An assisted death is likely to be quicker and easier than doing it yourself. But this doesn't mean a doctor has to do it on behalf of a state-backed service. It is not such a technical procedure that non-medics could not carry it out. Freedom Lovers could just have argued that each of us has a right to enter into a voluntary contract with another person to provide assistance in death – in which case nobody else should interfere. This seems to have been the original idea in Switzerland.

But in most places, campaigners don't argue for this minimal set-up. Apparently, they prefer the creation of an entire service integrated within a wider health system. They want professional medical involvement and a complex bureaucratic infrastructure. This is unlikely to keep busybodies – if that is how you regard people interested in controlling whether you live or die – out of your private arrangements. On the contrary, it invites them over the threshold.

One reason many Freedom Lovers seem keen on Big Assisted Death is that they see the attendant bureaucracy as protection for the individual. They assume that in private arrangements it is easy for one person to fall victim to the sinister machinations of another, and for autonomy to be violated instead of enhanced. In full-blown assisted death services, complete with lots of regulations and checking procedures, there may be less chance of this. As former Director of Public Prosecutions Max Hill, KC put it in 2025, in a statement intended to be supportive of Kim Leadbeater's bill:[1]

> [T]here is really very little point in scrutinising and looking for bad cases after the death has occurred. What is the point of an investigation, even a prosecution, after someone has been coerced into ending their life ... why are we doing that only after the fact? That is what's happening under the law at the moment.

To continue the metaphor: big fences maintained by lots of other people might seem stronger than your own puny ones. So let's see if that is true.

Not ideal

First, though, we should note a self-defeating tendency in popular versions of (hyper)liberalism. People who talk about freedom and rights are often very focused upon best-case scenarios, and unconcerned about how their preferred arrangements play out in practice. This tendency is apparent in other social debates: dreams of decriminalising prostitution, built upon the image of the middle-class student dabbling in escort work rather than the poverty-stricken mother standing on the street corner. Or, in discussion of how to medically treat minors confused about gender, visions of kids who will never regret hormones and surgeries in future – as opposed to the thousands for whom it turns out to be a phase. Academics, especially in the humanities, are some of the worst culprits here, unconcerned about how their imaginary social systems might work in the complex world we live in, full of moving parts.

Idealised thinking is also present in some defences of assisted death. In their enthusiasm for the UK's Terminally Ill Adults Bill, its sponsors often seemed unmoved by the fact that the NHS and social care services are already overstretched; that waiting lists for surgery are long and palliative care patchy; that mental health services can barely cope with the number of anxious and depressed people asking for help; and so on. Such facts could not fail to affect the way the law would operate, yet were treated by bill supporters as mostly separate issues.

A related point is that some prominent defenders of assisted death services seem – not to put too fine a point on it – quite rich. A number of prominent KCs publicly backed Leadbeater's bill. These included Lord Falconer, a former Lord Chancellor and Secretary of State for Justice under Tony Blair, who has brought several similar bills to parliament himself in the past. Television celebrities Dame Esther Rantzen and Dame Prue Leith were also among the bill's high-profile supporters. When the bill was first announced, Prime Minister Keir Starmer welcomed the news, saying he had previously 'made a promise' to Dame Esther that he would allow time for a debate and a vote. At the third reading, he voted for the bill himself.

With ample resources and powerful connections at one's

disposal, the legalisation of assisted death perhaps looks risk-free: a convenient 'good-to-have' to add to a range of services one can already access. In a gilded world, it may be easy to assume the future presence of loving partners or relatives who will never take advantage of ageing and fragile people; or benevolent, near-omniscient doctors who only want the best for their patients.

Actually, I don't think that's true for anyone. Either way, it seems we might need a refresher course in the varieties of human nature.

'You thought you could get away from me, didn't you?'

In 2018, thirty-four-year-old Jessica Laverack — known to family and friends as Jessie — tragically ended her life. After being strangled and stalked by a violent ex-partner, she had moved to a new town, but then was stalked by the same man again. Terrified and feeling helpless, she had eventually fallen into deep despair. Writing what is known as a 'Prevention of future deaths' report, the coroner at Jessie's inquest in 2022 identified 'a need for the recognition of the link between domestic abuse and suicide', also noting that '[p]rocesses and policies do not seem to include this serious area to the extent that is required'.

Since that moment — the first time the connection had ever been made in an English coroner's report — there has been heightened focus on the relation between intimate partner violence and suicide. It seems likely that previous numbers have been underestimated. For instance, a 2024 report found ninety-three 'suspected victim suicides following domestic abuse' in England and Wales for the period March 2022– April 2023, alongside more than a hundred homicides by partners or other family members.² In both cases, most victims were female.

But while this important discussion was starting to reach public consciousness, in a parallel world parliamentary supporters of the Terminally Ill Adults Bill were acting as if it was non-existent. Remember Labour MP Rachel Hopkins, imagining herself as an applicant for an assisted death and saying 'It is none of your business why I want to pursue this legal course of action'? It seems unlikely she would have said the same about the suicide of Jessie Laverack, whose final act of despair was also perfectly legal. Along with fellow supporters of an assisted death service, Hopkins apparently presumed dark aspects of human relationships were of little relevance: as if, once a person becomes terminally ill, they gain immunity from victimisation.

In fact though, terminally ill people are *more* vulnerable to coercion than many others. Their energy reserves are often depleted, and their psychological defences down. People in groups already prone to victimisation – for instance, the physically disabled, or those with learning disabilities or a history of mental illness – can become terminally ill too. And sensing new weakness in an ill partner or relative can bring out fresh sadistic tendencies, if a person is toxic and disordered enough.

And, of course, whether death looks attractive depends on the alternative. The most common relationship between suicide and coercion is *indirect*. For Jessie Laverack, life had become so terrible there seemed to her no other way out. It is easy to see how someone in her situation, once presented with a terminal diagnosis, might turn to an assisted death service as a means of quick escape. One survivor of intimate partner violence told a researcher about a previous suicide attempt:

> The moment that I knew that things were very, very wrong, was when I was regaining consciousness in hospital. I was

waking up and he was beside my bed, and he was stroking the side of my temples with his fingers. He was smiling, like smiling the most evil smile I've ever seen in my life. And he said, 'You thought you could get away from me, didn't you? You thought you could leave me.' That was the moment that I knew that I was in real trouble.[3]

As this suggests, solo suicide attempts don't always work, a fact that may well enhance the appeal of an assisted death service. For there is no legal requirement that your partner be informed of your decision to have an assisted death – including, of course, your coercive and abusive partner.

During parliamentary discussion, it also seemed to be a fantasy of bill supporters that no one could ever be directly coerced into doing something as drastic as taking their own life. But this too is easily disprovable. In 2021 in Boston, USA, a woman was sentenced for manslaughter, after her boyfriend killed himself just before his graduation. In court she admitted to 'escalating and unrelenting verbal, physical and psychological abuse', including sending forty-seven thousand text messages over a seven-week period, many urging him to take his life. According to the District Attorney's Office, 'suicidality began only as a result of ... near constant abuse'.[4] Admittedly, coercing someone into taking their own life, directly, is usually difficult: recall the common fear of self-injury described in Chapter Two. But the whole point of an assisted death service is that doctors make it very easy: no 'working up to it' required.

Some campaigners for assisted death services assume that nobody close to a terminally ill person would ever actively want to drive them to an early death for personal gain. *Guardian* journalist and campaigner Polly Toynbee has scoffed at the idea: 'That oft-quoted risk of death by relatives over-eager to grasp an inheritance always looked utterly implausible: they couldn't wait another month or two instead risking prosecution and a fourteen-year sentence for coercion?'[5]

Yet the criminal courts are very familiar with people who forge wills, steal from bank accounts, or physically abuse or kill elderly relatives for gain or kicks. To think that such characters would not take advantage of an assisted death service is – to put it frankly – delusional. A clinician acquaintance of mine, in a senior role at a US organisation managing care for 350,000 elderly or frail individuals, tells me: 'Here in NYC we deal with family members coveting apartments of the elderly.' Their targets are especially vulnerable, she notes: 'A third of the poor at end of life have no one to support them, living by themselves, overwhelmed by the minutiae of managing day to day life.'[6] The goal of a coercer might be financial: to acquire assets, or to save money on care. Or someone might have an unpaid role in caring for the ill or disabled person and just be fed up with doing it. Alternatively, the motive might be malice and spite arising out of poisonous relational dynamics. This is not an exhaustive list.

We should also remember that the majority of people with terminal diagnoses are elderly. Old age brings with it increasing susceptibility to coercion, abuse, and neglect; including frailty, confusion, memory loss, a retreat into the home, and the inability to look after bodily needs. Some of these things also make it less likely that an elderly person will be able to clearly articulate to a professional what is happening, should anyone ask. As the British Geriatrics Society reminded us in their position statement on Leadbeater's bill in 2024, older people are 'among the most vulnerable in society'.[7]

Sometimes suicide pacts are struck between older couples; rare, but made much easier by the existence of an assisted death service. Or – more precisely for our purposes – assisted death services can facilitate what from the outside look like mutual agreements, but in fact are one-sided decisions, made by half of a couple in the name of both. For a person intent on dying with their partner, an assisted death service might look like the most convenient way, assuming the pair both have qualifying health conditions. Research suggests that where this occurs, the dominant partner in the relationship introduces the idea and encourages it; and that 'the presence of cluster B personality traits such as narcissistic or borderline is of particular relevance in the dominant partner, while in the submissive one, dependent personality traits are more frequent'.[8] In 2022, fifty-eight cases of 'duo euthanasia' were recorded in the Netherlands, a number that is going up each year.[9] Of course, nobody can ask the 'submissive' partner about the true circumstances of the decision in retrospect.

But it is not just the elderly who are especially vulnerable to coercion. People with learning disabilities such as Down's syndrome are too. And they are not exempt from eligibility for an assisted death. A government equality impact assessment, published in May 2025, makes this clear: 'persons with learning disabilities ... may struggle to understand the information provided to them in written or oral form' and so should be provided with 'information in an accessible format'.[10]

As we know, campaigners for assisted death services tend to place a great deal of emphasis on autonomous choice. But the concept becomes quite hazy when it comes to those with cognitive disabilities. A default assumption is that most people possess the intellectual and emotional wherewithal to make good decisions for themselves; so that, if they do not in fact make good decisions, the moral responsibility lies only or mostly with them. But with someone who has systematic deficits in abstract thinking, social judgement, memory, and/or information retention, it is harder to maintain that their 'autonomous' – as in, 'self-governed' – decision-making should always be facilitated, especially when it comes to matters of life and death. The trusting behaviour of those with Down's or other similar impairment has been recognised as a worry when it comes to the possibility of undue influence. People with learning disabilities are particularly vulnerable to sexual exploitation, for instance, and can be more easily influenced to offer false confessions in a judicial context. Yet there is little sign this information is permeating the assisted death discourse.

The possibility that state health services might participate in a coerced death is a terrible prospect, to be ruled out if at all possible. The question is: how? In policing contexts, it is recognised that what the Crown Prosecution Service calls 'coercive or controlling behaviour' (sometimes 'coercive control' for short) is hard to spot. A coerced person can be very unwilling to discuss it. They may hide their true situation because they are frightened of the consequences of talking. They may tell a professional they agree to some particular decision, apparently convincingly; repeat the same point several times to different people; give reasonable-sounding explanations; yet all the while some other person is speaking through them.

Even where they apparently agree to something, a victimised person might have chosen differently if she hadn't been menaced or pressured by a hidden third party. According to the CPS, coercive control can include physical attacks, threats, isolating a person from their friends and family, limiting their income, monitoring their whereabouts electronically, making all daily life choices for them, and verbally humiliating them. Those subjected to such frightening treatment over a long period may end up so intimidated they can barely think straight.

Let us agree, then, that there is no reason to think these sadly familiar behaviours won't interact with assisted death provision. No magical transformations must occur in a relationship after a diagnosis of serious illness. Already vulnerable people stay vulnerable, and probably become even more so. Ill people, technically eligible for an assisted death, can still be victimised by partners, carers, or their own children. They too can start to long for death, not as an escape from disease but from a distressing future at the hands of others. They too can be made to fear life more than they hate death, or to think of themselves as a burden because other people are manipulatively telling them so. And a terminally ill person can go along with a partner's suicide plan for them both, not because she independently wants to, but because she feels unable to say no.

Ruling out coercion?

Against the backdrop of this troubling discussion, let's now look at actual assisted death services. How well do they detect any of this? The answer is: not very well at all.

There are of course safety protocols. Attempts are made to ensure that only people with severe enough illness or disability get access, according to whatever local terms are mandated. Doctors are required to declare they have seen sufficient evidence that health criteria have been met before signing off requests. If they don't have relevant expertise in the particular condition in question, they are supposed to seek it from another specialist.

Such rules, though imperfect in practice, are important. But for those who value autonomy, the most crucial protocols should involve checking that someone applying for an assisted death really wants to die. Diligent assessors will wish to satisfy themselves that coercion is absent. The trouble is, it is not very clear how they can reliably know.

Let's take the proposed UK system, vaunted by some of its champions as 'the safest in the world'.[11] Encouragingly, it stipulates that doctors are given special training about domestic abuse, including coercive control. There is also a plan to establish two new offences related to 'dishonesty, coercion and pressure' and 'falsification or destruction of documents', which might act as a deterrent. But at what points in this process can trained professionals exclude the suspicion of duress? Let's take the stages one by one, bearing in mind that safeguarding involves planning for the worst, not hoping for the best.

First, there is a preliminary discussion with the applicant. Here the doctor is required only to discuss the person's diagnosis and prognosis, any remaining treatment options, appropriate palliative alternatives, and possibilities for psychological support. There is no requirement to discuss why this person wants to die (here or at any later stage). At this initial point, then, opportunities to spot lurking coercion are limited, and nothing compels a doctor to delve deeper. And if the person is 'unwilling or unable' to conduct the preliminary discussion, all the doctor has to do is 'direct them to where they can obtain information and have the discussion'.[12]

Next, the applicant must make a 'first declaration', in writing, of their 'request for assistance'. This must state that the request to die is being made voluntarily, and that the applicant understands they may cancel at any time. Equally, though, another person – a proxy – can be appointed to make this declaration instead. They can intervene wherever the applicant 'declares to a proxy that they are unable to sign their own name ... by reason of physical impairment, being unable to read *or for any other reason*' (my italics). So, in theory, a person coercing an applicant from behind the scenes can tell officials they are going to act as proxy, stating that the applicant has already indicated an inability to sign; and the applicant would only have to give relatively minimal verbal or other signs of assent to the switch.

Either way, this declaration has to happen in front of the doctor in charge of the process (the 'co-ordinating doctor') and an independent witness. Doctor and witness must be unrelated to the applicant, and unlikely to benefit financially from the death. After that, there are two separate in-person assessments: one with the co-ordinating doctor, and the other with another doctor not already involved in the applicant's care. Officially, each of these clinicians should be independent of the other in terms of personal connections or professional hierarchies (though in fact this is unlikely, in any place where the lion's share of assisted death work goes to a relatively small number of doctors). There should be a gap of at least seven days between the appointments. Each doctor must assess the applicant for mental capacity, and check the first declaration was made voluntarily.

But two appointments with separate people does not offer much opportunity to get to know an applicant, or to look for telling signs of anxiety or fear. Though one of the doctors might have been involved in the applicant's care beforehand, this is not a given – and especially not in a pressured NHS. So both doctors might be meeting the applicant for the very first time. If appointments take place by video link, access to potentially instructive body language is also reduced.

Equally, there is no requirement to make strenuous investigations into an applicant's background. In forming their judgements, the two doctors are required to examine only those parts of the applicant's medical records that appear 'relevant', which means they can legitimately ignore large chunks. They are only required to 'make such enquiries' of other health or social care professionals as they consider 'appropriate' – which in practice means they don't have to make any at all. They don't have to talk to the applicant's family, nor make enquiries with the police. As with every assessor, at every stage, they don't have to raise any questions about why the applicant wants to die. Given the lack of concrete information, it's unclear how training to detect coercion would help.

And if assessors do have suspicions and refuse the application on that basis, they don't need to record them in much detail. So if the applicant tries again, there need not be a paper trail.

The final major stage of the process is consideration by a three-person panel comprised of a social worker, a lawyer, and a psychiatrist. This panel is not supposed to be adversarial, with two sides making a case, for or against, but more like a gentle conversation. The panel inspects the paperwork and hears from the applicant over video or audio link in a single meeting. Since no member of the panel will have encountered the applicant beforehand, here too there is limited opportunity to assess body language and demeanour (and even less so, if audio only). Under 'exceptional circumstances' the panel need not hear from the applicant at all.

The panel also has to 'hear from' the doctors involved in the assessment, and though they 'may question' them, they do not have to. Panel members have no special powers to order the disclosure of background information, or to compel witnesses; no enhanced access to medical or social care records; like the doctors, no requirement to engage with family members who might have useful insight; no access to potentially relevant material about wills or financial records. The people they talk to are not under oath, and the meeting is private. As one sceptical Conservative MP, Danny Kruger – the son of Prue Leith – put it during parliamentary scrutiny: 'It is a panel with judicial power to approve life-or-death decisions, but it is without a judge or the normal judicial processes that would happen in a tribunal or court.'[13]

If satisfied, the panel will sign a 'certificate of eligibility'. There will then be a second period of reflection, lasting either fourteen days or forty-eight hours, depending on whether natural death looks likely to occur very soon. After this, the applicant or the proxy makes a second declaration, again witnessed by a doctor and an independent witness. The doctor confirms the second declaration; at which point what is euphemistically called the 'provision of assistance at the end of life' can be made.

Despite the surface rigour, the proposed UK assessment process is not well set up to uncover background coercion. If a person with a terminal diagnosis repeats with enough apparent sincerity their wish for an assisted death, that will be deemed good enough. There is a general impression of the system doing the minimum rather than exerting officials to do the maximum. This stands in stark contrast to the state's attitude to unlawful killing in other contexts. That the state could actively participate in a coerced death would normally be disturbing to everybody. But where the terms 'freedom' and 'mercy' are being bandied about in the name of the interests of the individual, moral antennae seem to go haywire.

Services in other countries suffer from similar blind spots. On the homepage of US organisation Death with Dignity, you can find the rather hubristic assessment: 'Proven safe, effective, and above all, meaningful, the Oregon Death with Dignity Act works exactly as intended and exactly for whom it was intended, without fail.'[14] Yet according to one expert observer, 'the Oregon Public Health Division simply does not collect the information it would need to effectively monitor the law'.[15] And even so, there have been several suspected or documented cases of coerced death for financial gain, with one involving criminal mistreatment.[16] In the Australian state of Victoria, according to a former attorney general there, training for doctors in spotting coercion totals five minutes, while the use of video link worsens the 'difficulties of detecting mental illness, coercion or other family pressure'.[17] In Western Australia, out of 1,851 eligibility assessments the 'acting voluntarily and without coercion' test did not succeed in screening a single applicant out.[18] In Canada, out of 19,660 requests for assisted death during 2023, only forty-one were turned down because of the perception of involuntariness or coercion. In the Netherlands in 2025, six cases out of 9,958 people who died by euthanasia were referred to the public prosecutor for possible criminal charges, all due to 'procedural errors'.[19] Only someone quite naive could think that this represented the true picture.

Listening to UK MPs during parliamentary scrutiny, it was at times hard to countenance their complacency. The discussion seemed completely out of step with thinking now going on about coercive control in policing and social care. Along with Rachel Hopkins's 'none of your business' comment, this attitude was summed up in a confident dismissal by Labour's Jack Abbott. In response to a colleague's suggestion that doctors should be required to ask an applicant why they wanted an assisted death, he said: 'I gently suggest ... the "why" is that people with a terminal diagnosis, with six months to live, would like a course of action to end their lives in a pain-free way and to have the autonomy to do so.'[20]

Here again we find the attitude that once a diagnosis of terminal illness is made, normal moral considerations should not apply. Traditionally, the state's job is to protect the freedom of its citizens against unlawful aggression, including against killing or coercion. Where an assisted death service makes little effort to root these things out in advance, effectively it becomes a partner in crime with abusers. It is likely that struggling victims will be sent to preventable, unfree deaths at the hands of doctors – and relatively undetectably so, since the victim's silence is assured.

Genuine Freedom Lovers, whether radical or moderate, should care about this. And so for that matter should careful Merciful Helpers. Those in favour of assisted death services tend to rely heavily on the idea that the individual who chooses to die is responsible for their decision, even if a doctor assists. But assisted death is a joint project by definition. If the system fails to provide proper scrutiny and a coerced person dies, the doctors concerned will have unwittingly participated in something deeply immoral, if not an actual crime.

Controlling life and death

During the inquiry that followed the conviction of Dr Harold Shipman in 2000 for murdering fifteen of his patients, the presiding judge estimated that the GP had in fact killed at least 215 people, and perhaps as many as 250. Most of his victims were female. The crimes for which he was convicted concerned women ranging between the ages of forty-nine and eighty-one.

Shipman carried out murders in victims' homes and, occasionally, in his surgery office. His modus operandi was to tell a patient she looked pale and so should have a blood test. She would roll up her sleeve and look away; he would administer a fatal dose of diamorphine and watch her die. Afterwards, he would alter medical records to suggest prior ill health, sign the death certificate himself, and wherever possible talk relatives into an early cremation without post mortem.

Reflecting on this atrocious case from the vantage point of 2020, the prosecuting trial barrister recalled that the motive had not been financial but simply 'exercising the ultimate power of controlling life and death'. Malign actors as extreme as Shipman are highly unusual in a health service, but no idealiser should deceive herself that lightning cannot strike twice. Indeed, Shipman arguably had a predecessor, the Eastbourne GP Dr John Bodkin Adams, believed by some to have killed hundreds of his patients from the 1920s onwards.[21] You might naively presume that for a psychopathic health professional with a God complex, fascinated by 'exercising the ultimate power of controlling life and death', there would be little thrill in working in proximity to an assisted death service, where it is already explicit that doctors may participate in voluntary killing. Actually, I suspect this is exactly where you might find such a person.

Most doctors and nurses enter their profession sincerely set on doing good. Outsiders cannot properly imagine the intensely demanding situations that they have to face. To point out the possibility of bad apples says nothing about the well-intentioned, dedicated, and highly capable majority. But safeguarding involves thinking about worst-case scenarios. One can easily imagine a situation where a Machiavellian doctor or nurse finds it exciting to illicitly influence a terminally ill person's decision-making processes; conjuring detailed pictures of inevitable pain and suffering to come, should they wait; or subtly suggesting it would be easier for all if they opted for death. Perhaps the doctor secretly dislikes a particular identity group and targets them especially. Or perhaps they just like playing with people's lives. This scenario may seem outlandish, but so did the Shipman case at first. What is less easy to imagine is how the authorities would ever find out – for many of the standard ways of detecting professional malpractice just don't apply here.

The Shipman public inquiry identified several means by which unscrupulous doctors, intent on hastening patients' deaths, might be more quickly identified in future. These measures were also supposed to act as deterrents. One pivotal reform was better monitoring of GP records in order to look for high death rates. There was also increased oversight of prescriptions; tightening up death certification; giving coroners enhanced powers to investigate deaths and hold inquests; and the introduction of a system of medical examiners to independently scrutinise deaths not investigated by a coroner.

But none of these can have much bearing on the detection of malign doctors in the context of an assisted death service.

By definition, death rates are going to be high. A national database of controlled substances won't help when lethal substances are already sanctioned to end people's lives. Writing on the death certificate that someone's death was 'assisted' will cause no alarm bells to ring. And inquests will normally be deemed unnecessary, since their results look like foregone conclusions. Indeed, in May 2025, a former chief coroner of England and Wales, His Honour Judge Thomas Teague, KC, complained in a letter to *The Times* that 'by removing any realistic prospect of an effective inquest, such a dispensation would magnify, rather than diminish, the obvious risks of deception and undue influence' since 'the coroner's statutory duty to investigate all unnatural deaths, irrespective of whether any misfeasance is alleged, provides a powerful deterrent against wrongdoing'.[22]

There are always those who minimise such issues. In his defence of assisted death in the US, philosopher Gerald Dworkin protested that '[i]f a physician can manipulate the patient's request for death, he can manipulate the patient's request for termination [i.e. withdrawal] of treatment'.[23] This is true, perhaps; but it doesn't follow that we should throw up our hands and blithely usher in more opportunities for coercive manipulation. It always perplexes me when people respond to the identification of one harmful thing by defensively pointing out some other harmful thing. Why not try to eliminate both?

The fact that two doctors separately assess the applicant lessens the risk of a rogue doctor, but doesn't suppress it entirely. The involvement of a panel also constitutes something of a check. But still, we should not fantasise. In a haphazard, time-pressured system requiring only a few short interviews and inspection of paperwork, an applicant's faulty reasoning about the consequences of their own condition – a subtly misleading interpretation, maliciously fostered for Shipmanesque kicks – might remain undiscovered.

'The very best work I've ever done'

And this is not the only potential danger to patients from clinicians. In nearly every profession, you find enthusiasts – and assisted death services are no different. Doctors who don't like the process tend to vote with their feet, leaving the field clear for those with fewer qualms. Over time, a service is likely to become monopolised by clinicians who feel it is their special vocation.

Once again, Canada points the way. Some of the Canadian doctors who offer assisted death seem thoroughly delighted with their jobs. 'I find that the act of offering the option of an assisted death is one of the most therapeutic things we do,' says Dr Stefanie Green, an obstetrician who also specialises in euthanasia, and who describes both kinds of procedures she offers as 'deliveries'. Interviewed by the *New Atlantis* in 2023, Green said she had carried out more than three hundred assisted deaths at that point. She has also written a book about it, subtitled 'A doctor's story of empowering patients at the end of life'. Prominent in various medical bodies advocating for assisted death, Green advertises her services as a public speaker and gives regular interviews about her work. Safe to say, then, she is a fan.

Another Canadian doctor, Dr Ellen Wiebe, has participated in at least 430 assisted deaths, according to testimony she gave to a parliamentary committee in Canada in 2022. Since then, Wiebe has been involved in many more, though is reluctant to say the exact number. She has described her work as 'rewarding' and 'about honouring people's wishes, empowering people to have control over their own lives – it's wonderful that I have the opportunity to do that'.[24] A heavily circulated clip from a 2024 BBC documentary fronted by the British actress Liz Carr shows a wide-eyed, highly enthusiastic Wiebe telling a sceptical Carr that assisted death work is 'the very best work I have ever done' on the grounds that 'nobody is more grateful than my patients'.[25]

In late 2024, a temporary court injunction was issued to stop Wiebe euthanising a mentally ill woman, whose condition was expected by other doctors to resolve within months. The procedure was allegedly approved by Wiebe after a single Zoom meeting.[26] (Wiebe would not comment on the case other than to say that she has never violated Canadian assisted death laws and does not know of any provider who has.[27]) And in a leaked audio recording, reported on in 2023, Wiebe described how she had euthanised a man already deemed ineligible for an assisted death in a different Canadian province. Medical assessors in the applicant's home province had judged that he did not meet the criteria for assisted death and also lacked the capacity to make informed decisions, though a psychiatric report on his file disagreed and assessed him as having capacity. Wiebe, by her own admission in the recording, assessed the applicant virtually and found him eligible, along with another local doctor who agreed with her. 'And he flew all by himself to Vancouver,' she said. 'I picked him up at the airport, um, brought him to my clinic and provided for him.'[28]

This is known as 'doctor shopping' – persisting with a request until you can find a doctor who agrees to do what you want. In the audio recording, Wiebe related how the applicant just described was put in contact with her through the Canadian organisation Dying with Dignity. It is easy to see how this can happen, and perhaps even impossible to stop in a place where an assisted death service exists. Where something is a benefit, the thinking goes, where is the harm in making sure as many get access to it as possible? In the UK system too, this is bound to happen. Certain doctors will become known for being especially good at their jobs.

The idea of assisted death as a benefit, to which all

terminally ill people should have access, also lies behind the idea that a doctor should be able to bring up the idea of assisted death during a consultation, even if the patient has not mentioned it before. This point was repeatedly insisted upon by Leadbeater during scrutiny of her bill, facing down attempts by critics to amend wording so that only a patient could legitimately mention the matter first. In the end it was stipulated that while doctors were under no positive duty to bring the matter up, nothing prevented them from doing so, even multiple times.

Some groups – most obviously, those with Down's syndrome and similar learning disabilities – are more vulnerable to suggestion than others, as we have seen. But most of us are somewhat susceptible to medical authority, particularly when ill and anxious. We are used to deferring to expertise about decisions involving the body and health – indeed, we are encouraged to do so. They are supposed to have the detailed knowledge, not us. The aftermath of the Shipman inquiry led to much soul-searching in the UK about how to reduce medical paternalism and increase patient autonomy. Even so, it is usually impossible to eliminate the knowledge imbalance between doctor and patient. If they didn't know more than you, there would be little point in consulting them.

Campaigners for assisted death like to promote the fiction that an applicant must already have a clear and settled intention to die before they make an application. All the doctor really does is give the applicant what they already want. But with such a big decision, there is no reason to think that is true; and especially not where an enthusiastic doctor has raised the possibility of an assisted death first. In that context, the suggestion might easily seem like a helpful steer or recommendation. Equally, even where it *was* the patient who initiated the conversation, she might still be in two minds. Some might be absolutely certain of their decisions, but others are bound to feel hesitant and tentative. And in the latter case, it will make a difference if the applicant encounters a doctor sensitive enough to gauge latent hesitation, or, alternatively, one who railroads them through.

Some researchers usefully distinguish between 'desire to die' statements and a request for assisted death. As one analysis puts it, the former is 'death talk' and 'suicide talk' from a patient in the presence of a doctor, which 'may represent a desire for a hastened death' but equally 'may represent an expression of psychosocial distress or a passing comment without literal intention'. The worry is that, where a patient is engaging in desire-to-die statements, gung-ho doctors may not notice the difference.[29] In 2025, Canadian palliative care specialist Dr Leonie Herx told a podcast of the time the assisted death team at her hospital was called for a female in her fifties with a history of depression and a potentially reversible heart condition. She had been admitted with breathing difficulties, was panicking, and was heard saying 'I can't live like this.' As Dr Herx recalled: 'The cardiologist says, I'd better call the MAID team because I'm going to be accused of blocking access to assisted death if someone doesn't come and talk to them.' By the next day, before anyone had had a chance to offer medical alternatives, the patient had been euthanised.[30]

Does such influence count as coercion? Not strictly speaking, I don't think. There is no force or threat involved, and – with the exception of those with learning disabilities, who don't have sufficiently independent judgement – the applicant still technically has a choice. Unless these enthusiastic doctors flout the law, there is no criminality. And certainly, there is an important moral distinction between the merely keen provider of assisted death and the malevolent Shipman type. But still there is a troubling sense that, in the presence of a doctor who displays missionary-like zeal for the process, an applicant's decision to die may not be fully their own. Had they met different doctors, they could have decided differently and been alive months or even years later.

Freedom for all is expensive

We are lucky enough to live in a society that, theoretically at least, considers every life important. When an unidentified body turns up, efforts are made to identify it. If a death looks suspicious, it is investigated. Cold cases stay open, and there is always the possibility of a crime being solved years after the event. Once Shipman's heinous crimes were discovered, there was a public inquiry, and an attempt to learn lessons by those who had missed the signs. It is easy to take this attitude for granted, but it doesn't have to be this way. Plenty of societies have treated some kinds of human life as expendable.

Most of this chapter has been concerned with ways in which bad actors might covertly interfere with the provision of an assisted death service, both in the personal realm and occasionally in the medical one. So what might a safe, responsible assisted death service look like, in line with the attitude officially taken to life and death elsewhere?

The answer is: very expensive and time-consuming. There would have to be in-depth investigations before every decision, with officials given enhanced inquisitorial powers to draw upon a large range of evidence. There would also be secondary requirements: dedicated training and skills testing for all involved, regular audits, scrupulous record keeping, and so on. And there would have to be enhanced managerial oversight of any doctor–patient relationships, though how to achieve this is unclear.

Spelling this out perhaps makes clear why legislators don't seriously try to address the issue. Namely: they know they can't possibly afford to. Most health services are already overstretched. There aren't enough doctors to do the job, let alone social workers, lawyers, or judges, on top of the demanding roles they already have. Investigations into criminal backgrounds or financial records would also be a strain. Even worse, in places where assisted death services are already in place, the numbers of users tend to increase each year. Should assisted death become suddenly very popular, there would not be remotely enough capacity to cope.

Indeed, in Switzerland, where there is currently a mandatory investigation into every assisted suicide, there is growing unease about the financial cost. The obligation to investigate is enshrined in a law which dictates that there must be an investigation for every unnatural death. As a result of the growing costs of investigation, some pro-assisted death organisations are lobbying for assisted suicide to be treated as a special class of unnatural death, for which investigation is not required.[31] (Belgium, in contrast, treats an assisted death as a 'natural' death, defining the need for automatic investigation out of existence.[32])

The conclusion is inescapable. No assisted death service subject to realistic time and resource constraints can reliably deliver freedom for all its users. In some cases, it is bound to deliver quite the opposite. Though it might have seemed at first that a big system has sturdier fences, instead we have found that the bigger and more sprawling the system, the bigger the gaps.

Some supporters would simply price in the likelihood of coercive death for other unlucky people. Henry Marsh, a prominent British neurosurgeon in favour of such services, once remarked: 'Even if a few grannies are bullied into committing suicide, isn't that a price worth paying so that all these other people can die with dignity?'[33] More recently, Marsh seems to have moved to a position of denial: assisted death laws, he says, are 'not a slippery slope to killing off old people, vulnerable people ... it doesn't happen, you have legal safeguards'.[34] Personally, though, I preferred his earlier stance. Callous as it may have sounded, at least it was in touch with human nature.

6

A Humiliating Dependency on Others

Not worth living

As we know, supporters of assisted death services often assume that life with a terminal illness is not worth living. But why? Being terminally ill is not inevitably full of suffering, yet such narratives barely break through. As we've just seen, lobbyists rarely worry about worst-case scenarios when it comes to safeguarding an assisted death service. But when picturing experiences of dying, they hardly do anything else.

One word used a lot is *dignity*. Dying supposedly involves losing dignity quite radically, in a way that can be restored by an early death. Supportive organisations often have it in the title: Switzerland's Dignitas; Canada's Dying with Dignity; the US's Death with Dignity; and the UK's Dignity in Dying (formerly the Voluntary Euthanasia Legalisation Society). The Oregon statute pertaining to assisted suicide is called the Death with Dignity Act and specifies the right of a person to make a 'request for medication to end one's life in a humane and dignified manner'. Numerous similar US statutes also refer to it as a pivotal concept.

In short, dignity is a big rhetorical hitter. It has a long intellectual history, but is also quite a nebulous idea. It is rarely defined and often seems to refer only to an entirely subjective feeling. People are usually more able to identify a loss of dignity than the possession of it. So let's see what it might mean.

Kant can't help

When dignity came into vogue in the nineteenth century, it was broadly understood as an inalienable worth that each person inherently possessed – one that mandated mutual recognition and respect. The concept became prominent in the Catholic tradition, where humans are supposed to have a special standing because God has made them in His image. But there were also secular influences. The eighteenth-century Prussian philosopher Immanuel Kant – although himself a Protestant believer – provided an important account of dignity which did not depend on God for its success.

For Kant, human dignity is essentially bound up with the possession of autonomy: the capacity for self-government and 'owning' oneself and one's decisions that we met in Chapter One. He thought of autonomy as essentially involving the exercise of reason. The capacity to make freely willed, rational decisions on behalf of oneself gives a person inherent worth. In my dealings with you, I should respect your dignity – i.e. your capacity for rational self-government – just as you should respect mine. Doing so is incompatible with instrumentally treating others as a 'mere means' to your own selfish ends: selling them, enslaving or coercing them, sexually subjugating them, deceiving them, and so on.

Dignity, in this expansive sense, became a cornerstone of the rejection of previously entrenched social hierarchies. Eventually it came to underpin arguments for democracy and equal treatment for every citizen. By 1948, the Declaration of Human Rights was affirming 'the dignity and worth of the human person' and using the concept as a springboard to argue for a raft of universal rights.

In the contemporary context, there are those who see an assisted death service as an application of what is sometimes called 'patient autonomy'. Once I am terminally ill, they reason, I should be able to choose to die if I think this outcome is best for me; and a doctor should act as the instrument through which my autonomous decision is achieved. Some doctors think of themselves this way too: as when Dr Stefanie Green wrote of ending the life of a woman called Edna: 'I had to remind myself it was Edna's disease that was killing her and my role was only to facilitate her free will.'[1]

In fact, in tying dignity to autonomy and vice versa, Kant was not suggesting we should each be empowered by others to do whatever we want. Overall, he was more concerned with immoral and abusive things that should *not* be done to fellow humans because they count as violations of autonomy and dignity, rather than things to be positively done *for* them. In a medical context, respecting patient autonomy means not imposing treatments against a patient's will, rather than positively supplying them on demand. And Kant would have also pointed out that doctors like Green are not simply blind instruments of their patients' wishes, but rational people with autonomous projects of their own. They can't just shrug off their moral responsibility by claiming someone else's will is acting through them.

But perhaps the most basic problem with leaning on Kantian dignity to support assisted death is that Kant thought that *every* rational human had dignity – healthy, ill, dying, or otherwise. (There is a complication here about groups of people presumed to lack rationality, but let's leave that aside for now.) You can't lose dignity just by being seriously ill or dying, or by having bodily complaints that make you feel humiliated and ashamed. It's not that ephemeral. In the liberal tradition, dignity isn't really about the state of your body or feelings at all. It is much more profound and elemental: effectively, a replacement for the Christian value of 'sanctity of life' in a secular world.

Indeed, very much like more traditional Christians at the time, Kant was against suicide in nearly all forms. He thought that to choose it was to treat the self as a passive 'thing' to be got rid of; to renounce one's own agency and so one's own dignity too. Not mincing his words, he wrote that the person who attempts suicide 'sinks lower than the beasts'. He assumed that when you let things like pain, fear, or feelings of humiliation overwhelm you, your decision is the *opposite* of acting autonomously. Feelings, he argued, are not quite rational; so if feelings are in the driving seat for decision-making, it probably means the autonomous self is not.

We don't have to agree with him about all of that. But it does seem as if one of dignity's most prominent philosophical champions is not going to help much with the cause of assisted death.

Assistance for all or for none

Similar issues crop up with other liberal-egalitarian interpretations. During the eighteenth century, one definition of dignity was having a noble social position, or 'rank of elevation' as Samuel Johnson put it in his dictionary. The idea goes back to Roman times: the ideal of a well-bred, 'great-souled' nobleman, as opposed to the common herd. Early liberal thinkers such as Mary Wollstonecraft repurposed this old idea of dignity to apply it to all humans. But we meet the same problem, assuming we are trying to use the retention of dignity as a defence of assisted death. Wollstonecraft's dignity was supposed to be something that every human had, irrespective of their bodily state. It was supposed to do away with hierarchies, not create new ones.

To corroborate the thought that terminal illness involves a loss of dignity, it might seem more promising to look towards pre-Enlightenment and indeed pre-Christian traditions. One obvious candidate is the ancient Stoic view. The Stoic philosophers – including Seneca, whose thoughts on suicide we briefly met in Chapter One – conceived of dignity (or something a bit like it, anyway) in functional terms, partly tied to your bodily state. One of the contexts in which Stoics allowed that suicide may be justified is during severe illness and/or serious bodily debilitation, making it impossible to pursue a virtuous life.

The Stoics believed that living virtuously and in tune with nature requires being able to use reason to achieve one's ends; for man's reason is part of a world that is rationally ordered, indicating its divinity.[2] Sometimes the gravely ill and suffering body can no longer act in accordance with reason, in which case it is more admirable to choose departure. A suicide carried out merely because of the presence of pain and suffering would be neither dignified nor admirable; in his letters to Lucilius, Seneca is very clear that we should not let such 'trivial' things overcome us. But it is a different matter to leave life because your deteriorating bodily state means you can no longer achieve your rational goals.

We can perhaps see affinities here with modern support for assisted death. Some people define the possession of dignity in terms of having what clinicians refer to as 'functionality' – meaning, being capable of performing daily tasks and activities. Terminally ill people often lack functionality, at least without the right kind of help. And another train of thought ties dignity to bodily control: if illness means you have lost control of your bodily functions, then you lack dignity in this sense too.

But there is a problem with applying this ancient thought to the present context. The Graeco-Roman philosophy of suicide was concerned with what an individual should do – stick around, or find an exit – and there was little question of demanding another person or institution help you bow out. Indeed, given the famous Stoic emphasis on self-sufficiency, the idea that people might routinely think of themselves as dependent upon the assistance of others in order to die would have been treated with amazement.

In contrast, assisted death services provided by the modern state involve many people, and carry with them social consequences that go far beyond whatever benefits they provide to individuals (or not). One such consequence is an institutionalised message communicated to the wider world about the value of lives spent under certain bodily conditions. If 'dignity' is officially construed in terms of functionality and/or bodily control, it will turn out that anyone who lacks these capacities will lack dignity too.

Now, this might be a good result if you are narrowly focused on acquiring access to an assisted death. But it is not a good result for people in a similar position who want their life to be valued, and to be supported by others. While you are dying, you are still living – sometimes for quite a long time. There are many in this situation who don't want to die unnaturally early, and who reject the idea that their life is lacking in worth.

The general shape of the problem can be put like this. Eighteenth- and nineteenth-century liberal-egalitarian conceptions of dignity are pretty abstract, tied to general human qualities and not to concrete bodily conditions. That makes them hopeless for justifying assisted death for any human group. But if instead you define 'dignity' in terms of specific bodily capacities, you end up detrimentally shifting social norms about the value of lives that lack those capacities. Once this sort of definition is embedded into a formally organised service, delivering assisted death at scale – in which the absence of certain bodily capacities is presented as a good reason to help end someone's life – people will start to believe that *anyone at all* who lacks those capacities lacks dignity.

In vain might you protest that the absence of certain bodily capacities only takes your dignity *sometimes*; or it only makes life unbearable if you, personally, can't bear it and so consent to your own life ending. This is far too nuanced a message for a big impersonal system to get across. To grant assisted death only to a restricted group of people – even where they are consenting – clearly implies there is something awful about those lives. I am not saying that society will immediately start euthanising everyone in a supposedly 'undignified' position; but that there will now be an explicit excuse for disvaluing that kind of life.

In 1997, a disability activist organisation in the US made exactly this point, arguing against legalising assisted death on the grounds of 'dignity'.[3] Members of Not Dead Yet offered lawmakers a stark challenge: either allow assisted death for every adult who has mental capacity, or ban it completely. What was not acceptable, according to them, was to decide that only people with certain bodily complaints should have access. This challenge cleverly exposed the inconsistency of those who argue for assisted death only for some groups, yet do so on the supposed grounds of freedom and autonomy. If assisted death services really were interested in providing these things, there would be no implicit value judgements about which lives were 'unbearable'; but only an exit route available to all.

The implication should be looked squarely in the face. Judgements about lives that supposedly lack dignity, applied to terminally ill people who cannot carry out daily tasks or lack control over their bodily functions, are judgements about the value of certain kinds of human life. Lives with these complaints are judged less valuable than healthy ones. And those judgements extend to anyone at all in the same boat, whether they hate their life or absolutely love it.

Not dead yet

Perhaps you are wondering why we should sacrifice the interests of terminally ill people who long for an assisted death in order to protect the interests of those who want to go on living. It's a reasonable question. Put like that, though, it doesn't capture all that is at stake. For defining a lack of dignity in terms of a lack of bodily capacities doesn't just have a negative effect on terminally ill people. It adversely affects physically disabled people without terminal diagnoses too.

Not Dead Yet – whose name comes from a Monty Python sketch – has also made this argument. Its founders were first galvanised into action by the repeated reluctance of officials to prosecute Jack Kevorkian. Members were particularly concerned by the fact that some people dying with the help of Kevorkian's Thanatron were not terminally ill, only disabled. Their stated aim was, and still is, to fight assisted death laws and services in the US as they affect disabled people in particular.

In 2003 a UK chapter, Not Dead Yet UK, was founded by the disability rights activist Jane Campbell, now a life peer. Diagnosed with spinal muscular atrophy as a child, Baroness Campbell has been fighting for disability rights for decades. She features in the 2024 BBC TV documentary *Better Off*

Dead?, telling her fellow activist Liz Carr that 'people look at us and think we're in need of care, and we're weak and vulnerable. We are not! We are probably the toughest, toughest people out there, because we have to problem-solve every day of our lives.'[4]

A simple and effective point made by Not Dead Yet is that terminal illness and physical disability tend to overlap in their effects. The bodily conditions cited as justification for offering a terminally ill person an assisted death are the same ones that many non-terminal disabled people live with for years. Chronic pain, loss of control over bodily functions, and incapacity to do daily tasks unaided are often present with non-terminal disability too. So once a health service starts helping terminally ill people to die because of these supposed indignities, a wider negative message is communicated. In *Better Off Dead?* Jane Campbell tells Liz Carr that she herself has been judged terminally ill in the past, once receiving a 'Do Not Resuscitate' order when unconscious in hospital with a chest infection, before her husband managed to get it rescinded.

On the strength of such logic, the same service may eventually start to assist disabled, non-terminal people to die as well. For evidence that this is not just paranoia, we have Canada. The original 2016 law restricted assisted death to people whose deaths were 'reasonably foreseeable' – itself a vague category, potentially covering a lot of disabled people. But in 2017 two plaintiffs, themselves disabled, successfully challenged the legislation. Eligibility conditions were widened to include those without terminal diagnoses too.

This change didn't just enable depressed, poor, or unsupported disabled people to apply for assisted death in a spirit of hopelessness. It also challenges disabled people in general. In plain sight, Canada's medical services are now treating serious bodily disability as a good enough reason, on its own, to end someone's life. As Liz Carr points out in her programme, where an able-bodied person and a seriously disabled person are both suicidal, the Canadian system says to one of them, 'stay', and to the other, 'go'.

Not Dead Yet argues that such a negative judgement on the value of physically disabled life permeates the whole of society, undermining attempts to help disabled people live more comfortably and meaningfully. Indeed, in the same year as the Canadian law expanded to include physically disabled people, a report published in the *Canadian Medical Association Journal* found that 'doctor-assisted death could reduce annual health-care spending across the country by between $34.7 million and $136.8 million', with savings dwarfing direct costs.[5] There are multiple reports from Canada of disabled people asking for social support and having assisted death suggested to them by clinicians instead. And this is not unexpected: once an early death is formally treated within a system as a benefit – even a 'medical' solution – it follows that clinicians in charge of your care are bound to start weighing it up as a potentially reasonable approach.

None of this is especially merciful – quite the opposite. In Chapter Three we looked at information collected from Canadians choosing to die. Many of the reasons offered refer to aspects of physical disability: for instance, 'loss of ability to engage in meaningful activities'; 'loss of ability to perform activities of daily living'; 'loss of independence'; and 'loss of control of bodily functions'.[6] For disabled people, at least some of this suffering might be alleviated with access to consistent, high-quality medical and social support; but of course, that would be more expensive. True mercy would be to seriously invest resources and effort into making those lives easier, so that early death doesn't look like the best option.

Trapped in the motte

As the Stoics loved to point out two millennia ago, for most people who wish to die early a variety of means are already available. Here is Seneca again, colourfully labouring the point:

> In whatever direction you may turn your eyes, there lies the means to end your woes. See you that precipice? Down that is the way to liberty. See you that sea, that river, that well? There sits liberty at the bottom. See you that tree, stunted, blighted, and barren? Yet from its branches hangs liberty. See you that throat of yours, your gullet, your heart? They are ways of escape from servitude. Are the ways of egress I show you too toilsome, do they require too much courage and strength? Do you ask what is the highway to liberty? Any vein in your body.[7]

An important source of ideological support for assisted death services comes from the perceived value of freedom and autonomy; yet as Seneca makes plain, able-bodied terminally ill people already have these things, technically speaking. Occasionally, you find a campaigner making the hyperbolic claim that terminally ill people are being 'forced into living' by the absence of an assisted death service in their neighbourhood. Thus the philosopher Christopher Belshaw writes of people being 'coerced or pressured into continuing with life, when what they really want ... is to die'.[8] But really, this just isn't true. The average able-bodied person is no more forced into living by the absence of an assisted death service than they are forced into starvation by the absence of a personal chef.

How, then, should assisted death services be generally justified – let alone publicly funded – when the means to die at a moment of one's choosing already lies within most terminally ill people's power, assuming they can bring themselves to do it?

Enter severely physically disabled terminally ill people, literally unable to end their own lives except with great difficulty. Such people are now suddenly crucial to defences of assisted death.

In medieval castles, there was often a tower called a motte, and a patch of harder-to-defend land around the motte called a bailey. A motte-and-bailey fallacy has come to refer to a deceptive argument form. This alternates between venturing out to a relatively expansive, controversial conclusion (the bailey) then retreating to a narrower, somewhat easier-to-defend one (the motte), trying to convert listeners' support for the latter into support for the former, hoping they don't notice the difference. For us, the motte is assisted death services for physically disabled, terminally ill people 'trapped' into living, while the bailey is assisted death services for terminally ill people in general.

The most persuasive Freedom Loving case for an assisted death service – still insufficient but at least consistent – would be one that offered it *exclusively* to people who are genuinely so incapacitated they are unable to end their own lives. Yet to my knowledge, campaigners virtually never restrict their support for an assisted death service only to such cases. And I find that telling. Influencing the modern, secular sense of 'dignity', Kant urged us not to treat fellow humans as merely instrumental means to our own selfish ends. Using the plight of severely disabled people to railroad through assisted death services for a much wider group is in fact quite instrumental-ising, and shows little respect for the proper dignity of these people in Kant's foundational sense.

The particular hell of acquired disability

It will perhaps seem that I am trivialising the suffering of those with serious physical disability. As an able-bodied person, I have no real idea about what is like to be paralysed or otherwise unable to move around self-directedly; to be dependent on other people for most or all of my bodily needs; to have little control over bodily functions. I can try to imagine but I'm sure I will fail.

Tales of awful suffering must not be generalised to whole groups. What a disabled person feels about their life will depend on many contextual factors, and we should not make assumptions. But there is one sort of situation that seems virtually guaranteed to produce intense suffering: that is, where a person acquires severe physical disability through injury or sudden illness. Becoming permanently tetraplegic or quadriplegic, say – dependent upon others for nearly everything, when only days beforehand you were able-bodied – is a horrific blow. There is no gradual deterioration, but an absolute change of state from one day to the next, with memories of one's former life painfully to the forefront. The learning curve is steep, and grief for what has been lost overwhelming.

People who experience spinal cord injuries were often active, sport-loving people beforehand, especially valuing their strength and independence. Put in this suddenly devastating position, you are not necessarily terminally ill: you might have decades of life left to live, albeit with some difficult and unpleasant complications. In the depths of suffering, the thought of future longevity may seem more like a curse than a blessing. Some of the people in this situation really do feel trapped into living, with no real options for control: they can't move around, and there aren't obvious opportunities to shorten life by refusing medical treatment. A cruel twist of fate has conspired to cut the things that made life meaningful off at the root, or so it can seem. And the feelings don't necessarily go away. According to one 2024 study, persistent depression is found in a 'significant minority' of those with spinal cord injuries; while a 2023 study compared depression rates in those with acquired disabilities versus those with congenital ones, and found them higher in the former.⁹

We need not be absolutist. It is not wholly out of the question that in a particular situation – the details of which would have to be scrutinised at length by all involved – it might be merciful to assist someone who has become radically paralysed and is asking for help to end their own life. But this is a concession at the level of individual acts, not laws or medical protocols. The more pressing issue is whether there should be medical institutions whose rules formally make the 'indignities' of serious physical disability a justification for helping to end a life. And I still think there should not.

It is not just that depression can lift even for people in this desperate situation, and a sense of meaning and purpose return; or that helping someone to die forecloses possibilities of self-transformation. There are also more far-reaching consequences. Even if, very occasionally, an experience of terrible suffering justifies the provision of merciful release, that fact alone does not validate the creation of an entire assisted death service. There is just too much at stake to focus only upon matters at the individual applicant's level.

This conclusion may feel unfair, and I understand why. When legislating for the whole of society, not everyone's interests can be satisfied equally. Rather than trying to create unattainable Utopias, it is better to do the least socially destructive thing. In *Beyond Good and Evil*, Nietzsche wrote: 'The thought of suicide is a great consolation: by means of it one gets successfully through many a bad night.'¹⁰ Where a disabled, gravely suffering person does not have real access to that (perhaps) comforting thought, it is not up to society to formally step into the breach. Our institutions should not try to compensate for every cruel twist of fate in life by offering an early death as a good solution; not where doing so will make many other people's lives ultimately worse. Instead – though I grant it may feel like scant compensation – institutions should be investing serious resources and effort into improving the lives of physically disabled people, so they have better forms of support to live out their remaining lives.

To comfort and console

In a society which endorses the idea that terminally ill and severely disabled lives lack dignity, there are many negative consequences; but here is one in particular. It is deemed merciful – a 'release', or a 'deliverance', even – when such lives are ended. This value judgement results in a culture of leniency towards those who have participated in the death of another such person but without their obvious consent. Officially the law deplores the lack, but in practice seems relatively relaxed about it.

In a 2024 report, feminist campaigning group The Other Half collected several cases from the last three decades of men killing terminally ill or seriously disabled female spouses or relatives on the alleged grounds of providing 'mercy'. In each, it wasn't clear that the women had consented to their own deaths, either in timing or in manner. They included one woman being strangled with a dressing gown cord, another having her throat cut, and a third being thrown from a balcony. In every case, a sentence for manslaughter with diminished responsibility was handed down, often suspended.[11] The background moral calculus seemed to say: it is bad to kill people without their clear consent; but it is also good to kill people who lack dignity and/or are suffering unbearably. The wrongness of the former is somewhat mitigated by the latter.

The same logic seems to have been at work in a notorious case from the late 1970s involving what is now Dignity in Dying – at that time known as 'Exit'. From time to time, this organisation would get enquiries from members of the public. Sometimes Exit's general secretary, Nicholas Reed, would send another man, Mark Lyons, to visit those who had made enquiries. Lyons would 'help' them die with methods that included tablets, alcohol, and plastic bags. In court, Reed claimed he had no idea Lyons was helping people commit suicide, but thought he was sending him to 'comfort and console'; nonetheless the judge found Reed guilty on three counts of aiding and abetting suicide, and one of conspiracy to aid and abet.

As with those who met their ends at the hands of Kevorkian, some of the recipients of Lyons's services were neither in pain nor incurably ill. According to former *Guardian* editor Alan Rusbridger, who reported on the case, they included a 'depressed road accident victim', 'a suicidal twenty-five-year-old with drink problems', and 'a middle-aged agoraphobic with a paranoid personality disorder'.[12] There was (or should have been) considerable doubt about whether consent was meaningfully given in any of the deaths to which Lyons contributed, because of the testimony of a woman disabled by spinal injuries, who said Lyons had visited her and become abusive when she told him she had changed her mind. A taped phone call was played at his trial, in which he called her 'a bloody stupid bitch', 'scum', and recounted how he had told her 'I'm not risking my neck ... to get disobedience from you ... there will be no questioning of my commandment, none at all'. Even so, Lyons was charged and found guilty, not of murder or manslaughter, but only of seven counts of aiding and abetting suicides, as well as conspiracy to aid and abet. He was given a suspended sentence.[13]

To assume that the wrongness of killing a person without their consent is somewhat mitigated by the rightness of ending a suffering life without dignity is a dangerous logic for anyone physically incapacitated; but particularly for the severely disabled, often already the subject of the feverish projections of able-bodied people about the supposed intolerability of their lives. Put bluntly, such prejudices may make it easier to kill them and get away with it.

The lives that others fear

It is hard to shake the feeling that a lot of what energises campaigns for assisted death services is not altruistic concern for the ill or disabled at all, but rather the fearful preoccupations of healthy and able-bodied people.

During the committee stage of the Terminally Ill Adults Bill in 2024, some horrific descriptions of dying and death were offered by supporters of the bill. They sounded a lot like fear. Consider this lurid description by Reform MP Richard Tice in a newspaper piece:

> Imagine the news delivered by the doctor. Your illness is terminal. You have just a few months left to live. Sad, scary, grim. But then the brutal blow. You will most likely die by drowning in your own faecal vomit. The end will take between 5–8 hours of body wrenching struggle. No drugs, pain relief or surgery can prevent this. Your loved ones will be racked with guilt and horror.[14]

Similar stories were repeated in Parliament during debate. In vain did experienced palliative care doctors try to debunk the idea that faecal vomiting – let alone 'drowning' – is anything other than a highly exceptional occurrence, and certainly not something any doctor would predict. A later post on the phenomenon in the *British Medical Journal* forum, from a consultant in palliative medicine, described it as 'vanishingly rare'.[15] But it seemed that the minds of some bill supporters were so fixated on imagined horrors that a grip on more likely outcomes had been lost.

Meanwhile, in a striking sequence from *Better Off Dead?* Liz Carr and disabled friends cheerfully cite the numerous times they have heard some version of 'if I was as disabled as you, I would rather be dead'. As the late disability rights activist Harriet McBryde Johnson wrote in her memoir, 'We are living the lives that others fear.'[16] In the past, witty members of Not Dead Yet in the US have campaigned with placards that say 'Don't put me out of your misery'.[17]

Another piece of evidence for self-interested motives behind assisted death campaigns is that many of those backing a change in the law appear relatively indifferent to improving the lot of elderly, seriously ill, and disabled people in everyday life. There are numerous issues here that might be tackled politically: the inadequacy of the built environment, with broken lifts, too few ramps, narrow walkways, unusable toilets, and the like; an underfunded and understaffed care home sector in crisis, with 20% of homes ranked as inadequate or needing improvement; a stricken hospice movement; and so on. But some of those arguing for assisted death don't seem very interested in these specifics. And it is natural to wonder why.

What might be so frightening to able-bodied people about certain experiences, shared by some (but not all) gravely ill people and some (but not all) disabled people? Things like regular pain, a loss of control over bodily functions, and dependence upon others for daily needs. I'm not asking why such things are difficult and distressing; but only why they seem so awful that some would rather be dead than experience them. Obviously, this is a big question. A lot will depend on personal values and preferences; but that doesn't mean there aren't culturally salient factors in the background.

One part of the answer, I assume, is 'relative lack of familiarity'. Our culture does not see terminal illness up close very often, so the accompanying bodily experiences can seem especially frightening. Such things happen elsewhere: in hospitals, hospices, or the care homes in which old people are increasingly sequestered. Obviously, the older you get, the higher the chances of seeing a loved one in the last stages of terminal illness; but even for those that have done this, your experience of dying and death is unlikely to be particularly wide or varied. As with Richard Tice's febrile visions of faecal drowning, it is perhaps easier to imagine the very worst when you have only a narrow experience of watching someone die. Many of the most ardent supporters of assisted death have witnessed a loved one die in painful and distressing circumstances, and understandably want others to avoid that. But equally, one or two experiences does not represent a wide enough range of cases to draw a firm conclusion about what is the norm.

Palliative care specialist Dr Kathryn Mannix wrote her book *With the End in Mind* to better acquaint people with the mundane realities of ordinary death. In a widely circulated BBC video, she says that 'dying is probably not as bad as you are expecting'.[18] She goes on to describe the process of the final days and hours for most people dying of natural causes: more frequent sleeping periods begin to include periods of unconsciousness, unnoticed by the patient, which then get longer and put the body in a deep state of relaxation. 'By encountering death many thousands of times, I have come to a view that there is usually little to fear and much to prepare for,' she has written.

> The death rate remains 100 per cent, and the pattern of the final days, and the way we actually die, are unchanged. What is different is that we have lost the familiarity we once had with that process, and we have lost the vocabulary and etiquette that served us so well in past times, when death was acknowledged to be inevitable.[19]

Perhaps not surprisingly, among health professionals you find least support for assisted death services within specialties that have most familiarity with disability, ageing, and the natural dying process: clinical oncology, general practice, geriatric medicine, and palliative care. Conversely, the specialties where there is most support are anaesthetics, emergency medicine, intensive care, and obstetrics and gynaecology.[20]

There is also a lack of familiarity with disability. Unless you live with a physically disabled person, you are unlikely to meet one very often; for unfortunately the outside world is not particularly welcoming to them. Easy to imagine how unrelentingly terrible life is when you don't get to find out about the good parts as well as the bad. And there is also a widespread finding known as the 'disability paradox': people with first-hand experience of some particular condition tend to describe its effects as less disabling than those who have not. For instance, those with mastectomies or colostomy bags tend to rate the negative impact on well-being lower than those who haven't had them.[21]

Again, it may seem I am downplaying things, but that is not my intention. I don't doubt that disability can bring with it torment and despair. My point is that, as disabled people themselves tell us, this is not always the case. We are talking about introducing an official justification for offering assisted death to a particular cohort, partly based on the perception of able-bodied onlookers that terrible suffering is inevitably implied. That the picture is much more varied is surely worth explaining.

Familiarity with both dying and disability – which, to be clear, are two separate experiences though they sometimes have aspects in common – does not inevitably breed contempt. On the other hand, popular cultural attitudes towards health and fitness might.

The illusion of total control

As medical technologies have become more refined over the course of the twenty-first century, it is noticeable that the demand for assisted death has only increased. The more control we get, the more we apparently want. One influential factor is popular discourse about health, 'wellness', and control of the body. In a nutshell: the more actively responsible, proud, and self-congratulatory people are encouraged to feel about controlling their own physical good fortune, the more frightening and shameful the prospect of losing it seems.

Control over bodily processes is unprecedented. With enough resources and technology, you can fine-tune your body with surgery, pills, injections, exercise, sleep regimes, and diet. 'Biohacking' has now entered the lexicon. As I write this chapter, an article has just appeared in *The Times* describing a US woman who won't date a man without seeing a 'detailed assessment' of his health first, including 'checks on his gut, analysis of the toxins in his body, his nutrient levels and risk of inflammation'. Her own daily routine, which she does 365 days of the year, includes things like tongue-scraping, putting colostrum in her coffee, sessions with 'electromagnetic field therapy', spending hours in oxygen chambers, and – at precisely timed moments – spending time with whichever lucky man has fulfilled her exigent biometric requirements.[22]

But despite such exertions, bodily control can only be gained up to a point. You may feel proud of your heart and lung stats now, but they are bound to deteriorate over the next few decades. Death is also something that you can't avoid. Its presence in the world is beyond our control.

During periods when Christianity was in the ascendant, there was room in human minds for the acceptance of mortality – indeed, the fact was considered instructive and redemptive. In religious traditions such as Buddhism, there is also an acknowledgement that painful challenges in life are par for the course. But in a mostly secular age, bowing down to the inevitable is increasingly rare. Instead, we are encouraged to think it is all up to us. At the extreme end of this trend, there is even a nascent 'don't die' movement. Fronted by US venture capitalist Bryan Johnson, it attempts to find immortality via lifestyle changes. Johnson says he is developing virtual technology that will achieve this, and boasts that he personally has 'the best comprehensive biomarkers of anybody in the world'.[23] Explicitly, he treats the pursuit of health as a kind of competition, whose winners can take credit for controlling the outcome. 'I'm an Olympic gold medallist in health. It's a sport.'

Such ambitions are hubristic to the point of risibility. Still, Johnson articulates in exaggerated form an attitude widespread in modern life. I'm not just talking about a bit of fitness and sensible eating. I mean treating the physical self as an all-encompassing 'project', congratulating yourself for your effort and discipline, punishing yourself for transgressions, and flaunting the aesthetic rewards to provoke admiration and envy. Such trends suggest that, these days, the pursuit of health is a way to achieve moral superiority as well as bodily perfection.

The wellness discourse is also full of ersatz spiritual dimensions: the glorification of fasting practices; the ingestion of so-called pure foods; daily rituals of physical exertion; meditation and breathing exercises; the alleged self-healing of illnesses; the idea of a being on a journey; and so on. Gwyneth Paltrow once said: 'The point of life is not to have a perfect body, it is to have a healthy body.' At the time she probably thought she was casting shade on oppressive aesthetic norms for women; but really, she was just shifting the obsessive female quest for perfection to a new domain.

But where the pursuit of good health becomes figuratively infused with the possession of superior moral and spiritual value, it can only follow that those who don't have good health are symbolically associated with the opposite. The disabled, old, and seriously ill are increasingly viewed in our culture, at least unconsciously, as failures not successes; as tainted not purified. As well as having very scary implications for disabled people, these unconscious associations are bound to affect attitudes towards personal decline and mortality – which, I stress, are inevitable prospects. Old and ill people become uncomfortable reminders of what might happen to us if we let ourselves go.

Such implicit negativity will be vigorously denied by right-thinking people, even as they post proud pictures of their abs on Instagram, obsessively track stats, or mentally castigate themselves for gaining a few pounds. Nobody wants to admit they participate in a neurotic, narcissistic discourse which encourages such regressive ways of thinking. But many of us do, every day.

Feeling like a burden

According to information collected in Canada, Oregon, the Netherlands, and Australia, 'feeling like a burden' is a popular reason for choosing an assisted death. Feeling burdensome can also be a factor in solo suicide, so the connection is unsurprising. In their writings, John Donne and Thomas More distinguished between self-centred or worldly suicides, and more dutiful or Godly 'martyrdoms'.[24] Durkheim counted 'altruistic' suicide – chosen for the perceived good of others – as a major kind. It is fairly common for a suicidal person to feel their own ineffectiveness and uselessness are spoiling the interests of close others, and that it would be better for everyone if they were not around. Indeed, in his influential theory of suicide, Thomas Joiner hypothesises that 'perceived burdensomeness' is one of the two main factors behind suicidal thinking generally.[25]

Where the suicide chosen is an assisted one, altruistic motivations might include relieving carers from the task of looking after you, or reducing family members' anxiety about the vagueness of the time frame for your remaining life. Part of the loving empathy that connects us with fellow humans is sensing what they feel, and caring about that. They care about how you are feeling; watching you suffer makes them feel awful. Equally, you care about them; their suffering at the thought of your suffering makes you feel even worse.

On average, women are better than men at picking up cues about what others are feeling. The fact it is a stereotype doesn't mean it isn't true. Also stereotypically, women sometimes act like martyrs. An older female character in the BBC sitcom *Motherland* refuses to allow her daughter-in-law to do anything for her, shrugging off solicitous attention. When offered breakfast, she asks for a 'small piece of bread', adding 'just the heel will be fine ... don't waste a proper slice!' It's funny because we all know someone like this, who can't bear to be perceived as having interests of her own. And yes, such people are often women.

Martyrish tendencies become rather less amusing when they collide with assisted death services. Reporting from Canada tells us that while more men in 2023 received assisted death under Track 1 (men 51.6% vs women 48.4%), substantially more women than men received it under Track 2 (women 58.5% vs men 41.5%). Equally, a huge 49% of people on Track 2 cited being a 'perceived burden on family, friends and caregivers' as a reason for choosing death.[26]

One very obvious motive might be financial. Where money to be imminently taken by a care home has been earmarked as an inheritance for a child, early death may seem the self-sacrificing solution. Unpaid care is stressful and also means the carer taking time away from employment. In its 2025 report into the 'impacts' of introducing assisted death at scale, the UK government seemed well aware of such points, noting that 'providing unpaid care, particularly at higher intensities, is associated with negative bodily and mental health outcomes, and employment impacts'. The clear implication was that providing assisted death for terminally ill dependents might ease such burdens.[27]

Feeling like a burden is especially likely to be germane to dependent elderly people: a horrible feeling of shame and helplessness that descends like a cloud and lodges in your already uncomfortable body, compounded by the confusions of old age, the challenges of strange new environments and people, loneliness without good company, and neglect. You might feel like a burden diffusely, without having any particular people in mind; you might feel like a burden upon the entire world, even. You might experience shame for still living when others of your age have conveniently and discreetly given up the ghost. As the French medical ethicist Emmanuel Hirsch has put it: 'someone is cast out of the land of the living and then thinks that he, personally, wants to die'.[28]

So far, I have also been talking as if feeling burdensome is something separate to the arrival of an assisted death service in the neighbourhood, but that is not true either. Suddenly, every member of society who knows they meet the local eligibility conditions is confronted with a new and potentially tormenting decision: to stay or to go? And you can't just opt out: choosing not to use an assisted death service is still a choice. As J. David Velleman has observed: 'once a person is given the choice between life and death, he will rightly be perceived as the agent of his own survival'. He goes on:

The problem with this perception is that if others regard you as choosing a state of affairs, they will hold you responsible for it; and if they hold you responsible for a state of affairs, they can ask you to justify it. Hence, if people ever come to regard you as existing by choice, they may expect you to justify your continued existence.[29]

Velleman is focusing here on other people's perceptions; but equally you might just ask *yourself* why it's right to stick around, anticipating and internalising other people's potential judgements. Obviously, the same point extends to systems like Canada's where assisted death is accessible for non-terminal conditions too. Disabled daughters or sons may worry about negative effects on parents; disabled parents may feel guilty about negative effects on daughters or sons. You used to be able to console yourself with the thought that there was nothing socially acceptable to be done about it. But now there is.

Despite all the rhetoric around 'choice', then, being offered a choice to die is not an unalloyed good-to-have for everyone who is ill enough. For those who don't want to take that choice, but who also feel bad about the impacts of their illness on others, in a fairly direct way it makes things worse. People particularly susceptible to feelings of guilt will opt for early deaths for the presumed good of other people; others will live on, but feel even more horrible about it.

Callous or manipulative relatives may also deliberately play upon such feelings. And quite incredibly, some campaigners for assisted death services are also happy to leverage the guilt. In Chapter Two we heard about Dignity in Dying posters on the London Underground, showing a glamorous woman dancing energetically around her kitchen with the strapline 'My dying wish is my family won't see me suffer. And I won't have to.' In campaigns like this one, a terminally ill person's empathy is used against them, as it were. They are encouraged to think of their own early death as a mercy to spare loved ones' pain.

A familiar pattern in progressive discourse is, first, to deny that some problem even exists; and then, when confronted with evidence that it indeed does exist, to say this is a good thing, actually. Such was the way at the committee stage of Leadbeater's bill, when a supportive witness from the University of Western Australia, Professor Meredith Blake, denied that people were requesting assisted death in Australia because they felt like a burden. 'That is not the evidence that we have got,' she said. When then shown by MPs that 35% of people do in fact cite it as a reason, Blake moved to the inevitable justification: 'People can feel that they are a burden, and that is part of their autonomous thinking. People have their own views of their own life.'[30]

As usual, then, we meet a strategic transition: first, the supposed urgency of awful illness-related suffering and the desire to offer a merciful release; then, when pointed out that some people asking for death are suffering mainly from the secondary effects of those illnesses, a convenient switch to the stance of the Freedom Lover – people are free to do whatever seems best for them, and the details of why they want to die are none of our business. Having initially indicated the wish to be compassionate to suffering people, when confronted with evidence of an absence of compassion in practice, the argument seamlessly shifts to a dispassionate laissez-faire-ism.

Others just double down. Here is Polly Toynbee again: 'As for being a burden, yes, many don't want a humiliating dependency on others in their very last days – and for them, assisted dying is a reasonable choice.'[31] I never cease to marvel at the way that self-styled progressive thinkers like Toynbee, keen to take the side of the vulnerable in other areas of life, retreat to framing bodily incapacity and dependency as humiliating when trying to justify assisted death services. This implication – and especially when embedded within a society that agrees an early death is a good remedy for such 'humiliations' – cannot fail to have devastating consequences for physically vulnerable and dependent people elsewhere.

7

Human Beings as Units

The balance between input and output

The fact that assisted death services provide premature deaths for those worried about being burdensome is, for some, a black mark against them. For others it counts as a positive advantage. In a *Times* column in March 2024, former Tory MP Matthew Parris responded to the advent of the Scottish Parliament's Assisted Dying for Terminally Ill Adults Bill:

> As... the practice spreads, social and cultural pressure will grow on the terminally ill to hasten their own deaths so as 'not to be a burden' on others or themselves. I believe this will indeed come to pass. And I would welcome it... 'Your time is up' will never be an order, but – yes, the objectors are right – may one day be the kind of unspoken hint that everybody understands. And that's a good thing.[1]

Parris's background reasoning here was partly economic. He emphasised the cost to the public purse of an ageing population getting expensive medical and social care, and the savings that might accrue by allowing people to choose early deaths instead. But economic considerations on their own are not enough; they need a moral theory to justify them. The famous theory to which Parris seems most sympathetic is Utilitarianism.

Utilitarianism, which goes back at least to the eighteenth century, purports to offer a systematic basis for making morally correct decisions. There are several variations. Simply characterised, it names some ultimate goodness or 'utility' in the world – the nature of which I'll get to in a minute – and then tells us to maximise that, wherever we can. When working out what to do, you should compare the potential consequences of available actions and try to choose the one that makes for the most utility all round.

In the classical version of Utilitarianism brought to us by philosopher Jeremy Bentham, utility – that thing we all should be maximising in the world, as a moral imperative – was defined as the presence of pleasure, and the absence of pain. A world with more pleasure and less pain is better than a world with less pleasure and more pain – or so the intuitively attractive thought goes. Modern versions, struck by the difficulty of comparing hypothetical outcomes in terms of the amounts of pleasure and pain generated, sometimes define utility in terms of 'preference satisfaction' instead. Roughly: the more people get what they want, the better.

Steering clear of these differences, I will characterise utility broadly as determined by 'a person's positive conception of their own well-being'.[2] People usually positively conceive of their own well-being in terms of things like the presence of pleasure, absence of pain, and the satisfaction of preferences. So this covers a lot of the standard ground. It also has the advantage of emphasising a connection between Utilitarianism and liberalism, which became popular during the same historical period. Each of these outlooks tends to assume that value is – at least at the level of the individual – subjective; that the individual is the best judge of what is good for the self.

Still, it's also important to note that at the collective level, Utilitarianism may well recommend riding roughshod over some particular group's preferences in order to help a larger number of other people fulfil their own positive conceptions of the good. Notoriously, most versions of the theory are indifferent to how utility is distributed and only interested in maximising it overall. In this sense, a Utilitarian is quite unlike the two defenders of assisted death services we have met in this book so far, the Freedom Lover and the Merciful Helper. Utilitarians are not particularly bothered with prioritising either personal freedom or mercy for their own sake. They are interested in supporting freedom or prioritising mercy only if doing so contributes to maximising general utility. If, in some cases, this means showing indifference or contempt for certain people's freedom, or being spectacularly unmerciful to others, the average Utilitarian will put up with it.

Back now to Parris's column. Old age, he writes, is full of bodily and psychological pain: 'often characterised by immobility, ill-health and dementia' and with 'crippling degeneration, incapacity, indignity and ... suffering'. Assisted death can put a welcome stop to all that. The status quo without any assisted death service, he implies, reduces utility for taxpayers. Were they not being forced to pay so much for the NHS and social care, they could be spending it on things they prefer doing more. In future, he thinks, there will be a lot of pain for society generally, assuming it staggers on without an assisted death service. It may even collapse altogether, which won't be great for general preference satisfaction. 'For a society as much as for an individual, self-preservation must shine a harsh beam on to the balance between input and output,' says he.

Later in 2024, Parris's fellow newspaper columnist Sherelle

Jacobs added supplementary Utilitarian-style arguments.[3] An assisted death service would mean that public funds being hoovered up by 'palliative care for people in the final six months of their life' could be redirected towards drugs that improve life – those that slow down the advance of dementia, for instance. (Here we see in plain sight the assumption that early death is more expedient than palliation.) An assisted death service could also pass inherited wealth on to younger family members instead of forcing people 'to spend savings and sell assets to pay for end-of-life care'. Medical technology, she claims, is currently focused on combating diseases which shorten life expectancy rather than tackling chronic disease. This means old age will continue to be challenging, and 'society may soon be faced with a large number of very old people eking out miserable and painful lives'. If the wishes of some of these people to die early are not heeded, argues Jacobs, the NHS is likely to implode. Which means more pain for everybody, all round.

Life in Parris-world

Parris and Jacobs must know arguments like theirs are taboo. Existing norms make for a strong prohibition against treating killing as justified in the name of benefits for wider society, whether economic or otherwise. We don't even have the death penalty in the UK for criminals. And within the last decade we have been through Covid lockdowns, where prolonged socioeconomic damage was tolerated for the majority in the name of protecting the lives of the elderly and disabled.

These authors don't seem to care, though. They are effectively arguing that we should get rid of this taboo for the wider social good. And they are also apparently nonchalant about the dehumanising stance implicit in the idea that deaths might be socioeconomically beneficial. Jacobs talks of 'cold Utilitarianism' relatively approvingly. Parris writes that, though it may sound 'brutal', he doesn't 'apologise for the reductivist tone in which [his] column treats human beings as units – in deficit or surplus to the collective'.

There are of course historical precedents for such attitudes. Some Inuit cultures approved of ritual forms of suicide for elderly people; as did the ancient Scythians.[4] In his book on suicide, Durkheim lists many other cultures where self-sacrifice was encouraged for the good of the collective. So let us for a moment imagine the sort of world we might end up with, were Parris and Jacobs to get their way. In this hypothetical scenario, an assisted death service is already available. Quite a lot of people believe that the wider socioeconomic benefits brought by this service at least partially justify its existence. And such beliefs are not taboo, but mentionable in polite society.

This world – we might call it Parris-world – would surely inevitably lead to further changes in the perceived moral order. One obvious one would be the emergence of a public narrative about a positive duty to die, should you become terminally ill or elderly and therefore a drain on resources. Where some action is deemed socially beneficial, the *right* to do it – meaning, that you shouldn't be stopped from doing so – quickly morphs into a *duty*. Or as Hume, in some ways a proto-utilitarian, put it in his deliberately provocative essay 'On Suicide':

> But suppose that it is no longer in my power to promote the interest of society, suppose that I am a burden to it, suppose that my life hinders some person from being much more useful to society. In such cases, my resignation of life must not only be innocent, but laudable.

And Parris, it seems, agrees: 'If assisted dying becomes common and widely accepted, hundreds of thousands – perhaps millions – will consider choosing this road when the time comes; and in some cases, even ask themselves whether it would be selfish not to.'

But why stop there with our forecasting? If lots of people think there is a duty upon elderly terminally ill people to die early for the public good, then presumably there will spring up charities and campaign groups dedicated to trying to persuade them to do so. Influencers will make it their brand on social media. Celebrities might become involved. This is just what tends to happen when a moral cause catches the public eye. People who preach a doctrine of self-sacrifice for the greater good will accumulate prestige, which will incentivise others to join them. The effects of social contagion will exponentially increase the appeal of the idea.

Self-sacrificing heroes prepared to die early will be lionised, perhaps making public goodbye videos before they go. Families may be interviewed about how proud they are of a prematurely departing loved one. And, as people start to be socially rewarded for doing their 'duty', stubborn refusers will start to be blamed. Again, this is what tends to happen when a moral cause really gets going: a negative incentive to conform to popular opinion is generated alongside the positive ones.

One thinks of the dehumanising phrase 'bed blocker', already in the lexicon for an elderly person who would otherwise be discharged from hospital, but for whom no suitable follow-on care is available. In our scenario, similar stigma would start to attach to elderly people who continued to drain public resources, even when offered an easy opportunity to check out of life. Indeed, the fact that assisted death services are often presented as a more comfortable route than solo suicide would presumably get a new gloss here: the easier the journey, the more blame is directed towards those who don't take it.

Social stigma tends to infect those around you. Family members sensitive to its presence may be more likely to subtly or not-so-subtly encourage ageing dependents to take the plunge. Middle-aged people would start to fear old age and increased disability, knowing what disapproving pressures awaited them. Physically disabled people, sharing many bodily incapacities with the terminally ill and also perceived as costly to the taxpayer, would feel the weight of society's disapproval even more than they do now.

There would also be cultural shifts in how breaches of consent were treated. My evidence for this is the relatively lenient attitude already taken to so-called 'mercy killing', examined in the last chapter. Were the Parris-style view to be popularised, we would likely see increased tolerance of killings – even without consent – carried out in the name of those benefits. Here, too, it might be reasoned that the wrongness of killing without consent is softened by the rightness of furthering what is morally good – this time, for the group.

I could go on, but presumably you get the point. The existence of an assisted death service, in tandem with a widespread, openly voiced opinion that the early deaths of certain kinds of individuals are to be permitted for the positive good of society, could never be just a discrete event. Numerous other attitudes would also fundamentally change. You might insist my dystopian vision is improbably grotesque. But I'm afraid it is more likely than you think.

A new kind of Malthusianism

There is another aspect of Parris's general outlook on assisted death. It appears briefly both in the *Times* piece and in an earlier *Spectator* article, published in 2015, in which he argues for assisted death services on 'Darwinian' grounds.

According to him, 'tribes that handicap themselves will not prosper'.[5]

The idea seems to be that, since medicine has artificially prolonged life, the number of elderly people in the population should be reduced, otherwise the health of society will decline overall. Assisted death will bring society back to a more natural, vigorous state. With apparent envy, Parris writes of 'the raw and unbridled energies of an emerging, younger, nimbler and very different world, led by countries like China'.[6] He also seems to think that society is bound to naturally rebalance by introducing assisted death eventually: 'My opinions and my voice are incidental. This is a social impulse which will grow, nourished by forces larger than all of us. I don't exhort. I predict.'

Social Darwinism – that is, attempts to apply theories of natural selection and the survival of the fittest to the social realm – is largely discredited as a body of thought, and it's not clear exactly how those attempts mesh with Parris's brief reflections here. Though he thinks of his argument as Darwinian, he might just as well have mentioned Malthusianism. The idea that a society is made unhealthy by the over-representation of some particular cohort, in a way that will eventually precipitate some kind of 'rebalancing', predates Darwin and is reminiscent of the way the English economist Thomas Malthus used to think about the urban poor. During the nineteenth century, there was growing concern about the poor 'overbreeding'. Thanks to Malthus, the idea spread amongst polite society that a population was bound to grow until it outstripped available resources; at which point a natural event like a famine or plague would come along to recalibrate. Indulging in the naturalistic fallacy – i.e. 'what is natural is good' – some Malthusians concluded famines made society overall healthier. In this they were encouraged by Adam Smith's contention that the market was the best solution to high food prices.[7] One consequence was that when the Great Famine in Ireland caused millions of deaths, England offered relatively scant help.[8]

Of course, Parris is not the first to take a Malthusian line in defence of assisted death services. In Chapter Two we met Charles Killick Millard, the founder of the Voluntary Euthanasia Legalisation Society, who was very interested in population control. There were many others in the British establishment at the time who thought like him. But the problem with a Malthusian approach, as is evident from the disaster of the Great Famine, is that it can result in callous indifference to suffering and death. The idea of an economically 'well-balanced' society is one thing; but to say society is being made literally unhealthy by vulnerable people is dangerous indeed. And especially when an early death is proposed as a solution.

To put others down

A curious feature of Parris's and Jacobs's economic arguments is that they bear scant relation to the assisted death services being offered. Take Leadbeater's bill, where only people with a diagnosis of six months or less left to live are eligible for assisted death. It is predicted that the service will bring savings to the public purse, although the general picture is still unclear. The government's 2025 impact assessment anticipated savings in 'unutilised healthcare' between £5.84 million and £59.6 million within a decade.[9] Even so, financial benefits will be relatively limited, compared to what they might be.

Many terminally ill people will take up the offer of an assisted death only some months after first diagnosis, exploring other treatment options first. Were assisted death offered to those with a prognosis of twelve months, say, or even to physically disabled adults more generally, still greater savings could be made. According to a 2024 report, the cost of care for working-age adults and those with lifelong disabled conditions is now the largest area of expenditure in adult social care, taking up two-thirds of local authority budgets.[10]

Looked at from the point of view of frugality, the Canadian or Benelux systems are preferable: dispatching not just terminally ill people but also the disabled without terminal diagnoses who might have had years of treatment and care ahead of them. Including those who only have mental health conditions is an even bigger saving. And, of course, we could obtain the greatest savings of all, were authorities to get rid of the need for consent altogether. Rather than guilt-trip people into doing their duty, we could just force them.

Presumably, by now your flesh is creeping at my spelling out such economic incentives so baldly. But equally, a Parris or a Jacobs might protest: just because a Utilitarian defence is offered for assisted death does not mean that other moral traditions become inert. We would – and obviously should – still be keen on administering genuinely merciful death only for those whose severe suffering is irremediable, as well as requiring unforced consent. Moral values can be plural. Should we not stop severe and irremediable suffering, fully respect the autonomous decision-making of individuals, *and* save the NHS from collapse all at the same time? Can we not have it all?

I'm afraid not. Classical Utilitarianism only thinks of administering mercy and protecting personal freedom as important if they contribute to the maximisation of utility. If being merciless and/or coercive achieves better general results, that's the path that should be followed. Parris talks of human beings as 'units – in deficit or surplus to the collective', but at the same time confidently insists that '"Your time is up" will never be an order.'[11] But the whole point of treating humans as units is that, now and again, you are allowed to subtract a few from a particular column, if it means your sums work out better overall.

But let's allow for the sake of argument that in a Utilitarian system, protecting personal autonomy could operate as a side constraint on assessing who gets to live or die. Even so, there would still be certain groups omitted from this defence. People with severe dementia, for instance, have no 'personal freedom' or 'autonomy' in a sense relevant to independent decision-making. They can sometimes wander around freely, but that is not the same thing. The same applies to young children, and to some with severe learning disabilities. All three groups lack mature rationality, and so are usually thought to miss the bar for free, autonomous decision-making.

Another way of saying this is that such groups lack 'mental capacity'. For this reason, advanced dementia sufferers are ineligible for most existing assisted death services. Taking a precautionary stance, it is assumed that any person with dementia would have declined a premature death, had they been able to meaningfully choose. There are exceptions, though. In the Netherlands, Belgium, and Quebec, while still displaying mental capacity you can write an 'advanced directive', specifying that you wish to receive euthanasia later even when in the grip of severe dementia. Doctors are then supposed to be alert to any behaviour from the person concerned 'that may indicate resistance or objections to termination of life'; in which case they are supposed to ignore the directive and withhold an assisted death after all.[12]

The roots of our notion of mental capacity lie in an Enlightenment tradition strongly influenced by Kant. For him, in order to count as autonomous in the sense of being self-governing, you must be capable of exercising rationality in choosing what to do. Autonomy gives you dignity. But many scholars have since pointed out the troubling implications of Kant's view for how society acts towards those without rational capacities: neonates and young children, for instance; or those suffering from advanced dementia. Since it excludes some people, his view turns out to be a poor secular replacement for the Christian notion of the inherent sanctity of life.

Applied to our hypothetical assisted death service run explicitly along Utilitarian lines, we cannot be sure that its creators would automatically take a precautionary stance towards those with dementia. That is, we cannot be confident they would act as if, had these people been rational, they would have declined to use such a service. Parris himself mentions the cost of dementia as an apparently strong consideration for bringing in assisted death. And in 2008, the prominent British moral philosopher Baroness Warnock argued in an interview that people with dementia, specifically, should opt for assisted death. She was apparently undeterred by the fact they would have reduced autonomy:

> If you're demented, you're wasting people's lives – your family's lives – and you're wasting the resources of the National Health Service ... I feel there's a wider argument that if somebody absolutely, desperately wants to die because they're a burden to their family, or the state, then I think they too should be allowed to die ... I think that's the way the future will go, putting it rather brutally, you'd be licensing people to put others down.[13]

And what about the very young? Understandably, neither Parris nor Jacobs mention the costs to the state of seriously disabled children, facing a future of lifelong medical treatment and social care. I am sure that they both would be rightly horrified at the suggestion that any savings could be made here. It is easy just to assume that any Utilitarian-based assisted death service must, as a matter of decency, withhold eligibility from young children incapable of meaningfully consenting to their own deaths. But we should note that this is not even true for all existing services, right now; or at least, not where an additional Merciful Helper-style argument can be marshalled as well.

In the Netherlands, the requirement of mental capacity in order to get an assisted death is lifted for very young children who are not otherwise immediately dying, and who have 'hopeless and unbearable suffering with no prospect of improvement and no reasonable alternative to treat the suffering'.[14] Parental consent is also required. Initially this practice was relatively unregulated, but in 2005 what became known as the Groningen Protocol was introduced. As summarised in a 2023 overview, these regulations were 'intended for deliberate life-ending in stable neonates with sustained suffering in situations where continued treatments, including nutrition and hydration, are considered medically inappropriate and no life sustaining treatments are left to withhold or withdraw'.[15] The introduction of a formal protocol, with all cases referred to a pathologist's office for investigation afterwards, reduced the incidence to only two cases in five years. (Both involved lethal epidermolysis bullosa, an incurable disease which means the skin blisters under very small amounts of pressure, causing great pain.) In 2023, the protocol was extended to children under twelve, with the Dutch government estimating it would henceforth be used for between five and ten children a year.

The dominant impulse behind euthanising children is the provision of mercy. The belief is they are suffering dreadfully and permanently, in a way that cannot otherwise be relieved. In such terrible situations with no straightforward answers, the small number of cases perhaps suggests that careful and conscientious scrutiny of individual cases is occurring, as it absolutely should. But leaving aside the tortuous ethics of the act itself, we should at least note that this aspect of the Dutch system further confirms a general theme of this book. Namely:

appeals to freedom, rights, and personal autonomy are not the only justifications offered for the provision of assisted death, and sometimes drop out as totally irrelevant.

And this point is confirmed by a different aspect of the system in the Netherlands. According to a survey carried out at the request of a Dutch government commission in 1990, at least one thousand cases of non-voluntary euthanasia of adults – i.e. non-consensual killing – were carried out that year. Further analysis by legal scholar John Keown, based on interviews with doctors, suggested that at least 14% of these patients had full mental capacity and a further 11% had partial capacity. Reasons offered by doctors cited their own beliefs about the absence of possibility of improvement, the pointlessness of further treatment, and 'relatives' inability to cope'.[16]

All of this is (ostensibly, anyway) mercy-related; autonomy considerations have simply disappeared. Indeed, as Keown has pointed out, there is no logical reason why the principle of offering merciful help (as I call it) and the principle of enabling freedom/autonomy always have to go together as simultaneous justifications. They come from completely different directions, after all. Some advocates for assisted death insist that a person being helped to die must always consent to the process, even where mercy is the main justification. But they don't properly explain why. And as Keown intimates, if it really is morally urgent to end a severely suffering person's life, then it is unclear why those carrying out this mission of mercy should always acquire agreement from the suffering person first.[17] If you were on fire, I shouldn't have to get your permission to put the flames out.

Yet again, hidden tensions between the Merciful Helper and Freedom Loving ideals are revealed. But the pressing point is that, just as freedom and autonomy are sometimes treated as irrelevant in the Netherlands, they could conceivably become irrelevant in a Utilitarian cost-cutting scenario too. After all, wherever there is great suffering due to illness or disability for the Merciful Helper to worry about, there will also be the socioeconomic costs of care for a Utilitarian to worry about alongside. And two birds might be killed with one stone.

We should also remember what happened in the NHS with a notoriously inadequate palliative care protocol known as the Liverpool Care Pathway for the Dying Patient (LCP), phased out only in 2013. Initially designed to be used exclusively for an already dying patient, it was supposed to manage, among other things, the withdrawal of medical treatment, the use of sedation, and the application of Do Not Resuscitate orders. In practice, it was not always clear that alternative treatment paths had been tried, and half of those placed on the LCP were not told they were on it, let alone had consented.[18] The consequent savings to the NHS were also interpreted by some managers as a plus point. In fact, the NHS effectively *rewarded* managers for placing as many patients as possible on the LCP, giving millions to hospitals that met their targets.[19] As an occupational therapist who worked on a palliative care ward during the time of LCP wrote blackly about assisted death in 2024:

> You think the NHS isn't going to do that with assisted suicide? You think we won't package it up as end-of-life care and patient choice while counting the money saved by your convenient demise? Sign the form, kill yourself, protect the NHS.[20]

Accepting the status quo

Parris and Jacobs are correct that the costs of supporting elderly people are spiralling. Given advances in medicine and healthier habits, people are living longer and surviving former big killers like cancer and heart disease more often. But this comes at a cost. Old age makes you prone to injuries and chronic illnesses, and these are also expensive for the NHS to deal with.[21] Dementia is on the increase, now responsible for 11% of all deaths, as opposed to 3% in the 1950s. For those whose savings fall below the relevant threshold, dementia care is paid for by the state.

At the same time, birth rates are falling, which means fewer offspring to help with older people's care in the home. If current trends continue, the costs of supporting the elderly and disabled until their natural deaths will fall more heavily on fewer and fewer working-age adults, paying both for their pensions and for their medical and social care.

Nearly everybody acknowledges the NHS is in a terrible state. Funding is not keeping pace with demand for services, and especially not post-Covid. Waiting lists have increased by 52% since 2019.[22] Significant staff shortages and straitened resources are giving rise to poorer standards of care. Specifically in relation to the terminally ill, there is a shortage of palliative care. As we know, the hospice sector is facing a funding crisis: the government funds only 30%, with the rest reliant on falling charity donations.[23] The care home sector is also in disarray. As I write this in 2025, half of them have not been inspected by the Care Quality Commission since 2020.[24] Of those that have, one in five is rated as 'requires improvement' or 'inadequate'.[25] In light of such a depressing picture, it is not hard to see how already suffering people facing terminal illness may conclude it is high time to go.

But this book is not about what individuals should choose, once assisted death has been made available to them. It concerns what those in government or other relevant public bodies should choose, in deciding whether to make assisted death available for a given population *at all*. A government, unlike an individual, can do something about the systemic social challenges facing its citizens. It might put energy into finding political alternatives to premature death; incentivising a higher birth rate so that society gets rebalanced; finding efficiency savings in health services, or cutting rival areas; funding new and cheaper medical technologies for dementia; generally improving public health; restructuring the care sector to better provide for changing needs; or something else entirely. Offering death is not the only answer, however pleasingly simple and cheap it may seem.

To institute an assisted death service in response to such social challenges is to take the path of least resistance. So why are thinkers like Parris and Jacobs so keen on it? Recall that, broadly speaking, Utilitarianism defines utility – the thing that is supposed to be maximised as a moral requirement – in terms of subjective conceptions of well-being. People tend to conceive of their own well-being, or lack of it, in terms of the options they actually have in front of them. From the individual's perspective, it is usually pointless to dream of changing the system. So if society is offering a choice between a miserable remaining life and an early death, then people may well compare the pain of living to the cessation of pain brought about by dying, and conclude that the latter is in greater service to their 'well-being'. Granted, death is not normally described as a means of achieving well-being, but only because it doesn't count as a state of being at all. But it may look a lot better than the alternative.

We have seen that in the Canadian system, some people do indeed choose an early death over what they think of as an unacceptably miserable life, for reasons that go well beyond the pain of their illness or disability. They don't have access to the medical treatment they need, or supportive care at home; they are impoverished, or facing homelessness; they are lonely. Canada is not the only place where these issues crop up. In Australia in 2024, eighty-six-year-old Cyril Tooze chose an assisted death after waiting over nine months for home care assistance from the state, without which he could not live on his own.[26] Meanwhile, from Oregon we have the following description from a doctor about a patient opting for an assisted death: 'He had six months, but he probably had a good four months of quality time, and I asked ... "Why are you interested?" And he said: "I don't have any friends. I don't have any real quality of life – not because I'm ill, but for social-economic reasons."'[27]

Utilitarians are likely to take such feelings at face value. Indeed, some have it that minimising pain is more urgent a moral task than maximising pleasure, since the presence of pain is worse than the mere absence of pleasure. Philosopher Christopher Belshaw argues this point with respect to assisted death specifically, defending its provision on the grounds that it spares people morally repugnant suffering: 'Die too soon and you merely miss out on pleasure, too late and you suffer more pain.'[28] Matthew Parris's emphasis on the 'crippling degeneration, incapacity, indignity and often suffering' accompanying old age suggests he might agree.

Yet in deciding whether to provide an assisted death service or not, it is surely relevant that would-be users' options have been narrowed to one of two undesirable outcomes. If a system forces people to choose between unwanted circumstances, then what they choose cannot be taken as a measure of genuine subjective well-being, nor perhaps even what they 'really' want. If I'm stuck between the devil and the deep blue sea and choose the sea, it doesn't mean I think icy cold waves are good for me.

In other words: simply capitulating to people's feelings about the options they currently have, as the Utilitarian often does, tends to produce outcomes that are not to people's genuine benefit. It also encourages apathy about changing wider social systems for the better. In theory, Utilitarians could advocate for alternative solutions that would increase utility overall compared to the systems we actually have, but in practice they often do not.

Additional obstacles to agitating for social change under Utilitarianism are what are known as 'adaptive preferences'. Sometimes, when forced to opt for one of two evils, the chooser will be well aware that their eventual choice is only relatively desirable in the context of its alternative. But equally, sometimes people unconsciously 'adapt' their preferences, so that one of the two narrow and otherwise unpalatable options starts to genuinely look good. Or as economist and philosopher Amartya Sen puts it:

> The most blatant forms of inequalities and exploitations survive in the world through making allies out of the deprived and the exploited. The underdog learns to bear the burden so well that he or she overlooks the burden itself. Discontent is replaced by acceptance, hopeless rebellion by conformist quiet, and ... suffering and anger by cheerful endurance. As people learn to adjust to the existing horrors by sheer necessity of uneventful survival, the horrors look less terrible in the metric of utilities.[29]

Sen's subject in this passage is Bengali women tolerating high levels of malnutrition and disease without complaint. Translated into the context of assisted death, we can also see that even enthusiastic, heartfelt preferences for an early death might be an adaptation to grossly inadequate life circumstances. The Utilitarian has no easy way of dealing with this issue. Subjective conceptions of well-being just will not pick it up.

Not a real choice?

The complaint that assisted death services make people choose between an avoidably miserable life and an early death is a common one. In the context of capitalism, 'choice' is usually presented as something that must enlarge the consumer's possibilities in a positive way. The more choices you have, the better. For this reason, some like to say that assisted death does not offer real choice at all. Here, for instance, is Harriet McBryde Johnson:

> [C]hoice is illusory in a context of pervasive inequality. Choices are structured by oppression. We shouldn't offer assistance with suicide until we all have the assistance we need to get out of bed in the morning and live a good life. Common causes of suicidality – dependence, institutional confinement, being a burden – are entirely curable.[30]

Ironically, the assisted death lobby is also fond of complaining that certain 'choices' are in name only: for instance, their oft-repeated claim that those who wish for an assisted death are forced to either travel abroad to get one or die painfully and miserably at home. See this Dignity in Dying Facebook post from 2024:

> James' Mum travelled to Switzerland alone because assisted dying is illegal in the UK. She spent her life's savings and had to undertake the journey earlier than she would have liked to make sure she was well enough to travel. Dying people deserve a choice.[31]

In this context, at least, Dignity in Dying seems happy to allow that someone choosing the lesser of two unpalatable options is not really getting what they want, in a way that means they don't really have a meaningful choice at all. They envisage James's mum as having to choose between, on the one hand, a lonely, expensive, early death in Switzerland; and on the other, a continued miserable, terminally ill life in the UK. And so they argue for a third option, not yet on the table: an assisted death in the UK, surrounded by loved ones and costing far less.

Recall the old strapline from the US lobbying group Compassion and Choices: 'Too many suffer needlessly. Too many endure unrelenting pain. Too many turn to violent means at the end of life.'[32] Here too it was implied that desperately suffering people were being forced into a very limited choice: endure a miserable terminally ill life or embark on a violent solo suicide. So Compassion and Choices campaigned for a third option: assisted suicide.

Sometimes supporters of assisted death services blame opponents for being 'cruel' in wishing to withhold the choice of an early death from suffering people. But, of course, their preferred alternative is not the only one for which you might argue. In theory, Dignity in Dying could equally have argued for a better life during terminal illness for James's mum, so that an artificially hastened death doesn't seem like a desirable option. Compassion and Choices could have argued for better medical and social support for the terminally ill, so that they don't feel that a violent premature death is the only way out.

In other words: we can agree that under current circumstances, some people are faced with the awful dilemma of a miserable death versus a miserable continued life. Even so, society can respond either by improving the death bit, or the life bit. And when it comes to assessments of cruelty, I see no good reason why arguing for a better life for the terminally ill is any more cruel than arguing for a quick death.

Those steeped in the language of the Freedom Lover, whether supportive of assisted death services or critical of them, like to talk as if a lack of real choice means you are being coerced. They seem to think of the situation as roughly analogous to one where someone threatens that if you don't do such-and-such, something dreadful will be done to you. Who or what exactly is supposed to be doing the coercing here is slightly unclear. It's perhaps the set of political decisions that led to the limited options on the table, or maybe the relevant background socioeconomic conditions.

I have doubts about the wisdom of this framing. Not everything morally unacceptable in human life is the result of coercion. The fact that people are often keen to analyse awful social conditions in term of a loss of personal freedom only underlines how freedom is the principal articulable value in our hyperliberal world. Indeed, I would make the same objection against framing a wish to die prematurely, because of a background fear of being a burden to others, as involving your being 'coerced' by the emotional pressure of family or the state. Strictly speaking, emotional pressure on its own is not illegitimate force.

I grant that being stuck in a situation where, say, you only have a choice between assisted death and a miserable remaining life can *feel* coercive. It may well feel like someone is holding a metaphorical gun to your head. But nothing much is gained by diluting the meaning of the concept of coercion in this way, I think – not least because sloppy usage allows supporters of assisted death services to claim that, in the absence of such services, suffering people are being coerced into living. We should resist getting stuck in an ever-escalating competition of who is the least free.

We can still make the vital point, even without the talk of coercion – namely, a limited choice between a terrible life and a premature death is both morally and politically unacceptable. It is the responsibility of governments to broaden the field of choices for those who are terminally ill, elderly, or disabled, so that these are not their only practical options.

Those left behind

Let's return to the basic Utilitarian premise that an assisted death service will increase overall utility, understood in terms of reducing pain, increasing pleasure, and enhancing individual preference satisfaction. Even if we were to accept this as the right moral framework – which, to be clear, I do not – a simple Utilitarian story about the benefits of such services tends to leave out important negative aspects from the calculus.

We have explored many of these in earlier chapters. They include: the loss of meaningful and enjoyable time that might have been spent living, after the initial shock of diagnosis subsided; more widespread feelings of guilt or shame at being a burden, experienced by seriously ill or incapacitated people offered the supposedly 'easy' opportunity to depart prematurely; harmful messages conveyed to society about the humiliating indignity of serious disability, and the decreased value of lives spent under such conditions; an increased disgust for old age, and callousness towards the elderly. Each one of these effects is exacerbated by the fact an assisted death service causes many more people to die early than would have been the case if it hadn't existed – for it is a fantasy that all such people would have attempted solo suicide anyway. There are doubtless many other negative effects too. But one thing we haven't yet looked at are the interests of relatives – both those left behind by an assisted death and those who fear that their loved ones might receive one.

In Chapter One I argued that there could be no general 'right' to suicide, interpreted in the classical sense of imposing an automatic moral obligation upon others not to intervene in attempts to end your own life. The negative effects experienced by family members after a suicide are often too devastating to make it credible that you should never try to stop someone else from ending their life. For those left behind, there can be terrible shock, grief, trauma, and a plunge into financial chaos; plus a lifelong sense of failure in not having been able to change the outcome, or to have had a chance to say a proper goodbye. These things matter too.

Groups such as Dignity in Dying tend to present assisted death services as mitigating these awful consequences. In campaigning, they rely heavily on the symbolic power of children of terminally ill people arguing that they are on board with their loved one's desire for an early death. They are right that the shock of a sudden suicide can be lessened by an assisted version, assuming that loved ones are warned in advance. Unlike with a solo suicide, family can also be present at the death; an experience which for some (though not all) can be comforting and even uplifting. And where a terminally ill person is genuinely close to death anyway, and visibly suffering, there can be a lot of solace in knowing pain is at an end.

But as we know, it cannot be assumed that assisted death is provided only for those very near death, or who are suffering dreadfully from their illness. Far from it. And correspondingly, nor should we assume that loving family members will always agree with a suicidal person that it is the right time to go. It might still be a terrible shock. In most existing assisted death services, including Canada and the one proposed for the UK, there is no requirement that any relatives be informed about their family member's imminent death, let alone be consulted.

In her book *This Is Assisted Dying*, Dr Stefanie Green recounts how on one occasion she was about to euthanise a woman, but encountered the woman's 'nephew Andrew and his wife ... standing at the foot of her bed, pleading with her to reconsider'.[33] The nephew asked Green: 'How can it be possible that, as a close family member, my arguments won't be taken into account?' Green recollects with apparent equanimity that she 'assured him his arguments were important but only in relation to his own healthcare and no one else's'. Effectively, this is the Freedom Lover's position on assisted death writ large. It nods to the metaphysical background we met in Chapter One: the implicit assumption that each human is an autonomous, self-governing island, cut off from any ties of obligation or dependence towards other humans unless they are mutually agreed first.

Still, there is more than one kind of suffering to attend to. Here is Alicia Duncan, talking about the assisted death in Canada of her mother, granted by doctors as a result of 'self-starvation caused by untreated paranoia about heavy metals in food', and leading them to classify her as terminally ill, even though her condition was rooted in mental illness:[34]

> We tried to stop our mom's euthanasia, but with less than 16 'business' hours between finding out and her scheduled death, we were at a terrible disadvantage. We managed to get a warrant for her arrest under the mental health act to postpone it to buy us time, but instead my mom attempted to take her own life, which resulted in an involuntary hold for 48 hours. They killed her only four hours after being released. We didn't even know she had gone home ... My sister and I both have been diagnosed with PTSD now.[35]

And here is fellow Canadian Christopher Lyon, whose father had felt suicidal several times in his life, and who was on antidepressants at the time of receiving an assisted death. This was granted via Track 2 – where death is not 'reasonably foreseeable' – on the basis of arthritis, diabetes, and 'frailty'. Lyon and the rest of his family were informed only two days beforehand, and told by the doctor providing the death that if they wanted to see their father they would have to 'move quickly'. In a powerful interview, Lyon described having to attend his father's assisted death as 'the worst day of my life ... nothing compares to it. We were lost.' He went on:

> The people most affected by a MAID death before, during, and after, outside the person dying, are the family members. We're the ones who have to live with the grief, the anticipation of the upcoming death, the questions, especially if there's doubt about the qualifying illness, if we weren't consulted.[36]

And there is another deficit in general utility rarely talked about: the intense worry of parents of disabled children, who are themselves ageing, and who know they won't be around to protect and advocate for their offspring for ever. While alive and mentally competent, they are usually able to look after vulnerable children, fight against any attempt to devalue their lives from the medical or teaching professions, argue with local authorities for resources, or whatever the current struggle may be. But they know it won't be possible for ever. As Liberal Democrat leader Ed Davey wrote about his seriously disabled child John, describing his feelings along with those of his wife Emily,

> ... no amount of wealth or training or confidence can shift our anxieties about our children's future. It upsets Emily so much she can't discuss it. What happens to John when we're gone? ... [I]t's intense and acute and just so challenging. No one's going to love him, and hold him, like Emily and I do. He's so vulnerable, with special needs – it's just so raw.[37]

Such anxiety is bad enough, even without an assisted death service on hand. Its presence adds a whole new dimension of distress – and especially when you remember those with learning disabilities are extra vulnerable to the effects of coercion and illegitimate persuasion. As the government impact statement about Leadbeater's bill made clear, those who pass mental capacity tests will not be exempt from the proposed service.

From a Freedom Loving perspective, perhaps it makes sense to discount the worry of loving relatives about a particular assisted death, actual or anticipated. But from a Utilitarian perspective, the suffering of some relatives – both at the prospect of assisted death and in its aftermath – should surely be entered into the calculus of general utility, as a great debit to be weighed alongside the alleged credits.

The pleasure principle

We have looked at what assisted death services imply about the value of terminally ill and disabled lives. But there is also a deeper issue about what they say about the value of human life generally. This is most obviously true when backed up by Freedom Loving rhetoric. From this angle, an assisted death service gives the impression that a human life is only valuable if its owner thinks it is. If the owner's verdict is negative, nothing has been lost by ending things prematurely.

But even if we just stick to the more restrictive Merciful Helper attitude, this still confirms that suicide is an appropriate response to great suffering. This attitude, once firmly established in a society via the sanctioned presence of an assisted death service, will have implications that go far beyond those for the ill and the disabled.

Unfortunately, the option of solo suicide remains available for those ineligible for an assisted death: for all of us, in other words. Though every culture has solo suicides, some cultures have a lot more than others, and it is often partly because of an accompanying metaphysical attitude to the value of life, indirectly encouraging the trend. To take just one example: there was apparently an increase in the suicide rate during the Renaissance, due to 'the rebirth of classical learning and the popularity of authors such as Seneca, the birth of melancholy and an intense fascination with death, the newly emphasised role of the individual and personal responsibility and the depressing nature of the doctrines of Calvin'.[38]

In the present day, without a religious taboo against self-destruction, or an inherent positive belief in the sanctity of life – or even just in the inviolable dignity of the individual – there is already less to hold people back. Add in an assisted death service as the emblem of society's official attitude to dealing with personal suffering – i.e. 'get out when it gets too much, or whenever you personally feel like it' – and there are bound to be consequences for the way suicide is looked at in the round.

We cannot just assume that the pleasure of life will keep outweighing the pain for most. As Al Alvarez beautifully puts it:

> The pleasures of living – the hedonistic pleasure of the five senses, the more complex and demanding pleasures of concentration and doing, even the unanswerable commitments of love – seem often no greater and mostly less frequent than the frustrations – the continual sense of unfinished and unfinishable business, jangled, anxious, ragged, overborne. If secularized man were kept going only by the pleasure principle, the human race would already be extinct.[39]

Generally, we should not assume that future generations will always take the same attitude to life as we do; but it is also highly likely that theirs will bear a traceable historical relation to ours. What potentially destructive patterns are we initiating for our children? If we could start again and were being deliberate about it, what cultural attitude would we want to take to suicide, collectively?

This is a difficult thing to talk about, since it can be misconstrued as blaming people who have attempted to take their own lives. Still, it seems to me that it is very good to have a taboo against suicide generally; and that to cement that taboo, it would be good to develop compelling narratives about psychological resilience in the face of even great suffering. Again according to Alvarez, the great Russian poet Osip Mandelstam – facing Stalin's secret police once again, with vivid memories of the horrors of an earlier incarceration – still declined his wife's invitation that they take their lives together. 'Life is a gift that nobody should renounce,' he told her. Later that year he died in a forced labour camp. Such bravery in the face of the prospect of terrible affliction is inspiring. It conveys a vision of the human spirit as indomitable, that others may then aspire to live up to in their turn.

To repeat an insightful point from Seneca: 'We take our cue from people's thinking even in the way we feel pain.' An assisted death service tells each of us, with the stamp of social approval, that it is good to run away from it.

8

Slippery Slopes and Bottomless Pools

Slippery slopes, not staircases

Critics of assisted death laws argue that they are bound to lead to 'slippery slopes'. During the first phase of a slippery slope, some initiative is introduced with a defined set of consequences in mind, viewed as highly desirable by supporters and tolerable by neutrals. In the second phase, the initiative starts to have consequences much more undesirable than intended. These cannot now be easily controlled, given general acceptance of the first phase. There is a panicky sense of hurtling downwards to who knows where.

In the context of assisted death, critics predict that the introduction of a limited service in a new jurisdiction, with supposedly strict conditions of eligibility – usually, terminally ill adults only – places legislators on a slippery slope towards more permissive conditions later on. As we know, eligibility has widened in the Canadian system over time, from people who are terminally ill to physically disabled people who are not. As of 2027, eligibility is set to extend to people with psychological suffering but no accompanying bodily disorder. In the Netherlands and Belgium, laws started off by insisting that only adults could make the decision to die and ended up permitting euthanasia for babies and children.

But a slippery slope is also in the eye of the beholder. There are many who don't experience these changes as a frightening descent into the abyss, but rather as a thrilling ride on an arc bending towards justice. That is: they believe it is only right that initially strict laws should expand, as a matter of 'equality' or 'fairness'. And in countries where no assisted death service yet exists, there are usually campaigners who see the initial introduction of a limited service as a necessary staging post on the way to a more expansive one.

In 2007, for instance, the *New York Times Magazine* ran a profile of a former governor of Washington state, Booth Gardner, who was campaigning for a new assisted death law. It described him as someone who:

> sees [a restrictive law] as a first step. If he can sway Washington to embrace a restrictive law, then other states will follow. And gradually, he says, the nation's resistance will subside, the culture will shift and laws with more latitude will be passed.[1]

And Gardner turned out to be right. The law for which he was campaigning, to offer terminally ill people an assisted suicide, was introduced in Washington in 2008. And in 2023 the same law was expanded: reducing the fifteen-day waiting period to seven; allowing nurse practitioners and physician assistants as well as doctors to pronounce on eligibility; and authorising lethal substances to be mailed or delivered long-distance to patients.[2] These are small-scale expansions compared to those of Canada. Still, each was likely to bring significantly more people into the service than otherwise would have used it. Indeed, this is exactly what such changes were designed to do.

But not every supporter of assisted death services thinks that slopes towards greater expansion must be slippery. There are also those who insist that once a limited service is introduced, it will be easy enough to vote against any mooted changes later. So, for instance, Lord Falconer, the architect of several failed pro-assisted dying bills himself, argued in defence of Leadbeater's bill that:

> There is no slippery slope ... Our courts have made crystal clear that it is for our Parliament to decide the ambit of an assisted dying law.

And so did Lord Finkelstein:

> The 'slippery slope' argument in fact is a form of concession. It amounts to saying: 'I can't come up with an objection to the proposed law, so I'm going to vote against the legislation on the grounds of something that isn't in the bill, which no one is currently advocating and which I will have the chance to stop later if anyone does.'[3]

I disagree. With assisted death laws and services, sharp descents loom on every side in a way that doesn't tend to apply to more mundane legal initiatives. And they are indeed more like slippery slopes than refusable staircases.

Suffering expands

Experiences of fear, anxiety, and depression, prompted by the presence of serious illness or disability, used to be thought of as challenging but still bearable. Now they are tacitly viewed by some as unbearably horrific: so awful that they can only be relieved by death.

What this suggests is that 'suffering' and indeed 'unbearable suffering' are dynamic concepts that expand their terms of reference over time. In a series of articles published over the last decade, Melbourne psychology professor Nick Haslam has given us a helpful way to think about this. He has theorised the way some 'harm-related' concepts tend to 'creep' – that is, to cast a wider and wider net. Examples of creeping concepts discussed by him and his co-authors include 'trauma', 'abuse', 'addiction', 'bullying', and 'prejudice'. For a quick example, think of 'post-traumatic stress disorder' (PTSD). This used to be the sort of thing that only survivors of a prolonged and bloody war could get, having witnessed the action close up. These days, you can get it after a car accident in which nobody was hurt.

According to Haslam, harm-related concepts expand vertically, so that 'meaning extends downwards to encompass less extreme or intense phenomena than it did previously'. The concept is still being applied to the same kind of entity, broadly speaking, but whatever harm is involved is less severe. So – again according to Haslam – 'bullying' has come to include one-off actions rather than sustained campaigns; 'prejudice' is used for so-called 'microaggressions' as well as grave moral injuries; and 'autism' now includes high-functioning people with (what used to be called) Asperger's, as well as non-verbal people with multiple challenging sensory and behavioural issues.[4]

In her book *The Age of Diagnosis: How the Overdiagnosis Epidemic Is Making Us Sick*, neurophysiologist Dr Suzanne O'Sullivan argues that many chronic conditions are now being over-diagnosed:

> I have been a doctor for more than 30 years and a neurologist for 25 of those. I have recently grown particularly worried about the large number of young people referred to

me with four or five pre-existing diagnoses of chronic conditions, only some of which can be cured. Autism, Tourette syndrome, ADHD, migraines, fibromyalgia, polycystic ovary syndrome, depression, eating disorders, anxiety and many more.[5]

Another recent book, *The Care Dilemma* by David Goodhart, corroborates this with some jaw-dropping statistics about the apparent worsening of mental health in the UK. These include a rise in common mental disorders being self-reported by women aged 18–24, from 28% to 41% over eleven years. According to the Office for National Statistics, 7.1 million people in England and Wales now self-report having a mental health condition; the proportion of school-age children with special educational needs, including mental health, is 17%. Goodhart also notes that in 2023, the number of working-age people who self-reported a 'disability that restricts their daily activities' was 10.2 million, up from 6.6 million a decade previously.[6]

In her book, O'Sullivan argues that one explanation is that 'borderline medical problems are becoming iron-clad diagnoses and normal differences are being pathologised'. Philosopher Ian Hacking provided a framework to better understand the phenomenon years ago, when he described some psychological and psychiatric conditions as 'interactive kinds', exhibiting 'looping' behaviours across populations.[7] As some particular condition – autism, say – gets more widely known about in society, more people start to interpret their own symptoms and behaviour (or those of their children) in light of this new knowledge. An increasing number of people self-diagnose as having the condition in question, usually at the milder end of the spectrum of symptoms. Gradually, mental health professionals and their respective institutions start to widen their conception of the condition, at the very same time as they are diagnosing more people with it. Professional bodies formulate new diagnostic criteria in response to emerging trends and pressures, simplifying original protocols so that they can apply more widely. People who would previously never have thought of themselves as autistic can now do so, and will be backed up by the credentialled.

Opinions differ about whether vertical creep is a good thing. There are certainly those who believe it is. As a society, they think, we are getting better at detecting harm, which helps us to eradicate it. But I'm afraid I disagree, about both the presumed self-flattering motive and the overall social benefit.

In fact, vertical creep is making more and more people relate to themselves as passive victims or hopeless pathological cases. This is not good for them. It is also interfering with society's ability to see the impacts of more extreme instances of trauma, bullying, prejudice, autism (and so on), and to allocate material support to the people affected. Rapid expansion in the category of mental disability also means expansion in the category of disability more generally, which entails that the physically disabled are sometimes competing for resources with people fairly well adapted to life in comparison.

As for motive, I'm afraid I suspect that increased sensitivity to shades of harm on the part of modern language-users is not mainly altruistic, nor pursued in order to improve society, but rather is fuelled by self-serving power dynamics. To put it bluntly, contemporary social mores have incentivised people to claim passive victimhood. This means that the bar for such concepts has got lower over time, partly in order to give more relatively secure and functional people access to the social benefits of the label. My point is *not* that most people are cynically pretending such labels apply to their experiences in order to reap the benefits. Usually, they sincerely believe that the labels apply, and are backed up in their beliefs by authoritative-sounding professionals. Vertical concept creep is just what happens to a living and socially responsive language, given that self-interest plus social context has a lot of influence on how words get used.

Whether or not you agree with me about all that, perhaps we can at least agree that concepts related to the experience of suffering are definitely vertically creeping, whatever the background cause. Given wider social dynamics, they are expanding in ways we collectively cannot seem to control, and altering individual experiences as they go. There is not much point in introducing modifiers like 'unbearable', 'terrible', or 'awful' to try to specify more tightly what we mean, because they too will inevitably creep downwards to accommodate more and more trivial kinds of thing. The sources of today's unbearable, terrible, awful kinds of suffering don't seem trivial to us, not at all; but to our forebears, many surely would have done.

All of this is worrying. But in a context where the state provides an early death for unbearable suffering, it becomes positively dangerous.

Bottomless pools of suffering

In both the Netherlands and in Belgium, assisted death laws were designed relatively loosely from the start. Recipients of an assisted death did not have to be terminally ill, nor have any underlying bodily disorder. After decriminalisation in the 1990s, legislation passed in the Netherlands in 2002 focused on the alleviation of suffering that was judged 'lasting and unbearable'.[8] Case law dictated that this suffering must predominantly originate in a medically classifiable disease, but this could be a psychological one.

When it comes to discussing slippery slopes with respect to these countries, there is an understandable tendency to focus on the formal extension of euthanasia to children. But instead I want to draw attention to a more banal way in which the numbers of users of an assisted death service can expand over time. Even after years of relative stasis, a service can become suddenly popular. Perhaps this is best pictured as a bottomless pool rather than a slippery slope, but either way, the plunge appears out of control.

In both the Netherlands and Belgium, there has been a stark increase in people opting for an assisted death because of psychological suffering only, without any underlying bodily condition. In the first two decades after legalisation, the numbers of deaths by this route were tiny. But in 2023 in the Netherlands, 138 people were accepted, up 20% on the year before.[9] In 2024, there was a 60% increase again.[10] In Belgium too, there has recently been strong upward movement in numbers of users opting for death via this route.

What is happening? As in the UK, there are signs of a rising mental health crisis among Dutch people, especially young women.[11] In Belgium, rates of reported chronic mental health disorders also appear to be worsening, especially among teens and younger adults. This alone should give legislators pause for thought about the licensing of assisted death for psychological suffering. In both of these countries, young people can receive an early death from a doctor on the basis of diagnosed chronic conditions like autism, OCD, or borderline personality disorder, plus a finding of unbearable suffering with no hope of relief.

A 2023 study on Dutch 'euthanasia and physician-assisted suicide in people with intellectual disabilities and/or autism spectrum disorders' gives some chilling examples. They include a man under thirty who was euthanised on the basis that he was 'severely autistic and found this difficult to cope with'. Further description makes clear that he was verbal and could function independently at least to some extent, albeit with a self-reported feeling of great difficulty. A woman in her thirties who was given an early death by doctors is described as having autistic spectrum disorder, post-traumatic stress disorder, and borderline personality disorder, plus a history of sexual abuse in her teens. The 'core of her suffering', it was said by assessors, was 'an inability to love herself'. The studies' authors summarise: 'She suffered from fears, limited stress tolerance, being easily overstimulated, tormenting perfectionism and an inability to live independently or maintain relationships.' A second woman in her thirties, also euthanised, had complex comorbidities, including an anxiety disorder since early childhood, severe obsessive–compulsive disorder, a personality disorder, a psychotic disorder and Tourette syndrome. 'Her suffering consisted of continuous intrusive thoughts and compulsions' and she 'described her life as a succession of misery, ignorance, doubt and struggle'.[12]

More generally, the number of people using the Dutch service is also increasing, with a 14% rise in 2022 on the previous year, a 4% rise in 2023, and a 10% rise in 2024.[13] A similar trend is seen in Belgium. It seems likely that the concept of 'unbearable suffering' is creeping vertically over time to include less extreme or severe experiences, whether these be bodily or psychological. This in turn is widening the pool of people who count as eligible for an assisted death, and who view themselves as such. It also seems probable that vertical creep is causing changes in clinicians' perception of suffering, and so lowering eligibility thresholds for assisted death. Had such services been available decades ago, similar applications would presumably have been rejected outright.

The system beds down

Concept creep is not the only reason why a service can suddenly get more popular. Several causes might be operative at once, either working together or influencing different demographics in particular ways.

We know from our earlier discussion of Canada that where there is reduced access to goods like housing, subsistence, and adequate social and medical care, demand for assisted death will go up – just as during periods of austerity, the suicide rate goes up generally. Future economic downturns are bound to produce an uptick in assisted deaths. And thanks to growing individualism, changing family structures, and technological intrusion into the social world, loneliness and social isolation are also on the increase. This too is likely to make a difference to the numbers of assisted deaths in years to come. It will produce more of what Durkheim called 'egoistic suicides', or what Thomas Joiner calls suicides due to 'thwarted belongingness': cases where people feel rootless and alienated, assuming they don't much matter to anyone else, so don't really matter at all.

More concretely, a further factor related to growing numbers of users is how well recognised an assisted death service is by the general public. In existing services, numbers of users have increased over time as familiarity grows. In Switzerland, for instance, deaths have increased almost every year for twenty-five years, and in 2021 accounted for 2% of deaths overall.[14] In Belgium assisted deaths have increased sevenfold over twenty years, producing 2.4% of deaths in 2021.[15] In Canada, 4.7% of deaths in 2023 were assisted ones. As the practice gets assimilated by a culture, it becomes less intimidating and more mundane.

When the UK government tried to estimate how many users the new service described by Leadbeater's bill was likely to have, it estimated, rather conservatively, that there would be between 1,042 and 4,559 annual assisted deaths by Year 10.[16] The method used was simple: to take the proportion of assisted deaths in Oregon, relative to population – under 1% – and then apply this to UK population numbers. But this was to ignore a big difference between the UK and Oregon: namely, that we have a centrally controlled public health service, in which assisted death is intended to be provided free at the point of use. This means, among other things, that there will be no wrangling for the applicant about who is to pay for it, as there sometimes is in Oregon, with its dispersed and disjointed systems, multiple health providers, and complicated insurance processes.

Also unlike Oregon, a wide range of professionals across health and social care will be trained to be familiar with the process. There will be a legal obligation upon NHS doctors to offer information to any patient who expresses interest, and also to refer patients to a different doctor who can initiate the process, should the original be unwilling. The government has outlined a vast awareness campaign that will cost in the region of £550,000 to £850,000, stressing that 'there would likely be a need to provide information to a much wider pool of people, including all professionals who are providing or have recently provided health or social care to the person, as well as family members, friends, unpaid carers, and other support organisations and charities'.[17] Again, nothing like this is happening in Oregon. With this level of institutional backing filtering into every local care context, the popularity of assisted death is bound to get greater over time.

Death wishes are contagious

Social contagions are known to affect the popularity of solo suicide. In 1930s Japan, after a much-publicised suicide by a young woman who threw herself into an active volcano, there were 129 copycat suicides by volcano that same year, as well as six hundred attempts.[18] When Marilyn Monroe's cause of death in 1962 was listed as suicide, the suicide rate leapt by 12% in the United States the following year, and 10% in England.[19] More recently, internet culture has spawned the phenomenon of the pro-suicide website. Thousands of anonymous posters congregate in these virtual spaces, validating each other in suicidal feelings and talking about methods. One such site, based in the US, has been linked to more than fifty British deaths.

Platforms like Instagram and TikTok already act as a mechanism for the burgeoning numbers of self-diagnosed chronic conditions, as people create content about their supposed illnesses, which then causes other viewers to self-diagnose in turn – rightly or wrongly. Social media platforms are a conduit for the spread of what are known as 'psychogenic' or 'sociogenic' illnesses: where medically inexplicable symptoms rapidly spread in members of the same group, traceable to some particular aspect of the social environment. During Covid, for instance, exposure to social media content about Tourette's in young people apparently drove an increase in tic-like behaviour from people with no previous diagnosis.[20]

For some, death has always had a glamorous aura. In the interwar period, there was a huge vogue among students on the Continent for owning a plaster death mask of a young woman with a beatific smile, believed drowned and known as *L'Inconnue de la Seine*. Trawling through social media platforms, it is evident that similarly romanticised content is already being made about assisted death in a way that might help persuade others to take the same route.

A casual investigation of mine on TikTok in early 2025 found a young woman with her grandmother, larking about changing their outfits in order to go to a final dinner together, shortly before the grandmother's assisted death.[21] I also found a short clip of a young woman waving goodbye to the camera, suggesting she was about to be euthanised. And there was a lot of content about 'The Last Supper Project' by Ghanaian artist Joseph Awuah-Darko, who moved to the Netherlands in order to sign up for euthanasia via the psychological suffering route, and who was soliciting valedictory dinner invitations from strangers as part of an art project.[22]

As assisted death services deepen their hold on public consciousness, positive portrayals will become much more frequent. Regulators will have their hands tied: after all, the services themselves are legal and presented as a good thing. References to assisted death will be used by content-makers and influencers to get attention. They will sentimentalise and mythologise an early death, presenting it as a valid and even positively desirable response to the tragic messiness of life. Susceptible viewers who are otherwise eligible may get caught up in the fantasy. This isn't a dystopian novel, I'm afraid; this is likely to be real life.

How Canada fell down the slope

In the last few sections, we have been looking at the way social changes can result in increases in the numbers of people seeking an assisted death. But a service can also become more popular via explicit changes in the law. Where assisted death legislation formally names unbearable suffering as an object of relief, later updates to the law become likely to catch up with new or forgotten groups deemed to be suffering unbearably too. This is what has happened in Canada, where one of the key aims of original legislation was to alleviate 'grievous and irremediable' conditions causing 'enduring physical or psychological suffering that is intolerable'.

In the original version of the Canadian bill, a grievous and irremediable condition was defined as one in which, necessarily, natural death was reasonably foreseeable. But even this relatively lax condition was successfully challenged in

2021 in Quebec, under two sections of the Canadian Charter of Rights and Freedoms.[23] Soon afterwards, the law was updated to create Track 2 as a route to an assisted death for non-terminal disabled people, alongside Track 1 for the terminally ill. (The disturbing effects of this change were explored in Chapter Six.)

With respect to the constitutional 'right to life', the Quebec court found that the restriction of assisted death to terminally ill people infringed the right to life of disabled or ill people without any terminal diagnosis. It ruled that 'due to the prolongation of their life and the accompanying suffering, some patients will be inclined to end things prematurely, and often in a degrading or violent manner, before being in mortal agony, or having completely lost their dignity or being in the final stage of life'.[24] In a condensed form, here we find several assumptions rejected in the course of this book: that the only alternative to bodily pain in either illness or disability is an early assisted death, as opposed to improved medical or palliative care; that the only way to stop citizens carrying out violent, lonely suicides due to intense suffering is to offer them assisted deaths, rather than offering them more comfortable lives; and that severe incapacity and pain in disability must result in a loss of dignity, to be remedied only by an early death.

With respect to the constitutional right to 'liberty', meanwhile, the court ruled that the previous law was an infringement upon the freedom of disabled and ill people without terminal diagnoses. This was partly because it had deprived them 'of the opportunity to make a fundamental decision that respects their personal dignity and integrity'. In vain did the Attorney General of Canada try to point out an uncomfortable fact alluded to earlier: that, given the broad definition of disability, many people who count as disabled are in fact quite physically mobile; so that, in his words, 'nothing prevents them from exercising their autonomy, because they can end their own lives themselves, without any state intervention'.

Finally, the court ruled that the original law had created inequality in the form of unjustifiable discrimination between those whose natural death was reasonably foreseeable and those whose death was not, yet who met 'all the other legal requirements'. Effectively, the real justification for granting an assisted death was presumed to be the presence of grave suffering, whereas the diagnosis of terminal illness itself was deemed relatively unimportant.

As I write this chapter, a further legal challenge is under way in Canada, this time supposedly on behalf of the rights of the mentally ill. When the original law was expanded to produce Track 2 eligibility, this included people with only psychological or mental disorders but no underlying bodily condition, as in the Netherlands. In practice, a nervous government delayed implementation until 2027. But that delay is now being challenged. Applicants allege that denying assisted death to those suffering from mental illness is an infringement of the right of the latter to be treated equally under the law.[25]

Some equality-lovers would go even further. Among those who argue for extension of assisted death eligibility to the mentally ill are doctors – specialists in addiction, no less – who argue that eligibility for an early assisted death should also be formally extended to drug addicts on the grounds of equality. As Dr David Martell, physician lead for addictions medicine at Nova Scotia Health, said in 2023:

> I don't think it's fair, and the government doesn't think it's fair, to exclude people from eligibility because their medical disorder or their suffering is related to a mental illness. As a subset of that, it's not fair to exclude people from eligibility purely because their mental disorder might either partly or

in full be a substance use disorder. It has to do with treating people equally.[26]

Yet why stop there? There are lots of people suffering greatly for all sorts of reasons; and also lots of people who seem to think that, wherever great suffering exists and some kind of vaguely medical-sounding label can be attached to it, an early death could be a good answer.

The equality of mercy

So far in this book there has been a lot of discussion of freedom and mercy, but little about equality. Sometimes known as fairness, this is a value which often takes a starring role in politically liberal frameworks. It is also a prominent concern in modern healthcare. Most bioethicists agree that decisions should be a matter of balancing four fundamental principles: respecting autonomy, promoting welfare, avoiding harm, and attending to fairness and 'equal opportunity in treatment'. But when this familiar idea is applied to assisted death services, it is one of the main routes towards slippery slopes.

For simplicity's sake we can think of the equality dynamic as potentially playing out in one of two ways, depending on whether the thing to be distributed is thought of as merciful help or freedom. Where the goal of an assisted death service is understood as the helpful relief of unbearable suffering, groups can try to establish that they too suffer unbearably and deserve access to an early death. They are 'similarly situated', as the legal jargon has it. Health authorities with limited assisted death services are viewed as offering alleviation to one severely suffering group while unfairly withholding it from another in near-identical straits. Justice, the argument goes, would demand that they both get the same treatment.

Or, where the goal is to provide ill people with freedom or autonomy to make their own decisions about life and death, new groups can argue that they too should be given that very same freedom, as a matter of fairness. As the Canadian example suggests, attempts to expand existing laws tend to move between these two strategies, sometimes chasing freedom and sometimes chasing mercy.

There are also those who would take the approach further, arguing that health providers unwilling to share the alleged benefit of an early death to suffering people should be sanctioned. In the committee phase of the UK's Terminally Ill Adults Bill, Kit Malthouse appeared to suggest that hospices which tried to opt out of participating in assisted death services could be defunded.[27] This has already happened in Switzerland, where some cantons have started to compel hospitals and care homes to accept assisted suicides on their premises, or else lose access to state subsidies.[28] Such reasoning places even more pressure on existing assisted death services to expand.

And there is an accompanying factor, operating at the level of emotion rather than rational thought, which tends to supercharge equality arguments, as identified by psychiatrist and bioethicist Dr Scott Y. H. Kim.[29] Put simply, there is a longstanding taboo against the deliberate taking of life in nearly every Western culture. The taboo can be broken only in relatively exceptional, well-defined circumstances. So where a society agrees that offering assisted death is more important than respecting the taboo against killing, a symbolic line has been crossed. After a while, in order to retrospectively justify the transgression of the taboo, it starts to seem obvious that helping to kill suffering people must have been a goal of monumental moral significance all along. This in itself increases the chance of further expansions to new cohorts.

The thought process seems to go: that we were prepared to

go quite as far as we did, helping people to die because of their great suffering, demonstrates that the alleviation of suffering by death is something morally urgent. Hence, wherever we find new forms of severe suffering, it is extremely important that we alleviate that by offering assisted death there too.

Where safeguards become obstacles to freedom

In discussions of the Terminally Ill Adults Bill, a popular tack was to insist that slippery slopes would be avoided by the wording of the bill; and specifically, by the fact that it didn't mention unbearable suffering at all. Instead, as we know, eligibility was specified only in terms of a terminal illness diagnosis. Declared Lord Falconer:

> Where those laws start with terminal-illness-only provisions, that is where they stick. There is no slippery slope. That slippery slope occurs where the law is an unbearable-suffering law, and what constitutes unbearable suffering becomes a difficult line to draw. That is not this case.[30]

Unfortunately, though, there are two ways this looks alarmingly overconfident. The most obvious is that, even if it is not formally stated as such, a central rationale of Leadbeater's proposed service is still to relieve what is assumed to be terrible or unbearable suffering. Put simply, it is not a coincidence that assisted death is to be offered to the terminally ill rather than to the healthy. The assumption is that the former suffer dreadfully, whereas the latter typically do not.

With the alleviation of suffering as the implicit background rationale for an assisted death service, even if unstated, some of the dynamics described above are bound to still be in play. For instance: just because an assisted death law doesn't mention the alleviation of suffering as an explicit goal doesn't mean that pressure groups can't do so, or that politicians and judges won't eventually be swayed by public demands for 'equality' of treatment in this matter. It will still be argued: why should an assisted death service be confined to alleviating the sort of awful suffering associated, almost arbitrarily, with terminal illness? Isn't awful suffering an important thing to alleviate wherever it is found?

But let's leave aside the likelihood of pressure to make such big changes. Some slopes are gentle inclines rather than plunging mountain pistes, but even so, the gradients still add up. In other words: not every change to an assisted death law has to be a formal admission of some new and intensely suffering group as eligible. When the logic of equality meets the already conceded principle of offering assisted death, it becomes easier to make smaller changes. We can see the effects of this when we look at the government's equality impact assessment for Leadbeater's bill, released about a month before the final Commons vote.[31]

An equality impact assessment is required by law to consider potentially adverse effects of new legislation on protected groups. The statement's authors approached assisted death as a good thing, to which protected minorities might unfairly struggle to get access. It noted, for instance, that 'persons with learning disabilities ... are examples of disabled people who may struggle to understand the information provided to them in written or oral form', but – rather than concluding this factor should rule them out – determined that information would have to be given 'in an accessible format' instead. At another point, it was suggested that a basic safeguard against coercion – that of having two kinds of identity document, including photographic ID – might be lifted for disabled people and people from ethnic minorities, because members of these groups are less likely to possess the required kinds of identification.

Each of these so-called 'reasonable adjustments', offered in the name of equality, in practice made it more likely that undetectable coercion might occur. The background mentality seemed to be inherited from the framework of positive discrimination; as if we were talking, say, about lowering university entrance requirements for the underprivileged, rather than getting rid of basic protections against being coerced into an early death. In a grim twist, the application of this logic means that vulnerable groups such as the disabled will end up with *fewer* protections than the able bodied, not more. The queasy progressive-sounding branding was encapsulated in a post on social media by Sarah Wootton, the chief executive of Dignity in Dying. On the day of the report's release, she wrote with approval that 'The Bill is inclusive – it includes safeguards to protect people who may be more vulnerable, would apply equally to all sexes equally, may have a positive impact on those from lower socioeconomic backgrounds and does not discriminate against people with mental illness.'[32]

Overseas, assisted death services have followed a similar trajectory. Safeguards designed to protect the individual from coerced or unwise decisions have been treated as obstacles to dispensing either mercy or freedom. We saw another good example of this at the beginning of this chapter. The law in Washington state was amended in 2023 to remove what had originally been thought of as important safety features. The waiting period of successful applicants was reduced from fifteen days to seven. Health professionals who are not doctors were permitted to assess eligibility, raising the chances of medical confusion and error. And lethal substances could be mailed to patients, creating more opportunities for hidden coercion. As these expansions proceed, officials will be unlikely to find much evidence of harm. After all, the victims won't be around to speak out.

In other places too, safeguards set up to protect would-be users have been framed as undesirable barriers to access and removed. In Canada, the original ten-day reflection period was taken out completely in 2021 for those on the newly created Track 1. In the Australian state of Victoria, at first the law stopped doctors from bringing up assisted suicide with their patients, protecting the overly suggestible. Yet in 2025 this was styled as a 'gag clause' by critics, then removed on the grounds that it 'impeded access' to 'end-of-life choice'.[33]

And once an assisted death law *has* been expanded in the name of freedom, it creates pressure on legislators elsewhere. Oregon was the first US state to legalise assisted suicide for the terminally ill, in 1997. Until recently, some supporters of the Oregon model were proudly advertising that it had not changed its criteria in over twenty years. Campaigners for Leadbeater's bill were keen to stress that Oregon-style bills would not shift over time. Yet as I write, there is mounting pressure to remove existing safeguards, partly based on the fact that laws elsewhere have already expanded. A prominent group of doctors in Oregon is now arguing that the waiting period for an assisted death should be cut from fifteen days to forty-eight hours; and that, as in Washington, nurse practitioners and physician assistants should be allowed to oversee the process as well as doctors. Some supporters are reinstating familiar emotive rhetoric, grimly predicting that without legal reform to further open up access, ineligible suffering people will turn to 'do-it-yourself options'.[34]

Yet again, we see the collision of simplistic Merciful Helper and Freedom Lover discourses. The former urges us to simplify a system that cruelly excludes gravely suffering people for arbitrary reasons and makes them wait too long. The latter – at least in the radical guise, rather than the moderate one – refuses to countenance the idea that an individual self should not be given maximum control over its own destiny at all times. Any protests by careful Merciful Helpers get lost in the noise, as do concerns of moderate Freedom Lovers about checking for genuine autonomy.

There is also anecdotal evidence that viewing safeguards as unfair obstacles pressures doctors to sign off requests. Attempts by clinicians to slow down a person's determination to leap to the irrevocable endpoint can be interpreted by applicants and colleagues as hostile and regressive. One Canadian palliative care doctor, writing on X in 2025, said that a failure to immediately introduce the subject of assisted death to her eligible patients had been interpreted as unfairly blocking access.[35] An Australian palliative doctor chimed in to report that assisted death laws have 'introduced a perception that a person's autonomous wish should be acted on', meaning that attempts to gently push back are treated as obstructive.[36] In such a febrile context, it is understandable that a lot of medics are opting for a quiet life, and going along with whatever a patient wants.

Generally, professionals seem increasingly unable to say no. Perhaps they hope that higher-up managers, policies or laws will manage the conflict for them instead. In the UK, for instance, doctors now sign off ten million people as unfit to work each year, which seems likely to be significantly more than are literally unfit.[37] The idea that the very same GPs will suddenly become good at declining patients' fervent requests for their preferred exit route is hard to believe.

The difficulty of rolling uphill

We now have an answer to those who deny the possibility of slippery slopes. Limited laws don't just snowball on their own. They do so in tandem with burgeoning social currents, a vogue for simplistic ideological frameworks, and widely spread, seductive but fallacious ways of thinking.

The grand-sounding values that tend to dominate justifications of assisted death services – freedom, autonomy, mercy, dignity, equality, and so on – are all extremely abstract and can be interpreted in multiple ways. Their rhetorical malleability makes it easy to tell a simplified story about death as a benevolent state-sanctioned option – already an appealing vision when attempting to deal with entrenched human suffering and costly messiness. This story can quickly gather momentum, making it hard to notice inconsistency between rousing statements.

In theory, any proposed expansion of the law might be rejected. But the very nature of assisted death makes that less likely. People don't like to think much about dying and death. If they do, they often prefer fairy tales to concrete facts – whether horror stories or happily-ever-afters. And equally, assisted death eliminates what might have been a valuable source of information: namely, former users. When it comes to testifying about failures, there is very little lived experience, as it were. We can listen to the voices of those who changed their mind, or of relatives who were blindsided by the swiftness and impersonality of an unscrupulously run system. But we simply won't be hearing from anyone coerced into an early death; who had been given a faulty diagnosis or prognosis beforehand; who had not been sufficiently informed of relevant alternatives; or who did not, in fact, have mental capacity after all. They just won't show up.

Once introduced, getting rid of an assisted death system is very difficult. It is always hard to repeal a law. It is even harder where a repeal would retrospectively change the moral status of participation in the practice in question. Legality tends to make people stop worrying about morality, whereas illegality opens up painful avenues of thought. While, strictly speaking, participating doctors would not have done anything illegal in actively helping to kill people, repeal would make them consider whether they had in fact been doing something dramatically immoral. Equally, relatives and friends who had supported loved ones during over-hasty final journeys would have to reassess their involvement. Ten years after the introduction of an assisted death service, it is likely that everyone will know someone who has used it. The more users there are, the more incentive society has to let sleeping dogs lie.

Conclusion

Actually existing assisted death services – the real ones, not those in supporters' imaginations – fail to be reliable providers of either mercy or freedom. It is not that they never do; but that they often don't. This fact destroys the two main rationales offered for such services.

The impulse towards granting mercy and the impulse towards facilitating personal freedom point in two different directions. The former is essentially an interventionist stance; the latter an injunction to stay out of an individual's private business. Merciful Helpers try to justify the provision of early death only for particular gravely suffering cohorts. Freedom Lovers would like to offer an assisted death for everyone who wants one but can't defend why assistance must be provided by other people. They take considerations drawn from the non-interventionist discourse about solo suicide (e.g. 'I have a right to kill myself, if that's what I want!') and inappropriately translate them into discourse about assisted suicide services ('I have a right to your help in killing me, if that's what I want!')

Realistically, assisted death services can only be guided in their initial formation by concerns of the Merciful Helper. But this means they don't much advance the cause of freedom at all. They end up oriented only towards cohorts perceived to be suffering gravely or unbearably, which undermines the idea that they were ever aimed at the general 'right to die'. It is true that these services offer everyone who is eligible a new *choice*; but it is a choice that causes great problems for the many who don't wish to take it.

Not recognising the tension between mercy and freedom results in bad policy. Conscientious attempts to legislate for a truly merciful system get hollowed out by the individualistic idiom of freedom and autonomy: 'it's my choice', 'it's none of your business', and so forth. Legislators pay nowhere near enough attention to checking whether the suffering of applicants is genuinely severe, unrelenting, and irremediable, before death is provided as the simple-looking solution. And the rush to get death over and done with for a terminally ill or disabled cohort brings a loss of safeguards protective of autonomy, and an increased susceptibility to coercion and abuse for already vulnerable people.

Partly, the inability of assisted death services to simultaneously dispense mercy and protect freedom is born of conflicting internal aims. But this destructive dynamic is made worse by limits upon resources. Existing assisted death services simply don't have the time, money, or requisite number of professionals to seriously address the complexity of each new case. In the early twentieth century, when assisted death was first being debated, the classic example cited by the governing classes involved a family doctor who had known you most of your life. He would apply his understanding of your personal situation to notice when the moment was right – usually, when death was imminent, and bodily agony present or encroaching – and then put you 'quietly and undemonstrably out to sea', as Lord Horder described it to Parliament in 1936. Or at least that was the ideal. In the modern healthcare system, this model is totally inapplicable. The people who decide whether you live or die may never have met you before, and will probably devote less than an hour each to the decision.

CONCLUSION

No matter what their qualifications, doctors can get things wrong. The supporters of assisted death services want you to think of them as run by competent, well-rested, time-rich doctors who always know best; but life isn't like that. The title of this book is a quotation from a famous poem by Dylan Thomas. Thomas himself lived a chaotic life at various points, and eventually died in a New York hotel room in 1953, aged only thirty-nine, the apparent victim of medical incompetence. He had been injected with at least 30mg of morphine by his American doctor, who claimed it was a treatment for alcohol withdrawal – though accounts differ as to whether the poet was actually drinking heavily at the time, or simply suffering from bronchitis.[1] Either way, he sank into a coma from which he did not recover.

The champions of assisted death services want us to think only of a 'clean' applicant: a person with lots of irremediable pain in the final stages of life, in full control of their rational faculties, making a decision straightforwardly in their own best interests. But – as the case of Dylan Thomas also shows – human lives can be messier than this. We need to consider the sorts of case to which Professor Mark Taubert, a palliative care consultant in the NHS, drew readers' attention in a magazine article in May 2025:

> I am an NHS consultant working in frontline medicine. My patient, Allan, is 47 years old and has prostate cancer. He has suffered from alcoholism and substance abuse for much of his adult life, and is facing a custodial sentence. He has attempted suicide on four occasions. He has type-2 diabetes and a chronic lung condition, which makes it harder for him to breathe ... Ava, another patient, has stage-four breast cancer and is 21 weeks pregnant. She is facing eviction from her home, has an abusive partner and also a history of self-harm and anorexia nervosa ... Zain

has head and neck cancer, Down's syndrome, is non-verbal, has had substance-abuse issues and was sexually abused as a child.[2]

This is the reality of some people's situations. This, then, is the context in which assisted death will arrive as a formally organised practice. People like Allan, Ava, and Zain may long for self-annihilation at times, or at least say they do. Each will likely find a clinician prepared to diagnose them as terminally ill. How, then, are pressured doctors, social workers, or lawyers with limited information about these people's minds and lives supposed to decide whether they should carry on for more weeks or months, or die straight away?

The most likely outcome is that they won't try very hard to work out the answer: because they don't know on what grounds to object; because they don't have the time or resources to think about it; because they feel cultural pressure to say 'yes'; and because they can always mentally shift some responsibility for the decision onto other people and parts of the system. Once assisted death is embedded in a society, professionals in charge of decision-making will end up taking the path of least resistance. This may not be their intention – but it will happen nonetheless.

And there is another factor to consider. Throughout this book I have charitably assumed that, whatever the actual outcome, doctors providing assisted deaths wish to be merciful just as strongly as they wish to offer applicants 'freedom' and 'choice'. But actually, this may not be true. A senior clinician who manages the healthcare of elderly people in the US suggests to me that, in her experience, 'doctors in the business of assisted suicide/assisted death are very niche, mainly "Freedom Lovers" ... the "Merciful Helper" doctor is not what I would predict as prominent player'. Doctors temperamentally attracted to offering merciful help would, she thinks, tend to go into palliative care instead, or to some other area entirely. If she is right, assisted death services may disproportionately attract clinicians biased towards the crude idea that they are simply facilitating the applicant's autonomous wishes; whereas palliative care may be drawing those trying to attend to the precise nature of the suffering involved, in order to relieve it. Since the presence of an assisted death service tends to interfere with resourcing of palliative care services, this 'splitting' of doctor types is a troubling thought indeed.

When a system has early, non-natural death as a deliberate output – in other words, killing – it doesn't matter if that system sometimes gets things right, if it also often gets things wrong. If judgements are likely to be hit and miss, the service should not be there in the first place. In truth, delivering genuinely merciful help to someone who is suffering is a fine art, requiring close attention to personal circumstance. Mostly it will involve helping people to live their remaining natural life more comfortably, not helping to end things. Impersonal systems are hopeless instruments for deciding which is the more appropriate outcome, and even more so when they are financially straitened and managed by time-pressured strangers.

There are also wider social effects to consider. As assisted death becomes familiar, problems are not confined to applicants. The old, ill, and disabled implicitly get associated with the heading 'a fate worse than death', and in many cases feel extra guilty and burdensome as a result. The medical profession becomes more frightening to some, undermining trust and engagement. Public attitudes supportive of the prevention of suicide and coercive killing are confused. Some family members are blindsided and traumatised. And these are just the more predictable outcomes. Once people in power get accustomed to seeing a doctor-assisted killing as a simple, clean, officially sanctioned solution to suffering, who knows in what other freefalls we will end up.

Supporters of assisted death services sometimes challenge critics: under what circumstances would you agree to such a service, and with what safeguards exactly? If the critics don't concede the point at least a little, agreeing to the existence of a service albeit with restrictions, it is implied that they must be fanatically against assisted death no matter what. In this vein, British commentator David Aaronovitch, himself broadly in favour, asked opponents with apparent sarcasm on social media during fractious discussion of Leadbeater's bill: 'Just as a matter of interest, what possible safeguards could be introduced that would ever lead you to support an assisted dying measure?'[3] He seemed pretty sure that the answer must be 'none'. (Sometimes this comes with an additional insinuation: that the hidden resistance to assisted death must be religious in origin, which is presumed to make things even worse.)

But to argue that an assisted death service is morally unacceptable, given what we know about the society we live in, does not imply an objection to any form of assisted death whatsoever. As I hope I have made clear, I am not inevitably against the practice at the individual level. The scope of my argument has concerned assisted death as it plays out in realistic bureaucratic scenarios, not utopian ones: in the organised, large-scale forms we actually find in the world; alongside the economy and welfare states we have; with the overstretched, under-resourced health and social care sectors we know; with our own foibles and ideological blind spots, rather than fantasies about optimal levels of human reason and empathy.

Unlike many supporters of assisted death services, I am not constructing unrecognisable versions of these things – or just leaving out huge chunks of real-world information – then contemplating how smoothly assisted death services would work in that imaginary context. So when I say that assisted death services are morally unacceptable, I mean they have unacceptable consequences in the imperfect world we have. That is the context we should care about most. It is perfectly OK to say 'no' to assisted death services, full stop, without it implying that the secret background complaint must be about assisted death per se.

I believe that – at least occasionally – to help bring about someone else's death can be a morally appropriate response to extreme, unrelenting, and irremediable suffering: not obviously wrong, and perhaps even positively right. But this does not mean the practice of assisted suicide should even be decriminalised, let alone officially facilitated by doctors. At root, the law against it has a clear beneficial purpose: to deter people from coercing or killing their fellow humans for selfish reasons, including when they are gravely ill; and to make it easier to find and punish offenders when they do. We still need to see off the activities of rogue individuals like Jack Kevorkian, Harold Shipman, or Mark Lyons; not to mention opportunistic family members with an eye to financial gain, or spouses who engage in brutal 'mercy killings' under the guise of relieving suffering. Continued criminalisation functions as a deterrent.

Former Justice of the Supreme Court Lord Sumption has recently indicated he supports the legalisation of doctor-assisted suicide for terminally ill people, albeit that he finds Kim Leadbeater's bill 'seriously defective'.[4] But in a 2019 Reith Lecture, he argued that it was a good thing that there was a law against assisted suicide generally, but that this didn't mean it might not be right to break it sometimes:

> I'll tell you exactly what I think about this. I think that the law should continue to criminalise assistance in suicide, and I think that the law should be broken. I think that it should be broken from time to time. We need to have a law against

it in order to prevent abuse but it has always been the case that this has been criminal and it has always been the case that courageous relatives and friends have helped people to die, and I think that that is an untidy compromise of the sort that I suspect very few lawyers would adopt, but I don't believe that there is necessarily a moral obligation to obey the law and, ultimately, it is something that each person has to decide within his own conscience. That – that's something that I think. That is where it ought to be decided.[5]

I have no wish to encourage anyone to break the law; and I would also urge great caution and epistemic humility upon anyone considering ending the life of a suffering loved one at their sincere request. The stakes are very high, and the costs of getting it wrong are large. But broadly speaking, what Sumption says here is what I think too.

This means that, occasionally, someone who has done the right thing will nonetheless face the prospect of criminal prosecution. This cannot be avoided; for the alternative, removing the threat of prosecution altogether, destroys the law's entire rationale. Much is made by the assisted death lobby of relatives who wish to help a loved one die in good faith, but who feel anxious about facing criminal charges. While this is clearly a stressful situation, treating it as a top priority in radically reshaping our national legislation is surely overplayed. And that is not least because very few such criminal prosecutions ever take place.

In 2008, Sir Keir Starmer – now Prime Minister – was the newly appointed Director of Public Prosecutions. His first action was to introduce new CPS protocols which made assisted suicide more difficult to prosecute. As the *Guardian* reported at the time, 'Starmer's decision is a significant step towards official recognition that the law criminalising assisted suicide, which has not been changed since 1961, will not be acted upon by prosecuting authorities in cases of terminal or other serious illness.'[6] In 2024, another former DPP, Sir Max Hill, declared that out of twenty-seven cases that had crossed his desk between 2018 and 2023, only one of them had actually met the re-defined threshold for a prosecution.[7] Hill seemed to take this lack of historical prosecutions as a reason to decriminalise. But to me it suggests exactly the opposite. It surely cannot be reasonable to get rid of a criminal deterrent, useful in inhibiting coercion and abuse, on the grounds that people who are not coercive or abusive fear prosecution. In this case their fear, while understandable and presumably distressing, is not properly calibrated to likely outcomes.

Sometimes, there are legal grey areas. The existing law with respect to assisted death, in conjunction with a relatively lax attitude to prosecution in the case of terminal illness, creates one of them. Those who want to decriminalise it properly are trying to paint these grey areas black and white, pushing the activity of assisting in someone's death over the social line into officially acceptable behaviour, and so losing the enhanced judicial scrutiny. If they get their way, then given what human nature is actually like, a much greater number of people will meet coerced and unjust deaths than otherwise would have done. This is not a price a decent society should be willing to pay.

As I finish writing this book, Kim Leadbeater's Terminally Ill Adults Bill is passing through Parliament. Assuming it gets through the Lords, a lot about how it will work in practice is still undecided. Indeed, part of the bill as it leaves the Commons includes what is known as a 'Henry VIII' clause, granting ministers sweeping powers to determine key details in future, without seeking parliamentary approval. Whatever happens, it is certain there will be great pressure to reject further proposed safeguards – whether in this bill's lifetime, or that of another one with the same objective. That is just what happens when the goals of mercy and freedom collide.

During the bill's committee phase, despite the best attempts of dissenting members, the committee voted against a host of amendments designed to make it more attuned to granting genuine, careful mercy. Attempts to set up such a system were torpedoed by a first-personal, choice-obsessed idiom according to which – in the memorable words of Rachel Hopkins – it is 'none of your business why' someone else wishes to die. In relation to making sure that the suffering of applicants was genuinely severe, long-lasting, and irremediable, and that clinicians had tried other less drastic treatments and approaches first, the committee ruled against:

- requiring assessors to ask applicants why they wanted an assisted death
- requiring an applicant to meet with a palliative care specialist to hear about other options
- requiring an assessing doctor to meet with a specialist in the applicant's condition, to check there aren't other options
- requiring the assessing panel to actively question the assessing doctors about respective decisions (the present wording insists only vaguely that the panel should 'hear from' them)
- excluding from the definition of 'terminal illness' any diseases whose progress can be controlled or substantially slowed by medical treatment
- excluding from the definition of 'terminal illness' any bodily deterioration caused by not eating or drinking

Meanwhile, on the matter of excluding hasty, non-autonomous, or unduly influenced decisions, the committee voted against:

- requiring a higher threshold for decision-making than the minimal one given by the Mental Capacity Act
- making 'understanding care and treatment options' a requirement of demonstrating mental capacity
- requiring the applicant to speak to a mental health professional
- ensuring the applicant has 'no remediable risk factors for suicide' nor any 'impairment of judgement resulting from a mental disorder'
- providing special support for those with autism or learning disabilities such as Down's syndrome
- explicitly prohibiting 'encouraging' someone, 'manipulating' them, or exerting 'undue influence' upon someone to have an assisted death
- insisting that doctors may not bring up assisted death unless the patient does first
- insisting the assisted death process could not begin until twenty-eight days after diagnosis

So if the Leadbeater process is anything to go by, incoming assisted death laws are likely to end up representing the coinciding interests of radical Freedom Lovers and simplistic Merciful Helpers, to whom every case of suffering during grave or terminal illness – no matter what its origins, duration, or severity – potentially stands in need of an early death as a quick release. Perhaps this style of laissez-faire thinking works for decisions where the hoped-for outcome benefits the individual in a way everyone else can see. But opting to kill yourself when you could have gone on living is far from that.

And there is another, more pedestrian reason why amendments aimed at meaningful safeguarding are likely to be similarly rejected in future. An assisted death service cannot bring with it many safeguards, because the NHS simply cannot afford to have them. But in that case, I submit, we cannot afford an assisted death service at all.

Modern technology is able to prolong life in unprecedented ways, which don't always increase a patient's overall happiness. This problem is referred to as over-medicalisation. The processes themselves – intubation, ventilation, catheterisation, and so on – can be painful, disorienting, and traumatic. The hospital environment is peopled by strangers and full of jarring sensory experiences. Being ill in hospital can be desperately lonely.

Many who are gravely ill fervently wish to carry on living and are willing to put up with long hospital stays and invasive procedures because they increase the chance of that outcome. But others feel differently. From their perspective, it might seem that doctors and hospitals are holding them against their will; and so the cause of freedom requires that they, in particular, be released via the active supply of an early death.

The problem identified is real, and I don't make light of it. But the most obvious solution to over-medicalisation is not to empower doctors to actively help kill their patients. Rather, it is to get better at appropriately managing symptoms and – if necessary, and with the consent of the patient – withdraw treatment where it is no longer doing good. The hospice movement was founded precisely in order to move away from the idea that a patient's death is always a medical failure, to be put off for as long as possible no matter what. It offers the patient an alternative to the hospital-based version of dying and places an emphasis on palliation and holistic care. Palliative medicine itself has developed protocols for treating end-of-life suffering in a sensitive manner, attuned to the patient's needs and feelings. Though now underfunded, with proper political will, that issue could be sorted out.

Offering assisted death at scale is full of risk. To introduce a new technological approach to deal with the harmful consequences of an earlier technological approach is extremely unwise – and especially when the new technology is likely to set off a whole new chain of harmful consequences in its own right.

In different times and places, opinions have differed on what a human being essentially is: the 'person' or 'self', understood as bearer of moral significance. All such conceptions are guiding fictions or metaphors. They don't get discovered under microscopes but are created in stories we tell about ourselves, influenced by prevailing material and cultural conditions.

Modern hyperliberal times encourage us to think of the self as a thing with clean edges, metaphysically separated at birth from the vaguely threatening masses of other people. Global capitalism favours citizens who move around a lot, choosing where to put down their shallow roots according to the financial opportunities available. Technology mediates social relationships and keeps us physically apart. Popular culture encourages the rejection of unwanted responsibilities towards others, on the dubious grounds of personal liberation. We are supposed to view relationships as mostly contractual, and substantially justified by self-interest (or its updated version, 'self-care').

This wafer-thin picture of the self is now so endemic to contemporary discourse we barely notice, let alone contest it. Assuming you embrace the vision, you will end up ranking whatever the subjective self chooses fairly high up the list of moral priorities. After all, effectively you have already couched relationships with others as contingent and external to who you 'really are'.

And so we are sliding towards a wholly new way of being and relating to one another, which would have seemed alien to forebears only decades ago. The cultural descent into individualism is ironically a collective one. It is speeding up, and soon may be unstoppable. The clamour for assisted death services, emerging simultaneously across Western societies, is an outcrop of the underlying worldview. It acts as a resounding validation of individualistic thinking. For Freedom Loving supporters, an assisted death service encourages humans to fantasise that death is one more aspect of natural life over which they can have complete control. It fosters the idea that death is just a self-interested matter, rather than a potentially communal event. And it supercharges the thought that what matters about an individual life is entirely determined by what that individual *believes* matters. If you feel your life is worth nothing any more, then you are right.

Describing the 'egoistic' suicide characteristic of the hyperliberal predicament, Durkheim memorably wrote about how a disintegrating society can produce further despair, so producing more suicide:

> ... at the very moment when he is breaking away from the social environment, he is still subject to its influence. However individualized a person may be, there is always something collective that remains, which is the feeling of depression and melancholy that arises from this exaggerated individualism.[8]

The further we slide down the slope, the faster we go.

Yet at the same time we are social animals, a fact hard-wired into the species which enables its survival. Simply put, we could not thrive if we did not team up. The impulse to mercifully relieve the great suffering of others, in a way that goes beyond mere self-interest, is a sign of this aspect of our deep selves. The achievements of medicine in lengthening and improving the quality of human life are a stunning testament to the power of care. Even in the very desire to create assisted death services, we find evidence of a belief that humans should look after one another. The impulse is merciful; but the resulting process is not.

The growing energy of assisted death campaigns in the world confronts us with a series of stark questions. Do we continue to act as if every human life is valuable, no matter what its owner thinks? Or do we explicitly allow that some lives are not worth living? If the latter, have we really thought through the myriad consequences of this radical, probably irrevocable, shift? And ultimately: do we prioritise a vision of the self muscling through life alone, metaphysically unencumbered from connections to other people; or do we protest that our deepest selves are not in fact so existentially independent? Should we try – while we still can – to carefully get both life and death right for our fellow humans as well as for ourselves; or will we just opt for taking whatever each of us personally can get?

Do we go gentle into this frightening moral order? Or do we rage against the dying of a hard-won, precious attitude towards life's value, and what we owe one to another? I say we do not go gentle. I say we rage.

Notes

Introduction

1. 'Palliative and end of life care profile December 2023 update: statistical commentary', Office for Health Improvement & Disparities, updated 17 September 2024. https://www.gov.uk/government/statistics/palliative-and-end-of-life-care-profiles-december-2023-data-update/palliative-and-end-of-life-care-profile-december-2023-update-statistical-commentary
2. Kevin Yuill, *Assisted Suicide: The Liberal, Humanist Case Against Legalization*. Palgrave Macmillan, 2013.
3. Kim Leadbeater. Register of Interests. https://www.theyworkforyou.com/mp/26040/kim_leadbeater/spen_valley/register
4. Terminally Ill Adults (End of Life) Bill: impact assessment, 2 May 2025. https://www.gov.uk/government/publications/terminally-ill-adults-end-of-life-bill-impact-assessment
5. Terminally Ill Adults (End of Life) Bill (Sixth sitting). Hansard. Debated on Thursday 30 January 2025. https://hansard.parliament.uk/commons/2025-01-30/debates/895ba091-38d0-4162-8f79-40df9fae7e38/TerminallyIllAdults(EndOfLife)Bill(SixthSitting)
6. Alexander Murray, *Suicide in the Middle Ages. Volume I: The Violent against Themselves*. Oxford University Press, 1998.
7. Émile Durkheim, *Suicide: A Study in Sociology*. 1897. Trans. John A. Spaulding and George Simpson. Routledge, 1952.
8. 'Doctors offer some support to Kevorkian', *New York Times*,

5 December 1995. https://www.nytimes.com/1995/12/05/us/doctors-offer-some-support-to-kevorkian.html
9. 'Kit Malthouse: Legalising assisted dying will protect terminally ill people and improve end-of-life care', Conservative Home, 28 November 2024. https://conservativehome.com/2024/11/28/kit-malthouse-legalising-assisted-dying-will-protect-terminally-ill-people-and-improve-end-of-life-care/
10. Rowena Mason, 'MPs opposed to assisted dying criticise "distasteful" Esther Rantzen claims', *Guardian*, 16 May 2025. https://www.theguardian.com/society/2025/may/16/mps-opposed-to-assisted-dying-criticise-distasteful-esther-rantzen-claims
11. Nigel Biggar, *Aiming to Kill: The Ethics of Suicide and Euthanasia*. Darton, Longman & Todd Ltd, 2003.
12. James Rachels, *The End of Life: Euthanasia and Morality*. Oxford University Press, 1986.
13. Terminally Ill Adults (End of Life) Bill (Twenty-eighth sitting). Hansard. Debated on Tuesday 25 March 2025. https://hansard.parliament.uk/Commons/2025-03-25/debates/072fb172-50ba-42e5-bff5-e5899a834189/TerminallyIllAdults(EndOfLife)Bill(Twenty-EighthSitting)
14. 'The RCPsych cannot support the Terminally Ill Adults (End of Life) Bill for England and Wales in its current form', Royal College of Psychiatrists press release, 13 May 2025. https://www.rcpsych.ac.uk/news-and-features/latest-news/detail/2025/05/13/the-rcpsych-cannot-support-the-terminally-ill-adults-(end-of-life)-bill-for-england-and-wales-in-its-current-form
15. Trudo Lemmens, 'When death becomes therapy: Canada's troubling normalization of health care provider ending of life', *American Journal of Bioethics*, 23(11), 2023, pp. 79–84. https://doi.org/10.1080/15265161.2023.2265265

Chapter 1: Give Me Liberty and Give Me Death

1. '"I will probably not be given the chance to die in my favourite place": Esther Rantzen on the right to choose a good death', *Guardian*, 15 June 2024. https://www.theguardian.com/lifeandstyle/article/2024/jun/15/esther-rantzen-right-to-choose-a-good-death

2. 'Why British MPs should vote for assisted dying', *The Economist*, 23 November 2024. https://www.economist.com/leaders/2024/11/21/why-british-mps-should-vote-for-assisted-dying
3. Polly Toynbee, 'The right to die is about freedom – don't let those who see it as a line on a spreadsheet torpedo it', *Guardian*, 14 November 2024. https://www.theguardian.com/commentisfree/2024/nov/14/assisted-dying-bill-wes-streeting-mps
4. Andrew Copson, 'Assisted dying is about freedom to choose – and this is the case for it', *Evening Standard*, 16 October 2024. https://www.standard.co.uk/comment/assisted-dying-bill-parliament-kim-leadbetter-humanists-b1188256.html
5. 'The delicate task of granting a right to die', *Financial Times*, 10 November 2024. https://www.ft.com/content/c9c65997-0c98-4c05-b7f2-fcb2a50388a0
6. Seneca, *On Providence*, VI, 7–8.
7. Plato, *Phaedo*.
8. 1 Corinthians 6:19; Philippians 1:23.
9. Thomas Aquinas, *Summa Theologiae*. Benziger Bros, 1947.
10. John Locke, *Second Treatise of Civil Government*, Chapter 5.
11. Plutarch, 'The Life of Cato the Younger', *The Parallel Lives*.
12. Michel de Montaigne, 'A Custom of the Isle of Cea' (1588). Trans. Charles Cotton, c. 1686.
13. Jorge Luis Borges, 'Donne's *Biathanatos*', in John Miller (ed.), *On Suicide: Great Writers on the Ultimate Question*. Chronicle Books, 1993.
14. Quoted in introduction to John Donne, *Biathanatos: A Declaration of that Paradoxe, Or Thesis, that Self-homicide is not so naturally Sin, that it may never be otherwise*, 1648. Ed. Michael Rudick and M. P. Battin. Garland English Texts, 1982.
15. Margaret Pabst Battin, 'Assisted suicide: can we learn from Germany?', in *The Least Worst Death: Essays in Bioethics on the End of Life*. Oxford University Press, 1994, p. 261.
16. Thomas Szasz, *Suicide Prohibition: The Shame of Medicine*. Syracuse University Press, 2011.
17. Jeffrey A. Schaler, 'Kaddish for Thomas Szasz', The Thomas S. Szasz, MD Cybercenter for Liberty and Responsibility. https://web.archive.org/web/20191214095354/http://www.szasz.com/szaszdeath.htm

18. Thomas Szasz, *My Madness Saved Me: The Madness and Marriage of Virginia Woolf.* Routledge, 2006.
19. Thomas Szasz, *Law, Liberty, and Psychiatry: An Inquiry into the Social Uses of Mental Health Practices.* Routledge & Kegan Paul, 1990.
20. Thomas Szasz, *The Myth of Mental Illness: Foundations of a Theory of Personal Conduct.* Harper Perennial, 2010.
21. Olive Anderson, *Suicide in Victorian and Edwardian England.* Oxford University Press, 1987, p. 356.
22. Hannah McGreevy, 'Dan Walker: Strictly star spends morning "in tears" over reaction to emotional interview', *Daily Express*, 27 November 2021. https://www.express.co.uk/celebrity-news/1528026/Dan-walker-crying-gary-speed-death-strictly-come-dancing-news
23. Diogenes Laertius, *Lives of Eminent Philosophers*, vol. 2. Harvard University Press, 1925.
24. Schaler, 'Kaddish for Thomas Szasz'.
25. Alasdair MacIntyre, *After Virtue: A Study in Moral Theory.* Notre Dame University Press, 1981, p. 250.
26. Schaler, 'Kaddish for Thomas Szasz'.
27. Chris Kelly and Eric Dale, 'Ethical perspectives on suicide and suicide prevention', *Advances in Psychiatric Treatment*, 17(3), 2011, pp. 214–19. doi: 10.1192/apt.bp.109.007021
28. Faye Brown, 'Kim Leadbeater says legalising assisted dying won't lead to "slippery slope"', Sky News, 3 October 2024. https://news.sky.com/story/kim-leadbeater-says-legalising-assisted-dying-wont-lead-to-slippery-slope-13227215
29. 'Humanism can offer us answers in the assisted dying debate', *Observer*, 19 January 2025. https://www.theguardian.com/theobserver/2025/jan/19/humanism-can-offer-us-answers-in-the-assisted-dying-debate
30. Janet Eastham, 'The depressed should be allowed to end their life, says A. C. Grayling', *Sunday Telegraph*, 21 January 2024. https://www.telegraph.co.uk/news/2024/11/21/assisted-dying-bill-depressed-and-disabled-ac-grayling/
31. Written evidence submitted by Professor Anthony Clifford Grayling (ADY0202). https://committees.parliament.uk/writtenevidence/116195/pdf/
32. Alfred Alvarez, extract from *The Savage God*, in Miller (ed.), *On Suicide.*
33. Mahmoud Keyvanara et al., 'A qualitative exploration of

motives of suicide attempts among Iranian women', *Australian Journal of Psychology*, 72(2), 2020, pp. 133–44. https://doi.org/10.1111/ajpy.12277

34. S. Fischer et al., 'Suicide assisted by two Swiss right-to-die organisations', *Journal of Medical Ethics*, 34(11), 2008, pp. 810–14. doi: 10.1136/jme.2007.023887. Kaoru Uda, 'Membership in Swiss assisted-suicide organisations reaches record high', SwissInfo.ch, 18 March 2023. https://www.swissinfo.ch/eng/society/membership-in-swiss-assisted-suicide-organisations-reaches-record-high/48358502

35. 'Widespread public support for assisted suicide at end of completed life', *NL Times*, 8 November 2023. https://nltimes.nl/2023/11/08/widespread-public-support-assisted-suicide-end-completed-life

Chapter 2: Better Off Dead

1. Aristotle, *Rhetoric to Alexander*, Book II, Chapter 8, R.1385bl2-1.
2. *Catechism of the Catholic Church*. Our Sunday Visitor, 2nd edn, 2000.
3. Shawn Floyd, 'Aquinas and the obligations of mercy', *Journal of Religious Ethics*, 37(3), 2009, pp. 449–71. http://www.jstor.org/stable/40378115
4. Aquinas, *Summa Theologiae*.
5. 'Why I helped my daughter to die', BBC News, 1 February 2010. http://news.bbc.co.uk/1/hi/magazine/8481751.stm
6. Paul D. Green, 'Suicide, martyrdom, and Thomas More', *Studies in the Renaissance*, 19, 1972, pp. 135–55. http://jstor.org/stable/2857090
7. Memorandum by Dignitas. 28 October 2004. Select Committee on Assisted Dying for the Terminally Ill Bill. Minutes of Evidence. https://publications.parliament.uk/pa/ld200405/ldselect/ldasdy/86/5020307.htm
8. Ian Dowbiggin, '"A prey on normal people": C. Killick Millard and the euthanasia movement in Great Britain, 1930–55', *Journal of Contemporary History*, 36(1), 2001, pp. 59–85.
9. Ibid.
10. 'Archive, 1935: Newly formed society proposes first assisted dying bill', *Guardian*, 28 November 2024.

https://www.theguardian.com/society/2024/nov/28/archive-1935-newly-formed-society-proposes-first-assisted-dying-bill
11. Hansard, Voluntary Euthanasia (Legalisation) Bill Hl. Debated on Tuesday 1 December 1936. https://hansard.parliament.uk/Lords/1936-12-01/debates/38e7926b-07b7-4acf-b9cd-67fc10fce643/VoluntaryEuthanasia(Legalisation)BillHl
12. Dowbiggin, '"A prey on normal people"'.
13. Voluntary Euthanasia (Legalisation) Bill Hl.
14. Dignity and Choice in Dying. Company no. 4452809.
15. Dignity in Dying website, March 2024. https://web.archive.org/web/20250313071032/https://www.dignityindying.org.uk/
16. Written evidence submitted by Professor Anthony Clifford Grayling (ADY0202).
17. Linda Ganzini, Elizabeth R. Goy, and Steven K. Dobscha, 'Why Oregon patients request assisted death: family members' views', *Journal of General Internal Medicine*, 23(2), 2008, pp. 154–7. doi: 10.1007/s11606-007-0476-x. 'Fifth Annual Report on Medical Assistance in Dying in Canada, 2023', Government of Canada. https://www.canada.ca/en/health-canada/services/publications/health-system-services/annual-report-medical-assistance-dying-2023.html
18. 'Expert panels make for stronger, safer bill', Dignity in Dying press release, 12 March 2025. https://www.dignityindying.org.uk/news/expert-panels-make-for-stronger-safer-bill/
19. Cited in Yuill, *Assisted Suicide*, p. 41.
20. Vahé Nafilyan et al., 'Risk of suicide after diagnosis of severe physical health conditions: a retrospective cohort study of 47 million people', *Lancet Regional Health Europe*, 25(100562), 2022. doi: 10.1016/j.lanepe.2022.100562
21. Alvarez, extract from *The Savage God*.
22. Thomas Joiner, *Why People Die by Suicide*. Harvard University Press, 2007.
23. Durkheim, *Suicide*, pp. 216–17.

Chapter 3: Suffering What You Fear

1. Ana Worthington, Ilora Finlay and Claud Regnard, 'Efficacy and safety of drugs used for "assisted dying"', *British Medical Bulletin*, 142(1), 2022, pp. 15–22. doi: 10.1093/bmb/ldac009

2. 'The RCPsych cannot support the Terminally Ill Adults (End of Life) Bill for England and Wales in its current form'.
3. Terminally Ill Adults (End of Life) Bill. Written evidence submitted by the Complex Life and Death Decisions group, King's College London (TIAB109). https://publications.parliament.uk/pa/cm5901/cmpublic/TerminallyIllAdults/memo/TIAB109
4. Ibid.
5. Matthew Galkin (dir.), *Kevorkian*, HBO, 2010.
6. Michael Betzold, *Appointment with Doctor Death*. Betzold Momentum Books, 1993.
7. Ned Stafford, 'Jack Kevorkian', *British Medical Journal*, 342, 2011. doi: 10.1136/bmj.d4100
8. Kirk Cheyfitz, 'SUICIDE MACHINE, PART 1: Kevorkian rushes to fulfil his clients' desire to die', *Detroit Free Press*, 3 March 1997. https://web.archive.org/web/20110608173811/http://www.freep.com/article/20070527/NEWS05/70525061/SUICIDE-MACHINE-PART-1
9. Ibid.
10. Irene Tuffrey-Wijne et al., 'Euthanasia and physician-assisted suicide in people with intellectual disabilities and/or autism spectrum disorders: investigation of 39 Dutch case reports (2012–2021)', *BJPsych Open*, 9(3), 2023, e87. doi:10.1192/bjo.2023.69
11. Mary Glindon, 'Assisted dying bill: "Oregon is no assisted dying utopia"', *Labour List*, 28 November 2024. https://labourlist.org/2024/11/assisted-dying-bill-kim-leadbeater-oregon-mary-glindon/
12. Terminally Ill Adults (End of Life) Bill. Written evidence submitted by Dr Alex Hughes, King's College Hospital (TIAB119). https://publications.parliament.uk/pa/cm5901/cmpublic/TerminallyIllAdults/memo/TIAB119.htm
13. Maria Cheng and Angie Wang, 'Euthanasia doctors in Canada struggle with the ethics of killing vulnerable patients', *Independent*, 16 October 2024. https://www.independent.co.uk/news/uk/home-news/assisted-dying-canada-bill-uk-b2630209.html; 'Canadians with nonterminal conditions sought assisted dying for social reasons', *Guardian*, 17 October 2024. https://www.theguardian.com/world/2024/oct/17/canada-nonterminal-maid-assisted-death
14. Gabrielle Peters, 'Dying for the right to live', *Maclean's*,

12 November 2020. https://macleans.ca/society/dying-for-the-right-to-live/

15. Bryce Hoye, 'Winnipeg woman who chose to die with medical assistance said struggle for home care help led to decision', CBC News, 4 October 2022. https://www.cbc.ca/news/canada/manitoba/sathya-dharma-kovac-als-medical-assistance-in-death-1.6605754
16. Maria Cheng and Angie Wang, 'Private forums show Canadian doctors struggle with euthanizing vulnerable patients', AP News, 16 October 2024. https://apnews.com/article/euthanasia-ethics-canada-doctors-nonterminal-nonfatal-cases-dfe59b1786592e31d9eb3b826c5175d1
17. Flo Read, '"Why did Canada help my brother die?"', UnHerd, 18 October 2022. https://unherd.com/2022/10/why-did-canada-help-my-brother-die/
18. Holly Honderich, 'Who can die? Canada wrestles with euthanasia for the mentally ill', BBC News, 14 January 2023. https://www.bbc.co.uk/news/world-us-canada-64004329
19. Iain Brassington, 'Five words for assisted dying', *Law and Philosophy*, 27(5), 2008, pp. 415–44. https://www.jstor.org/stable/27652661
20. 'The interpretation and role of "reasonably foreseeable" in MAiD practice', CAMAP, February 2022. https://camapcanada.ca/wp-content/uploads/2022/03/The-Interpretation-and-Role-of-22Reasonably-Foreseeable22-in-MAiD-Practice-Feb-2022.pdf
21. Janet Eastham, 'Assisted dying row as patients given six months to live often survive for three years', *Daily Telegraph*, 21 January 2025. https://www.telegraph.co.uk/news/2025/01/21/assisted-dying-row-terminally-ill-patients-live-longer/
22. Lydia Treleaven et al., 'A review of the utility of prognostic tools in predicting 6-month mortality in cancer patients, conducted in the context of voluntary assisted dying', *Internal Medicine Journal*, 53(12), 2023, pp. 2180–97. doi: 10.1111/imj.16081
23. 'Letters: Lingering concerns about assisted dying bill', *The Times*, 19 May 2025. https://www.thetimes.com/comment/letters-to-editor/article/times-letters-lingering-concerns-about-assisted-dying-bill-9bqvjs3qd
24. 'RCP position statement on the Terminally Ill Adults (End of Life) Bill, 9th May 2025', Royal College of Physicians, 12

May 2025. https://www.rcp.ac.uk/policy-and-campaigns/policy-documents/rcp-position-statement-on-the-terminally-ill-adults-end-of-life-bill-9th-may-2025/
25. C. Killick Millard, *Euthanasia: A Plea for the Legalisation of Voluntary Euthanasia*. C. W. Daniel, 1931.
26. Elaine Scarry, *The Body in Pain: The Making and Unmaking of the World*. Oxford University Press, 1985.
27. Michel de Montaigne, 'Of Experience', *Essays*, Book 3, Chapter 13.
28. 'Media guidelines for reporting suicide', Samaritans. https://media.samaritans.org/documents/Media_Guidelines_FINAL.pdf
29. E. J. Cassell, 'The Nature of Suffering and the Goals of Medicine', *New England Journal of Medicine*, 306(11), 1982, pp. 639–45. doi: 10.1056/NEJM198203183061104
30. Alicia Krikorian et al., 'Suffering assessment: a review of available instruments for use in palliative care', *Journal of Palliative Care*, 16(2), 2013. https://www.liebertpub.com/doi/abs/10.1089/jpm.2012.0370
31. Paul Kioko and Pablo Requena, 'Towards a definition of unbearable suffering and the incongruence of psychiatric euthanasia', *British Journal of Psychiatry*, 212(4), 2018, pp. 247–8. https://doi.org/10.1192/bjp.2018.47
32. A. E. Ellis, *The Rack*. Vintage Digital, 2022.
33. Dr Alex Chula, private correspondence.
34. Henry James, *Notes of a Son and Brother*. Macmillan, 1914.
35. Cees D. M. Ruijs et al., 'Unbearability of suffering at the end of life: the development of a new measuring device, the SOS-V', *BMC Palliative Care*, 8(16), 2009. https://doi.org/10.1186/1472-684X-8-16

Chapter 4: Worse Than the Disease

1. Emily Dickinson, 'Pain—has an Element of Blank', in *The Complete Poems*. Faber, 2016.
2. Jessica Nutik Zitter, *Extreme Measures: Finding a Better Path to the End of Life*. Avery, 2017.
3. Cicely Saunders, 'Correspondence: distress in dying', *British Medical Journal*, 21 September 1963. https://www.bmj.com/content/2/5359/746.2
4. Quoted in Robert Twycross, 'A tribute to Dame

Cicely Saunders', Memorial Service, 8 March 2006. https://www.oxfordreference.com/display/10.1093/acref/9780191826719.001.0001/q-oro-ed4-00009140
5. Maryam Zavarmousavi et al., 'Gamification-based virtual reality and post-burn rehabilitation: how promising is that?' *Bulletin of Emergency and Trauma*, 11(2), 2023, pp. 106–7. doi: 10.30476/BEAT.2023.97911.1416.
6. Seneca, Letter LXXVIII.
7. John D. Otis, *Managing Chronic Pain*. Oxford University Press, 2007.
8. Terminally Ill Adults (End of Life) Bill (first sitting), 21 January 2025. Hansard. https://publications.parliament.uk/pa/bills/cbill/59-01/0012/PBC012_TerminallyIllAdults_1st-7th_Compilation_30_01_2025.pdf
9. Aesop, 'The Hawk, The Kite and The Pigeons'.
10. Khalil Gibran, 'On Pain', from *The Prophet*. Knopf, 1923.
11. Written evidence submitted by Professor Anthony Clifford Grayling (ADY0202).
12. Dr Alex Chula, private correspondence.
13. Scarry, *The Body in Pain*, p. 54.
14. J. David Velleman, 'A right of self-termination?', in *Beyond Price: Essays on Birth and Death*. Open Book, 2015.
15. Minurika Perusinghe, Kai Yang Chen, and Brett McDermott, 'Evidence-based management of depression in palliative care: a systematic review', *Journal of Palliative Medicine*, 24(5), 2021. doi: 10.1089/jpm.2020.0659
16. Ilaria Spoletini et al., 'Suicide and cancer: where do we go from here?', *Critical Reviews in Oncology/Hematology*, 78(3), 2011, pp. 206–19. doi: 10.1016/j.critrevonc.2010.05.005; Timothy V. Johnson et al., 'Peak window of suicides occurs within the first month of diagnosis: implications for clinical oncology', *Psychooncology*, 24 January 2011 (early release online); Nafilyan et al., 'Risk of suicide after diagnosis of severe physical health conditions'.
17. Geoffrey Walters, 'Is there such a thing as a good death?', *Palliative Medicine*, 18(5), 2004, pp. 404–8. doi: 10.1191/0269216304pm908oa
18. Kristin Wright, 'Relationships with death: the terminally ill talk about dying', *Journal of Marital and Family Therapy*, 29(4), 2003, pp. 439–54. doi: 10.1111/j.1752-0606.2003.tb01687.x
19. '"We tend to forget that life can only be defined in the present

tense": edited version of Melvyn Bragg's interview of Dennis Potter on March 15 1994. It was broadcast by Channel 4 on April 5 1994', *Guardian*, 12 September 2007. https://www.theguardian.com/theguardian/2007/sep/12/greatinterviews
20. Judgments – MH (by her litigation friend, Official Solicitor) (FC) (Respondent) v. Secretary of State for the Department of Health (Appellant) and others. 2005–6. https://www.bailii.org/uk/cases/UKHL/2005/60.html
21. Tad Friend, 'Jumpers', *New Yorker*, 5 October 2003. https://www.newyorker.com/magazine/2003/10/13/jumpers
22. 'Swiss doctors adopt tighter assisted suicide guidelines', SwissInfo.ch, 20 May 2022. https://www.swissinfo.ch/eng/society/swiss-doctors-adopt-tighter-assisted-suicide-guidelines/47610372
23. Oregon Death with Dignity Act, 2017 Data Summary. https://www.oregon.gov/oha/PH/PROVIDERPARTNERRESOURCES/EVALUATIONRESEARCH/DEATHWITHDIGNITYACT/Documents/year20.pdf
24. Cheng and Wang, 'Euthanasia doctors in Canada struggle with the ethics of killing vulnerable patients'.
25. Chelsea Roff and Catherine Cook-Cottone, 'Assisted death in eating disorders: a systematic review of cases and clinical rationales', *Frontiers in Psychiatry*, 15, 2024, 1431771. doi: 10.3389/fpsyt.2024.1431771
26. Tony Sheldon, 'The doctor who prescribed suicide: was the Dutch psychiatrist Dr Boudewijn Chabot right to help a sane, healthy woman to take her own life?', *Independent*, 30 June 1994. https://www.independent.co.uk/life-style/the-doctor-who-prescribed-suicide-was-the-dutch-psychiatrist-dr-boudewijn-chabot-right-to-help-a-sane-healthy-woman-to-take-her-own-life-tony-sheldon-reports-1425973.html
27. S. M. P. van Veen et al., 'Physician assisted death for psychiatric suffering: experiences in the Netherlands', *Frontiers in Psychiatry*, 13, 2022. doi: 10.3389/fpsyt.2022.895387
28. Ibid.
29. 'Euthanasia on solely mental health grounds increased in the Netherlands during 2023', Living and Dying Well. https://livinganddyingwell.org.uk/euthanasia-on-solely-mental-health-grounds-increased-in-the-netherlands-during-2023/
30. Bruno Waterfield, 'Dutch rethink euthanasia law after

60% rise in mental health cases', *The Times*, 24 March 2025. https://www.thetimes.com/world/europe/article/dutch-rethink-euthanasia-law-60-percent-rise-mental-health-cases-nbnmqvb6q
31. Bruno Waterfield, 'Number of Dutch people euthanised due to mental illness up 20%', *The Times*, 5 April 2024. https://www.thetimes.com/world/article/number-of-dutch-people-euthanised-due-to-mental-illness-up-20-percent-w0xmfz3s2
32. van Veen et al., 'Physician assisted death for psychiatric suffering'.
33. Waterfield, 'Number of Dutch people euthanised due to mental illness up 20%'.
34. Eugene S. Paykel, 'Basic concepts of depression', *Dialogues in Clinical Neuroscience*, 10(3), 2008, pp. 279–89. doi: 10.31887/DCNS.2008.10.3/espaykel
35. Paola Bozzatello et al., 'Gender differences in borderline personality disorder: a narrative review', *Frontiers in Psychiatry*, 15, 2024, 1320546. doi: 10.3389/fpsyt.2024.1320546
36. Ibid.
37. Monique Kammeraat et al., 'Patients requesting and receiving euthanasia for psychiatric disorders in the Netherlands', *BMJ Mental Health*, 26(1), 2023, e300729. doi: 10.1136/bmjment-2023-300729
38. Sidney Zisook and Katherine Shear, 'Grief and bereavement: what psychiatrists need to know', *World Psychiatry*, 8(2), 2009, pp. 67–74. doi: 10.1002/j.2051-5545.2009.tb00217.x
39. Hadley Freeman, 'As an anorexic, I'd have longed for assisted dying', *Sunday Times*, 2 March 2025. https://www.thetimes.com/comment/columnists/article/as-an-anorexic-id-have-longed-for-assisted-dying-qvxjlhvjh
40. Yoshiyuki Takimoto, 'Key components of the mental capacity assessment of patients with anorexia nervosa: a study of three countries', *Journal of Eating Disorders*, 10(1), 2022, 110. https://doi.org/10.1186/s40337-022-00633-7
41. Dawn I. Velligan et al., 'Why do psychiatric patients stop antipsychotic medication? A systematic review of reasons for nonadherence to medication in patients with serious mental illness', *Patient Preference and Adherence*, 11, 2017. pp. 449–68. doi: 10.2147/PPA.S124658
42. Scott Y. H. Kim, Raymond G. De Vries, and John R. Peteet,

'Euthanasia and assisted suicide of patients with psychiatric disorders in the Netherlands 2011 to 2014', *JAMA Psychiatry*, 73(4), 2016, pp. 362–8. doi: 10.1001/jamapsychiatry.2015.2887.
43. Tuffrey-Wijne et al., 'Euthanasia and physician-assisted suicide in people with intellectual disabilities and/or autism spectrum disorders'.

Chapter 5: A Few Grannies

1. The Other Half, X, 2 April 2025. https://x.com/OtherHalfOrg/status/1907448915755966464
2. Vulnerability Knowledge and Practice Programme, Domestic Homicide Project. https://www.vkpp.org.uk/vkpp-work/domestic-homicide-project/
3. Sam Corbishley, '"Hidden scandal" of domestic abuse-related suicides "needs urgent attention"', *Metro*, 26 February 2025. https://metro.co.uk/2025/02/26/hidden-scandal-domestic-abuse-related-suicides-needs-urgent-attention-22626526/
4. 'Young woman pleads guilty to manslaughter for her role in boyfriend's suicide', Suffolk County District Attorney's Office, Massachusetts, 24 December 2021. https://www.suffolkdistrictattorney.com/press-releases/items/inyoung-you-guilty
5. Polly Toynbee, 'The assisted dying bill has passed. At last: a decent life can end in a decent death', *Guardian*, 29 November 2024. https://www.theguardian.com/commentisfree/2024/nov/29/assisted-dying-bill-life-death-mps
6. Deborah Hammond, private correspondence.
7. 'BGS position statement on assisted dying (physician assisted suicide and voluntary active euthanasia)', British Geriatrics Society, 30 November 2024. https://www.bgs.org.uk/bgs-position-statement-on-assisted-dying
8. Benedetta Nardi et al., 'An attempted "suicide pact" in Covid-19 era – psychiatric perspectives', *BMC Psychiatry*, 22, 2022. https://doi.org/10.1186/s12888-022-04333-z
9. Senay Boztas, 'Duo euthanasia: former Dutch prime minister dies hand in hand with his wife', *Guardian*, 10 February 2024. https://www.theguardian.com/world/2024/feb/10/duo-euthanasia-former-dutch-prime-minister-dies-wife-dries-eugenie-van-agt

10. Terminally Ill Adults (End of Life) Bill: equality impact assessment, updated 26 June 2025. https://www.gov.uk/government/publications/terminally-ill-adults-end-of-life-bill-equality-impact-assessment/terminally-ill-adults-end-of-life-bill-equality-impact-assessment-html-version
11. Lewis Atkinson, 'Our assisted dying law will be the safest in the world', *Prospect*, 7 March 2025. https://www.prospectmagazine.co.uk/ideas/a-good-death/69484/our-assisted-dying-law-will-be-the-safest-in-the-world
12. Terminally Ill Adults (End of Life) Bill: impact assessment.
13. Terminally Ill Adults (End of Life) Bill (Twenty-third sitting). Debated on Wednesday 12 March 2025.
14. Death with Dignity. https://deathwithdignity.org/about/
15. 'Rapid response: would judicial consent for assisted dying protect vulnerable people?' *BMJ*, 351, 19 August 2015, h4437. https://www.bmj.com/content/351/bmj.h4437/rr-10
16. 'Some Oregon and Washington state assisted suicide abuses and complications', Disability Rights Education & Defense Fund. https://www.nycourts.gov/reporter/webdocs/some-oregon-and-washington.pdf
17. Terminally Ill Adults (End of Life) Bill. Further written evidence submitted by Hon. Robert Clark, a former Attorney-General and MP in Victoria, Australia (TIAB245(a)). https://publications.parliament.uk/pa/cm5901/cmpublic/TerminallyIllAdults/memo/TIAB245(a).htm
18. Terminally Ill Adults (End of Life) Bill. Written evidence submitted by The Other Half (TIAB104). https://publications.parliament.uk/pa/cm5901/cmpublic/TerminallyIllAdults/memo/TIAB104.pdf
19. 'Euthanasia cases rise 10%, more psychiatric-related deaths', Dutch News, 24 March 2025. https://www.dutchnews.nl/2025/03/euthanasia-cases-rise-9-more-psychiatric-related-deaths/
20. Terminally Ill Adults (End of Life) Bill (Twentieth sitting). Debated on Tuesday 11 March 2025. https://hansard.parliament.uk/Commons/2025-03-11/debates/a7b99ba9-554a-4eec-bf40-0527f3235500/TerminallyIllAdults(EndOfLife)Bill(TwentiethSitting)
21. Amanda Poole, 'Did Antrim's notorious "Doctor Death" go to his grave with 300 murders on his

conscience?', *Belfast Telegraph*, 22 May 2013. https://www.belfasttelegraph.co.uk/news/northern-ireland/did-antrims-notorious-doctor-death-go-to-his-grave-with-300-murders-on-his-conscience/29282190.html
22. Laurence Sleator, 'Assisted dying bill raises foul play risks, says ex-chief coroner', *The Times*, 6 May 2025. https://www.thetimes.com/uk/law/article/assisted-dying-bill-clause-coroner-inquests-r5j6r5gq2
23. Gerald Dworkin, 'Public policy and physician-assisted suicide', in Gerald Dworkin, R. G. Frey, and Sissela Bok, *Euthanasia and Physician-Assisted Suicide: For and Against*. Cambridge University Press, 1998.
24. Sharon Kirkey, 'This doctor has helped more than 400 patients die. A judge just blocked one of her cases', *National Post*, 6 July 2024. https://nationalpost.com/feature/canada-maid-assisted-suicide-doctor
25. Liz Carr and James Routh, *Better Off Dead?*, BBC/Open University, 2024.
26. Leyland Cecco, 'Canada judge halts medically assisted death of woman in rare injunction', *Guardian*, 31 October 2024. https://www.theguardian.com/world/2024/oct/31/canada-medically-assisted-death-judge-ruling
27. Elaina Plott Calabro, 'Canada is killing itself', *The Atlantic*, September 2025. https://www.theatlantic.com/magazine/archive/2025/09/canada-euthanasia-demand-maid-policy/683562/
28. Alexander Raikin, 'No other options', *New Atlantis*, 16 December 2022. https://www.thenewatlantis.com/publications/no-other-options
29. Peter L. Hudson et al., 'Responding to desire to die statements from patients with advanced disease: recommendations for health professionals', *Palliative Medicine*, 20(7), 2006, pp. 703–10. doi: 10.1177/0269216306071814
30. The Other Half, *Assisted*, episode 6. https://www.youtube.com/watch?app=desktop&v=i5YQvnN_odA
31. Marc Leutenegger, 'Switzerland no longer wants to foot the bill for "suicide tourism"', SwissInfo.ch, 21 February 2025. https://www.swissinfo.ch/eng/aging-society/switzerland-no-longer-wants-to-foot-the-bill-for-suicide-tourism/88896839
32. Ibid.
33. Zosia Chustecka, 'Renowned neurosurgeon on assisted dying

and his "suicide kit"', *Medscape*, 27 April 2017. https://www.medscape.com/viewarticle/879187
34. 'Dr Henry Marsh's opinion on the assisted dying debate', Audible Sessions, 12 January 2024. https://www.youtube.com/watch?v=jRKpSbXK1v4

Chapter 6: A Humiliating Dependency on Others

1. Stefanie Green, '"We're going to talk about death today – your death": a doctor on what it's like to end a life rather than extend one', *Guardian*, 15 March 2025. https://www.theguardian.com/society/2025/mar/15/were-going-to-talk-about-death-today-your-death-a-doctor-on-what-its-like-to-end-a-life-rather-than-extend-one
2. Miriam Griffin, 'Philosophy, Cato, and Roman suicide: I', *Greece & Rome*, 33(1), 1986, pp. 64–77. http://www.jstor.org/stable/643026
3. Brief Amici Curiae of Not Dead Yet et al., Vacco v. Quill, 521 U.S. 793 (1997).
4. Carr and Routh, *Better Off Dead?*
5. Kelly Malone, 'Medically assisted deaths could save millions in health care spending: report', CBC News, 23 January 2017. https://www.cbc.ca/news/canada/manitoba/medically-assisted-death-could-save-millions-1.3947481
6. 'Fifth Annual Report on Medical Assistance in Dying in Canada, 2023'.
7. Seneca, *De Ira*, III, 15, 3–4. *Essays*, I, pp. 294–5.
8. Christopher Belshaw, 'Assisted dying bill: why fears about coercion may be exaggerated – a philosopher's view', *The Conversation*, 22 January 2025. https://theconversation.com/assisted-dying-bill-why-fears-about-coercion-may-be-exaggerated-a-philosophers-view-246666
9. Brigida Molina-Gallego et al., 'Anxiety and depression after spinal cord injury: a cross-sectional study', *Healthcare*, 12(17), 2024, 1759. https://doi.org/10.3390/healthcare12171759. Angus M. Kim and Jae-Hyun Park, 'Depression and its associated factors: a comparison between congenital and acquired physical disabilities', *International Journal of Psychiatry in Medicine*, 59(6), 2023, pp. 655–69. doi: 10.1177/00912174231219037

10. Friedrich Nietszche, *Beyond Good and Evil*, trans. Helen Zimmern, 1906. Reprinted by Courier Dover Publications, 1997.
11. 'Safeguarding women in assisted dying: a rapid review to inform the debate on assisted dying in the UK', The Other Half, November 2024. https://theotherhalf.uk/safeguarding-women-in-assisted-dying
12. Alan Rusbridger, 'My father wanted to die – this is why the law should have allowed it', *Prospect*, 18 October 2024. https://www.prospectmagazine.co.uk/ideas/law/68264/my-father-wanted-to-diethis-is-why-the-law-should-have-allowed-it
13. Rosa Silverman, 'The sinister past of the group pushing for assisted dying', *Daily Telegraph*, 26 November 2024. https://www.telegraph.co.uk/news/2024/11/26/aiding-abetting-suicide-sinister-past-group-assisted-dying/
14. Richard Tice, 'I've witnessed full horror of death without dignity – we can't carry on like this', *Daily Express*, 27 November 2024. https://www.express.co.uk/news/politics/1981277/death-dignity-assisted-dying-bill
15. Tony Duffy, '"Faecal vomiting" – a case of frequently mentioned, but rarely seen', *Forum: BMJ Supportive and Palliative Care*, 8 April 2025. https://blogs.bmj.com/spcare/2025/04/08/faecal-vomiting-a-case-of-frequently-mentioned-but-rarely-seen/
16. Harriet McBryde Johnson, *Too Late to Die Young: Nearly True Tales from a Life*. Henry Holt and Company, 2005.
17. Robert P. Jones, *Liberalism's Troubled Search for Equality*. University of Notre Dame Press, 2007.
18. Dr Kathryn Mannix, 'Dying is not as bad as you are expecting', BBC, 29 March 2018. https://www.bbc.co.uk/videos/cx02l4p0e5wo
19. Dr Kathryn Mannix, *With the End in Mind: Dying, Death and Wisdom in an Age of Denial*. William Collins, 2017.
20. 'Physician-assisted dying survey', British Medical Association, 18 September 2024. https://www.bma.org.uk/advice-and-support/ethics/end-of-life/physician-assisted-dying/physician-assisted-dying-survey
21. Polly Mitchell, 'Adaptive preferences, adapted preferences', *Mind*, 127(508), 2018, pp. 1003–25. https://doi.org/10.1093/mind/fzy020
22. Sarah Rainey, 'How extreme is your daily routine? Ask

the new health-obsessed', *The Times*, 27 March 2025. https://www.thetimes.com/life-style/health-fitness/article/extreme-daily-routine-new-wellness-set-9pf97qrrs
23. Mel Ottenberg, 'Bryan Johnson wants you to have better boners', *Interview*, 28 January 2025. https://www.interviewmagazine.com/culture/bryan-johnson-wants-you-to-have-better-boners
24. Green, 'Suicide, martyrdom, and Thomas More'.
25. Joiner, *Why People Die by Suicide*.
26. 'Fifth Annual Report on Medical Assistance in Dying in Canada, 2023'.
27. Terminally Ill Adults (End of Life) Bill: impact assessment.
28. Emmanuel Hirsch, *Partir: l'accompagnement des mourants* (1986). The translation is Nigel Biggar's in his book *Aiming to Kill*.
29. J. David Velleman, 'Against the right to die', in *Beyond Price*.
30. Dan Hitchens, 'The assisted dying bill is becoming a car crash', *Spectator*, 8 February 2025. https://www.spectator.co.uk/article/where-is-the-scrutiny-over-the-assisted-suicide-bill/
31. Toynbee, 'The assisted dying bill has passed'.

Chapter 7: Human Beings as Units

1. Matthew Parris, 'We can't afford a taboo on assisted dying', *The Times*, 29 March 2024. https://www.thetimes.com/article/we-cant-afford-a-taboo-on-assisted-dying-n6p8bfg9k
2. Amartya Sen, 'Utilitarianism and welfarism', *Journal of Philosophy*, 76(9), 1979, pp. 463–89. https://doi.org/10.2307/2025934
3. Sherelle Jacobs, 'There is a strong economic case for assisted dying, but we daren't admit it', *Daily Telegraph*, 18 November 2024. https://www.telegraph.co.uk/news/2024/11/18/strong-economic-case-for-assisted-dying-taboo-britain/
4. Joiner, *Why People Die by Suicide*.
5. Matthew Parris, 'Euthanasia is coming – like it or not', *Spectator*, 31 March 2024. https://www.spectator.co.uk/article/matthew-parris-assisted-dying-lives/
6. Parris, 'We can't afford a taboo on assisted dying'.
7. David Wootton, *Power, Pleasure and Profit: Insatiable Appetites from Machiavelli to Madison*. Belknap Press, 2018.

8. Glenn Davis Stone, 'Malthusian thought', *Oxford Research Encyclopedia of Anthropology*, 25 March 2021. https://doi.org/10.1093/acrefore/9780190854584.013.312
9. Terminally Ill Adults (End of Life) Bill: impact assessment.
10. 'New analysis reveals two-thirds of social care commissioning budgets are spent on working age and disabled adults, as councils call for this "forgotten" group not to be overlooked', CCN News, 11 November 2024. https://www.countycouncilsnetwork.org.uk/new-analysis-reveals-two-thirds-of-social-care-commissioning-budgets-are-spent-on-working-age-and-disabled-adults-as-councils-call-for-this-forgotten-group-not-to-be-overlooked/
11. Parris, 'We can't afford a taboo on assisted dying'.
12. David Gibbs Miller, Rebecca Dresser, and Scott Y. H. Kim, 'Advance euthanasia directives: a controversial case and its ethical implications', *Journal of Medical Ethics*, 45(2), 2019, pp. 84–9. doi: 10.1136/medethics-2017-104644
13. Martin Beckford, 'Baroness Warnock: dementia sufferers may have a "duty to die"', *Daily Telegraph*, 18 September 2008. https://www.telegraph.co.uk/news/uknews/2983652/Baroness-Warnock-Dementia-sufferers-may-have-a-duty-to-die.html
14. Eduard Verhagen and John Lantos, 'The Dutch model for regulating paediatric euthanasia', *Archives of Disease in Childhood*, 6 December 2024. doi: 10.1136/archdischild-2024-326998. Epub ahead of print.
15. A. A. Eduard Verhagen, 'Neonatal euthanasia in the context of palliative and EoL care', *Seminars in Fetal and Neonatal Medicine*, 28(3), 2023, 101439. https://doi.org/10.1016/j.siny.2023.101439
16. John Keown, 'Euthanasia in the Netherlands: sliding down the slippery slope', *Notre Dame Journal of Law, Ethics & Public Policy*, 9(2), 1995. http://scholarship.law.nd.edu/ndjlepp/vol9/iss2/3
17. John Keown, 'The logical link between voluntary and non-voluntary euthanasia', *Cambridge Law Journal*, 81(1), 2022, pp. 84–108. doi:10.1017/S0008197321001057
18. Laura Donnelly, 'Half of those on Liverpool Care Pathway never told', *Daily Telegraph*, 1 December 2012. https://www.telegraph.co.uk/news/health/news/9716418/Half-of-those-on-Liverpool-Care-Pathway-never-told.html
19. Kat Lay, 'Give water to the dying, doctors told', *The Times*,

16 December 2015. https://www.thetimes.com/uk/healthcare/article/give-water-to-the-dying-doctors-told-2nx3xdmtx60
20. Sarah McCulloch, 'We already know how the NHS will misuse assisted suicide. Trust me, I work for it.' Conservative Home, 20 November 2024. https://conservativehome.com/2024/11/20/sarah-mcculloch-we-already-know-how-the-nhs-will-mishandle-assisted-dying-trust-me-i-work-for-it/
21. David Goodhart, *The Care Dilemma*. Swift Press, 2024.
22. 'Patients Association statement: NHS and social care system failing most vulnerable', Patients Association, 25 October 2024. https://www.patients-association.org.uk/news/patients-association-statement-nhs-and-social-care-system-failing-most-vulnerable
23. Harriet Sherwood, '"Hospices are in retreat": funding crisis squeezing UK palliative care providers', *Guardian*, 24 March 2025. https://www.theguardian.com/society/2025/mar/24/hospices-in-retreat-funding-crisis-squeezing-uk-palliative-care-providers
24. Lewis Denison, 'Thousands of care homes not had CQC inspection since 2020, data analysis finds', ITV News, 4 April 2025. https://www.itv.com/news/2025-04-03/thousands-of-care-homes-not-been-inspected-since-2020-data-analysis-finds
25. Giles Sheldrick, 'Fury as devastating figures show full scale of social care crisis', *Daily Express*, 7 April 2024. https://www.express.co.uk/news/uk/1885886/care-homes-crisis
26. 'Vale Cyril Tooze: the face behind the figure', National Seniors Australia, 15 November 2024. https://nationalseniors.com.au/news/latest-news/vale-cyril-tooze-the-face-behind-the-figures
27. Terminally Ill Adults (End of Life) Bill. Written evidence submitted by Michael W. Bien, JD, Dr Alan C. Carver, MD and Matthew P. Vallière (Patients' Rights Action Fund) (TIAB400). https://publications.parliament.uk/pa/cm5901/cmpublic/TerminallyIllAdults/memo/TIAB400.htm
28. Belshaw, 'Assisted dying bill'.
29. Amartya Sen, *Resources, Values, and Development*. Oxford University Press, 1984, p. 309.
30. Harriet McBryde Johnson, 'Unspeakable conversations', *New York Times*, 16 February 2003. https://www.nytimes.com/2003/02/16/magazine/unspeakable-conversations.html
31. Dignity in Dying Facebook page, 17 May 2024. https://

www.facebook.com/story.php?story_fbid=854978296660743&id=100064457423406
32. Yuill, *Assisted Suicide*, p. 41.
33. Green '"We're going to talk about death today – your death"'. Extract from *This Is Assisted Dying: A Doctor's Story of Empowering Patients at the End of Life*. Simon & Schuster, 2025.
34. Terminally Ill Adults (End of Life) Bill. Written evidence submitted by Alicia Duncan (TIAB220). https://publications.parliament.uk/pa/cm5901/cmpublic/TerminallyIllAdults/memo/TIAB220.htm
35. Alicia Duncan, X, 12 March 2025. https://x.com/aliciaduncan_xo/status/1899912666791243889
36. Christopher Lyon, 'Not Maid for this: Christopher Lyon's story'. https://www.youtube.com/watch?v=cbAmI_yjtCs
37. Ed Davey, 'What happens to our disabled son when we're gone?', *The Times*, 30 April 2025. https://www.thetimes.com/uk/politics/article/ed-davey-disabled-son-t7h59qw29
38. Patrick Henry, 'The dialectic of suicide in Montaigne's "Coustume de l'Isle de Cea"', *Modern Language Review*, 79(2), 1984, pp. 278–89. https://www.jstor.org/stable/3730012
39. Alvarez, extract from *The Savage God*.

Chapter 8: Slippery Slopes and Bottomless Pools

1. Daniel Bergner, 'Death in the family', *New York Times Magazine*, 2 December 2007. https://web.archive.org/web/20170201033933/https://www.nytimes.com/2007/12/02/magazine/02suicide-t.html
2. Eric Tegethoff, 'WA lawmakers update state's medical aid-in-dying law', Public News Service, 13 April 2023. https://www.publicnewsservice.org/2023-04-13/health/wa-lawmakers-update-states-medical-aid-in-dying-law/a83996-1
3. Danny Finkelstein, 'There's no "slippery slope" to assisted dying', *The Times*, 19 November 2024, https://www.thetimes.com/comment/columnists/article/theres-no-slippery-slope-to-assisted-dying-rcjzppkjh
4. Nick Haslam and Melanie J. McGrath, 'The creeping concept

of trauma', *Social Research*, 91(1), 2024, pp. 311–34. https://dx.doi.org/10.1353/sor.2024.a923123
5. Suzanne O'Sullivan, *The Age of Diagnosis: How the Overdiagnosis Epidemic Is Making Us Sick*. Hodder & Stoughton, 2025. Extracted in the *Guardian*, 1 March 2025. https://www.theguardian.com/society/2025/mar/01/the-number-of-people-with-chronic-conditions-is-soaring-are-we-less-healthy-than-we-used-to-be-or-overdiagnosing-illness
6. Goodhart, *The Care Dilemma*.
7. Ian Hacking, 'Kinds of people: moving targets', *Proceedings of the British Academy*, 151, 2007, pp. 285–318. https://doi.org/10.5871/bacad/9780197264249.003.0010
8. 'Dutch law on Termination of life on request and assisted suicide (complete text)', WFRTDS. https://wfrtds.org/dutch-law-on-termination-of-life-on-request-and-assisted-suicide-complete-text/
9. 'Euthanasia on solely mental health grounds increased in the Netherlands during 2023'.
10. Waterfield, 'Dutch rethink euthanasia law after 60% rise in mental health cases'.
11. 'Mental health problems among Dutch teens remain high', Utrecht University, 27 June 2003. https://www.uu.nl/en/news/mental-health-problems-among-dutch-teens-remain-high
12. Tuffrey-Wijne et al., 'Euthanasia and physician-assisted suicide in people with intellectual disabilities and/or autism spectrum disorders'.
13. 'More euthanasia cases in 2022, 29 couples helped to die', Dutch News, 5 April 2023. https://www.dutchnews.nl/2023/04/more-euthanasia-cases-in-2022-29-couples-helped-to-die/. Senay Boztas, 'Death by euthanasia in the Netherlands increased 10% in 2024, figures show', *Guardian*, 24 March 2025. https://www.theguardian.com/society/2025/mar/24/euthanasia-death-increase-netherlands
14. 'Le suicide assisté en Suisse', Alliance Vita, 20 October 2023. https://www.alliancevita.org/2023/10/le-suicide-assiste-en-suisse-3/
15. Jacques Wels and Natasia Hamarat, 'Incidence and prevalence of euthanasia in Belgium. A study using administrative data on all cases of euthanasia reported between 2002 and 2023', medRxiv, 17 October 2024. doi: https://doi.org/10.1101/2024.10.16.24315619

16. Terminally Ill Adults (End of Life) Bill: impact assessment.
17. Ibid.
18. Cezary Jan Strusiewicz, 'The lesbian romance that inspired a string of volcano suicides', Tokyo Weekender, 2 May 2025. https://www.tokyoweekender.com/art_and_culture/japanese-culture/the-lesbian-romance-that-inspired-a-string-of-volcano-suicides/
19. Mary Anne Walling, 'Suicide contagion', *Current Trauma Reports*, 7(4), 2021, pp. 103–14. doi: 10.1007/s40719-021-00219-9
20. Jessica Frey, Kevin J. Black, and Irene A. Malaty, 'TikTok Tourette's: are we witnessing a rise in functional tic-like behavior driven by adolescent social media use?' Psychology Research and Behavior Management, 15, 2022, pp. 3575–85. doi: 10.2147/PRBM.S359977
21. Ali Tate Cutler, TikTok. https://www.tiktok.com/@alitatecutler/video/7234358189611961642
22. Angelina Mo, 'Joseph Awuah-Darko: the art of living, the act of dying', Sleek, 6 March 2025. https://www.sleek-mag.com/article/joseph-awuah-darko-the-art-of-living-the-act-of-dying/
23. Constitution Act 1982, Government of Canada. https://laws-lois.justice.gc.ca/eng/const/page-12.html
24. Truchon v. Canada (AG) decision. https://www.thaddeuspope.com/images/Truchon_English_2019qccs3792.pdf
25. Luc Rinaldi, 'They're suing the government for the right to die', *Maclean's*, 24 February 2025. https://macleans.ca/longforms/canada-maid-mental-illness/
26. 'Canada considering euthanasia for drug addicts', Care, 27 October 2023. https://care.org.uk/news/2023/10/canada-considering-euthanasia-for-drug-addicts
27. Terminally Ill Adults (End of Life) Bill (Twenty-fifth sitting). Debated on Tuesday 18 March 2025. Hansard. https://hansard.parliament.uk/Commons/2025-03-18/debates/5c370560-a5bd-46c6-b2d5-8203523db8a9/TerminallyIllAdults(EndOfLife)Bill(Twenty-FifthSitting)
28. 'Assisted Suicide in Switzerland', Alliance Vita, 20 October 2023. https://www.alliancevita.org/en/2023/10/assisted-suicide-in-switzerland/
29. Scott Y. H. Kim, 'What does true equality in assisted dying require?', *American Journal of Bioethics*, 23(9), 2023, pp. 1–4. doi: 10.1080/15265161.2023.2244318

30. 'The assisted dying debate: Charles Falconer and the Observer's Sonia Sodha tackle the issues', *Observer*, 17 November 2024. https://www.theguardian.com/society/2024/nov/17/the-assisted-dying-debate-charles-falconer-and-the-observers-sonia-sodha-tackle-the-issues
31. Terminally Ill Adults (End of Life) Bill: equality impact assessment.
32. Sarah Wootton, X, 3 May 2025. https://x.com/sarah_wootton/status/1918622475358703696
33. Benita Kolovos, 'Victoria scraps "gag clause" banning doctors from raising voluntary assisted dying with patients', *Guardian*, 20 February 2025. https://www.theguardian.com/australia-news/2025/feb/20/victoria-scraps-gag-clause-banning-doctors-from-raising-voluntary-assisted-dying-with-patients
34. Jake Thomas, 'Senators hear passionate arguments over how terminally ill patients end their lives in Oregon', The Lund Report, 4 March 2025. https://www.thelundreport.org/content/senators-hear-passionate-arguments-over-how-terminally-ill-patients-end-their-lives-oregon
35. Dr Leonie Herx, X, 5 February 2025. https://x.com/LeonieHerx/status/1887147554535772196
36. Dr Leeroy William, X, 22 February 2025. https://x.com/drleeroyw/status/1893314687493636210
37. Fit note reform: call for evidence. UK Government, 25 April 2024. https://www.gov.uk/government/calls-for-evidence/fit-note-reform-call-for-evidence/fit-note-reform-call-for-evidence#fn:4

Conclusion

1. Theodore Dalrymple, 'The death of Dylan Thomas: a conspiracy theory', *BMJ*, 341(7773), 2010, pp. 609–9. http://www.jstor.org/stable/25738196
2. Mark Taubert, 'Take it from a doctor, this assisted-dying bill is dangerous', *Spiked Online*, 14 May 2025. https://www.spiked-online.com/2025/05/14/take-it-from-a-doctor-this-assisted-dying-bill-is-dangerous/
3. David Aaronovitch, X, 22 March 2025. https://x.com/DAaronovitch/status/1903409427677430187
4. Jonathan Sumption, 'I can't rejoice at this assisted dying bill.

Where is the humanity?', *The Times*, 30 November 2024. https://www.thetimes.com/uk/healthcare/article/i-cant-rejoice-at-this-assisted-dying-bill-where-is-the-humanity-9bsx0dfwp

5. Jonathan Sumption, 'Lecture 1: Law's expanding empire', The Reith Lectures 2019: Law and the Decline of Politics, BBC Radio 4. https://downloads.bbc.co.uk/radio4/reith2019/Reith_2019_Sumption_lecture_1.pdf

6. Afua Hirsch and Robert Booth, 'CPS will not prosecute relatives who help terminally ill to die', *Guardian*, 10 December 2008. https://www.theguardian.com/society/2008/dec/10/assisted-suicide-daniel-james-cps

7. Jon Ungoed-Thomas, 'Suspects in assisted dying cases wait far too long on prosecution decision, says ex-DPP', *Guardian*, 21 September 2024. https://www.theguardian.com/society/2024/sep/21/suspects-in-assisted-dying-cases-wait-far-too-long-on-prosecution-decision-says-ex-dpp

8. Durkheim, *Suicide*, p. 230.

Acknowledgements

The arguments of this book have benefited immensely from the scrutiny of several learned, wise, and generous people. Huge thanks to: Sallie Baxendale, Alex Chula, Pallavi Devulapalli, Mark Fiocco, Deborah Hammond, Rob Hopkins, Allan House, Derek Matravers, Charlie Robinson, Lucy Thomas, David Wootton, and Kevin Yuill. I am particularly grateful to Paul Sagar, who disagreed with most of it yet still took the trouble to tell me why.

Many thanks, too, to my agent Caroline Hardman; to my editor Sameer Rahim at The Bridge Street Press; and to Zoe Hood and Zoe Gullen, also at Little, Brown. Love and hugs to M. and A. for being so encouraging; and to G. for keeping me cheerful. And finally: endless love and gratitude to Laura, for everything. I simply could not have written this book without our life-sustaining conversations.

Index

Aaronovitch, David 244
Abbott, Jack 147
Adams, John Bodkin 148
adaptive preferences 204
addiction 32–4, 40, 73, 112, 218, 229
Adkins, Janet 80, 84
advanced directives 196
Aesop 110
afterlife 29, 77
Alvarez, Al 43–4, 65, 213–14
Alzheimer's 80, 84
anorexia 82, 122–3, 129–30, 241
anti-depressants 113, 125, 210
anti-emetics 108
anxiety 9, 58–9, 61, 70, 72, 93, 96–7, 99, 106–7, 126–8, 144, 211, 217, 219, 223
  anti-anxiety medication 113
Aristotle 48
arthritis 121, 210
Asperger's 218
Association for Palliative Medicine 108
attention-deficit hyperactivity disorder (ADHD) 131, 219

Australia 3–4, 59, 82, 120, 146, 180, 184, 203, 235–6
Austria 3
autism 82, 126, 130–1, 218–20, 222–3, 249
Awuah-Darko, Joseph 227

Belgium 3–4, 82–3, 120–1, 125–6, 154, 195–6, 216, 221–4
Belshaw, Christopher 168, 203
Bengali women 204
Bentham, Jeremy 187
bereavement 76, 94, 129
  see also grief
Better Off Dead? 165–6, 175
Biggar, Nigel 13
biohacking 178
birth control 52
birth rates, falling 201
Blake, Meredith 184
blindness 82
borderline personality disorder (BPD) 128, 131, 222–3
Borges, Jorge Luis 29
Boston 138

Brassington, Iain 88
British Geriatrics Society 139
British Medical Journal 105–6, 174
Buddhism 72, 100, 179
bullying 218, 220
burdensome, feeling 180–6, 207
burns victims 107
Burton, Robert 119

Calvin, John 213
Campbell, Jane 165–6
Camus, Albert 31
Canada 3–4, 18, 59, 61, 82–4, 88–9, 92–4, 102, 116, 125, 146–7, 151–2, 154, 224, 235–6
   and disabilities 120–1, 166–7, 228–9
   expanding eligibility 215–16, 227–9, 231
   and family members 209–11
   and feeling burdensome 180–1, 183
   and social conditions 202–3
Care Quality Commission 201
Carr, Liz 151, 166–7, 175
Cassell, Eric 97
Cato the Younger 26, 31
Chabot, Boudewijn 125, 129, 132
China 193
Christianity 12–13, 24–5, 29, 48–9, 51–3, 55, 72, 91, 178
   and sanctity of life 159, 161, 197, 213
Christie, Agatha 9
Cobain, Kurt 26, 31–2, 65

coercion 136–48, 154, 207, 247
   proposed safeguards 142–8
Colombia 3
compassion 5, 19, 22–3, 45–54, 61–3, 80, 85–6, 106, 117, 184
Compassion and Choices 63, 206
Complex Life and Death Decisions group 77–8
concept creep 218–21
Conservative Home website 9
Copson, Andrew 23
Covid 82, 189, 201, 226
Cox, Sarah 108–9
Crown Prosecution Service 141, 246–7

Davey, Ed 211
Dawson, Lord 54, 57
death penalty 289
death rates 1, 82, 93, 126
Death with Dignity 146, 158
dementia 4, 188–9, 196–7, 201–2
depression 2, 9, 32–4, 43, 58–9, 61, 70, 72, 75, 81–3, 85, 93, 96–100, 106–7, 109, 116–18, 125–9, 135, 154, 166, 170–1, 173, 217, 219, 252
diabetes 82, 121, 123, 210, 241
diamorphine 148
Dickinson, Emily 104
Dignitas 3, 42, 51, 67, 158
dignity 158–65, 169–75
   and bodily capacities 163–5
   and functionality 162–3
Dignity in Dying (formerly

Exit) 5, 13, 42, 52, 54–5, 62, 158, 172–3, 183, 205–6, 209, 234
disability 2, 4, 18, 180, 183, 202, 207–8, 211–12, 215, 217, 222, 233–4, 240, 243, 249
  acquired disability 170–1
  and Canadian law 120–1, 166–7, 228–9
  and coercion 137, 139–42
  and dignity 164–7, 169–75
  disability paradox 177
  learning disabilities 82, 130–1, 137, 140–1, 153–4, 196, 211, 233, 249
  mental disabilities 219–20
  and psychological suffering 59–60, 73, 96–7
  and reflection period 120
  and talking therapy 113
  and terminal diagnoses 90, 92–4
  and 'unbearable suffering' 102–3
  and Utilitarian arguments 189, 192, 194–7, 200–1
doctor–patient relationships 148–55, 240–3
  'doctor shopping' 152
  and patient autonomy 153, 160
'don't die' movement 179
Donne, John 29, 53, 180
Dostoevsky, Fyodor 30
Down's syndrome 140, 153, 242, 249
Duncan, Alicia 210
Durkheim, Émile 8, 30–1, 39, 55, 71, 180, 190, 224, 252
Dworkin, Gerald 150
Dying with Dignity 152, 158
dyspraxia 131

eating disorders 121–2, 128, 219
  see also anorexia
Economist, The 23
Ecuador 3
Ellis, A. E. 99
empathy 37, 39, 48, 81, 181, 183, 244
Epicurus 37
epidermolysis bullosa 198
equality arguments 230–6
Erskine, Major General Sir William 26, 31–2
eugenics 52
European Convention on Human Rights 27
euthanasia 3, 7, 40, 44, 46, 51–4, 74, 79–80, 94, 121, 129, 147, 151, 196, 210
  active and passive 14
  for babies and children 216, 222
  'duo euthanasia' 140
  non-voluntary 4, 199
  'psychological' 110–11
Evening Standard 23
Exit, *see* Dignity in Dying
eyes, post-mortem changes in 79–80

faecal drowning 174, 176
Falconer, Lord 135, 217, 232
feminism 26
fibromyalgia 219
Finkelstein, Lord 217

France 3
Freedom Lover archetype
    21–3, 26–8, 31, 33–5,
    37–8, 40–7, 49, 54–7, 60,
    66–7, 70, 73, 85, 116,
    119, 122–4, 126, 132–4,
    147, 184, 188, 206, 210,
    235–6, 239, 242, 249, 252
Freeman, Hadley 130
Friedrich, Caspar David 38

Gardner, Booth 216
George V, King 54
Germany 3
Gibran, Khalil 110
Gilderdale, Kay 50–1, 61, 87
global capitalism 251
Goodhart, David 219
Grayling, A. C. 42–3, 60, 68,
    110
Green, Stefanie 151, 160,
    209–10
Greenwich, Alex 8
grief 8, 37, 43, 58, 94, 100,
    113, 129, 170, 209, 211
    see also bereavement
Groningen Protocol 198
Guardian 23, 53, 138, 173,
    246

Hacking, Ian 219
Haslam, Nick 218
health and wellness 178–80
hearing loss 83
Herx, Leonie 154
Hill, Max 134, 247
Hinduism 100
Hirsch, Emmanuel 182
HIV 121
Hommay, Victor 30

Hopkins, Rachel 8–10, 117,
    124, 137, 147, 248
Horder, Lord 54, 57, 240
hospices 91, 105–6, 108, 114,
    120, 175–6, 201, 231, 250
human rights 23, 27–8, 68, 72
Hume, David 37–8, 53, 190

individualism 30–1, 38–9, 224,
    240, 252
informed consent 75–8
inheritance 15, 138, 182
inquests 149–50
Inuit cultures 190
Iranian women 43–4
Irish famine 194
Italy 3

Jacobs, Sherelle 189–90,
    194–5, 197, 200, 202
James, Henry 100
Japan 225
Jefferson, Thomas 28
Johnson, Bryan 179
Johnson, Harriet McBryde 175,
    205
Johnson, Samuel 161
Joiner, Thomas 64–5, 181, 224
Julius Caesar 26
Jung, Carl 72

Kant, Immanuel 159–61, 169,
    196
Keown, John 199
Kevorkian, Jack 9, 79–81, 84,
    165, 173, 245
Kim, Scott Y. H. 231
Kruger, Danny 145

Laverack, Jessica 136–7

Leadbeater, Kim 4–8, 13, 16–17, 23, 42, 52, 59, 74, 77, 90–1, 93–4, 117, 122–4, 134–5, 139, 153, 184, 194, 212, 217, 224, 232–3, 235, 244–5, 247, 249
Leith, Prue 135, 145
lethal drug complications 75–6
liberalism (and hyperliberalism) 22, 27, 39, 55, 134, 161, 207, 251
and Utilitarianism 187–8
L'Inconnue de la Seine 226
Listowel, Earl of 53
Liverpool Care Pathway 200
Locke, John 25, 28
London Underground 62, 183
Luxembourg 3–4, 126, 195
Lyon, Christopher 210–11
Lyons, Mark 173, 245

MacIntyre, Alasdair 39
Malthouse, Kit 8–10, 231
Malthusian League 52
Malthusianism 193
Mandelstam, Osip 214
Mannix, Kathryn 176
Marsh, Henry 156–7
Martell, David 229
Melzack, Ronald 106
mental capacity 76–7, 93, 116–17, 152, 164, 196–9, 212, 249
mental disorders (mental illness) 17, 30–5, 40, 43, 73, 112, 126, 129–30, 132, 137, 146, 152, 210, 219, 222, 229–30, 234
mental health services 135

Merciful Helper archetype 45–7, 52, 54–7, 60–1, 66–8, 73, 84–7, 89, 94, 108, 114, 116, 118, 122–4, 132, 147, 188, 198–200, 212, 235–6, 239, 242, 249
'mercy killing' 49–51, 61, 192, 245
microaggressions 218
migraines 219
Mill, John Stuart 25
Millard, Charles Killick 52–3, 57, 94–5, 194
Monroe, Marilyn 225
Montaigne, Michel de 28–9, 96
morality 12–13
More, Thomas 51, 53, 71, 180
morphine 32, 50–1, 107, 148, 241
Motherland 181
motor neurone disease 82
muscle relaxants 107

National Health Service (NHS) 5, 16–17, 122, 135, 144, 188–9, 195, 200–1, 225, 241, 249
neonates 197–8
nerve blocks 108
Netherlands 3–4, 44, 59, 82–3, 121, 125–31, 140, 147, 180, 195–6, 198–9, 216, 221–3, 227, 229
neuropathic agents 107
New York state 3
New Yorker, The 119
New Zealand 3–4
Nichols, Alan 83–4, 89, 92, 116
Nietzsche, Friedrich 171

Nonconformists 51
Not Dead Yet 102, 164–7, 175

obesity 121
Observer 42
obsessive–compulsive disorder (OCD) 131, 222–3
opioids 107, 111
Oregon 4–5, 16, 61, 75, 82, 93, 120–1, 146, 158–9, 180, 203, 224–5, 235
organ harvesting 80
O'Sullivan, Suzanne 218, 219
Other Half, The 172
over-diagnosis 218–19
over-medicalisation 250

pain and pain relief 15, 60–1, 69, 100, 105–12, 120, 174
  'gate control' theory 106–7
  and 'psychological euthanasia' 110–11
  refusal of relief 110–12
  see also palliative care
palliative care 66, 69, 71, 81, 87–8, 99–100, 105, 108–12, 120–1, 135, 143, 154, 174, 176–7, 189, 200–1, 228, 236, 241, 243, 248, 250
palliative sedation 15–16
Paltrow, Gwyneth 179
paralysis 42, 50, 170–1
Parkinson's 75
Parris, Matthew 186–95, 197, 200, 202–3
patholysis 9
peripheral nerve stimulation 106
personality disorders 82
  see also borderline personality disorder
Plath, Sylvia 104
Plutarch 26
polycystic ovary syndrome 219
Ponsonby, Lord 53
Portugal 3
positive discrimination 234
post-traumatic stress disorder (PTSD) 126, 210, 218, 223
Potter, Dennis 115
preference satisfaction 187
prostitution, decriminalisation of 134–5
psychogenic (sociogenic) illnesses 226
psychological suffering 58–63, 70–3, 83, 87–8, 93–9, 216, 222, 227
  of family and friends 62–3
  'psychiatric' suffering 125–32
  and terminal illness 113–18

Quebec 3, 196, 228

Rachels, James 14–15
Rantzen, Esther 13, 22, 90, 135
Rawls, John 39
Reed, Nicholas 173
religion 12–13, 79, 96, 99–100, 213, 244
  see also Buddhism; Christianity; Hinduism
Revolutionary War 22
rights
  claim rights 27–8, 68–72
  inalienable rights 27
  and individualism 38–9

INDEX

negative rights 27–8, 67–8, 72
positive rights 68
'right to die' 21, 23, 26–8, 41–2, 44, 66–8, 72–3, 240
'right to life' 28, 60, 68, 70, 228
see also human rights
Romantics 30
Royal College of Physicians 91
Royal College of Psychiatrists 17, 77
Rusbridger, Alan 173

St Augustine 24
St Christopher's Hospice 105–6
St Paul 24
St Thomas Aquinas 25, 37, 49–51
Samaritans 97
Saunders, Cicely 105–7, 113, 117
Scarry, Elaine 95, 112
schizophrenia 35
Scottish Parliament 6, 186
Scythians 190
secularism 12–13, 25, 49, 52, 55, 119, 159, 161, 169, 179, 197, 213
self-care 251
self-diagnosis 226
self-harm 64–5
self-sacrifice 190–1
Sen, Amartya 204
Seneca 24, 41, 107, 162, 168, 213–14
Shakespeare, William
Hamlet 18
The Merchant of Venice 48

Shipman, Harold 148–50, 153–5, 245
slippery slope arguments 215–17, 236
see also equality arguments
Smith, Adam 193
social care 74, 93, 135, 144–5, 147, 186, 188, 195, 197, 201, 225, 244
social conditions 9, 30–1, 68, 82–3, 93–4, 107, 175, 207, 224
and Utilitarian arguments 202–4
social Darwinism 192–3
social media 191, 226, 234, 244
Socrates 24
Spain 3
Speed, Gary 37
spinal cord stimulation 106
Starmer, Keir 135, 246
steroids 107
Stoics 24, 28, 162–3, 168
subjectivity 55, 99, 101, 123, 159, 188, 202–3, 251
suicide 24–32, 34–8, 40–4, 63–6, 70–3
altruistic 180–1, 190–1
'anomic suicide' 71–2
decriminalisation 41
and domestic abuse 136–8
'egoistic suicide' 30, 71, 224, 252
Freitod 30
Graeco-Roman philosophy of 162–3
and healthcare professionals 74–5, 78–9
Hume and 37–8, 53, 190

suicide – *continued*
  impact on others 37–8, 73, 208–12
  Kant's opposition to 161
  Nietzsche and 171
  pro-suicide websites 2, 226
  rates 71, 213, 224–6
  rates and gender 128–9
  and refusal of pain relief 111
  Seneca and 24, 41, 162, 168
  and social contagions 225–6
  suicidal mindsets 93–4, 97
  suicide pacts 139–40
  'suicide talk' 154
  suicidal thinking 64–6, 75, 100–1, 114, 118–20, 181
  'suicide machine', *see* Thanatron
  terminology 8–11
  and value of human life 212–14
  variety of motives 43–4
suicide prevention 8, 31–2, 34–6, 41, 83, 97, 100
suicide watches 36
Sumption, Lord 245–6
Switzerland 3, 11, 16, 44, 67, 120, 133, 156, 205–6, 224, 231
Szasz, Thomas 31–6, 38, 40

Taubert, Mark 241
Teague, Thomas 150
Ten Commandments 24
TENs machines 106

ter Beek, Zoraya 126–7
terminal diagnoses 89–94
terminal illness, definitions of 4–5, 89, 121–2, 246
Terminally Ill Adults (End of Life) Bill 4–8, 13, 16–17, 23, 42, 52, 54, 62, 74, 134–5, 153, 174, 184, 217, 231–5, 244–5, 247–9
  assessment process 142–8
  and coercion 137–9
  definition of terminal illness 121–2
  economic arguments 194–5
  equality impact assessment 233–4
  'Henry VIII' clause 247
  and horror stories 174–6
  and mental capacity 77, 93, 117, 212
  projected uptake 224–5
  and terminal diagnoses 90–1, 93–4, 123–4
Thanatron (suicide machine) 80, 84, 165
Thomas, Dylan 19, 241
Tice, Richard 174, 176
Tooze, Cyril 203
torture 112
Tourette syndrome 219, 223, 226
Toynbee, Polly 23, 138, 184
transfusions 80
treatment, withdrawal of 14–15

'unbearable suffering' 4, 19, 23, 42, 56, 59, 97–103, 118, 125–6, 129, 164,

198, 218, 221–3, 227, 230, 232
Unitarianism 52
Universal Declaration of Human Rights 68, 160
US Declaration of Independence 28
Utilitarianism 187–90, 195–7, 200, 202–4, 208, 212

Velleman, J. David 112, 182–3
Victoria (Australia) 59, 146, 235
Voluntary Euthanasia (Legalisation) Bill 52–4
Voluntary Euthanasia Legalisation Society (VELS) 52, 194

Walker, Dan 37
Wall, Patrick 106
Warnock, Baroness 197
Washington state 216, 234–5
Western Australia 146
Wiebe, Ellen 151–2
Wollstonecraft, Mary 162
Woolf, Virginia 26, 31–2
Wootton, Sarah 62, 234

Yellowstone 47, 50, 61, 85, 87
Yuill, Kevin 3, 63

Zitter, Jennifer Nutik 105